CAMBRIDG

Shakespeare

Coriolanus

S0-BOI-287

Edited by Rex Gibson

Series Editor: Rex Gibson
Director, Shakespeare and Schools Project

DISCARD

CAMB
UNIVERS

PUBLISHED BY THE PRESS SYNDICATE OF THE UNIVERSITY OF CAMBRIDGE
The Pitt Building, Trumpington Street, Cambridge, United Kingdom

CAMBRIDGE UNIVERSITY PRESS
The Edinburgh Building, Cambridge CB2 2RU, UK   http://www.cup.cam.ac.uk
40 West 20th Street, New York, NY 10011–4211, USA   http://www.cup.org
10 Stamford Road, Oakleigh, Melbourne 3166, Australia
Ruiz de Alarcón 13, 28014 Madrid, Spain

First published 1999

Printed in the United Kingdom at the University Press, Cambridge

Typeface Ehrhardt 11½/13pt *System* PageMaker®

A catalogue record for this book is available from the British Library

Library of Congress Cataloguing in Publication data applied for

ISBN 0 521 64863 7

Prepared for publication by Stenton Associates
Designed by Richard Morris, Stonesfield Design
Picture research by Callie Kendall

Thanks are due to the following for permission to reproduce photographs:

28, 222*l*, Angus McBean/photo courtesy of Shakespeare Centre Library, Stratford-upon-
Avon; 42, Douglas Jeffery; 55, 126, 141,156, 184, 206, 214, 233, 235, Donald Cooper ©
Photostage; 62, © Vera Tenschert, Berlin; 97, 251, Reg Wilson Collection/photo courtesy
of the Shakespeare Centre Library, Stratford-upon-Avon; 112, 170, Alastair Muir, London;
134, Joe Cocks Studio Collection/photo courtesy of Shakespeare Centre Library, Stratford-
upon-Avon; 148, © Shakespeare Centre Library, Stratford-upon-Avon; 222*r*, Topham
Picturepoint; 249, Photo: Will Gullette/courtesy of The Old Globe Theatre, San Diego,
California

Contents

Cambridge School Shakespeare

This edition of *Coriolanus* is part of the *Cambridge School Shakespeare* series. Like every other play in the series, it has been specially prepared to help all students in schools and colleges.

This *Coriolanus* aims to be different from other editions of the play. It invites you to bring the play to life in your classroom, hall or drama studio through enjoyable activities that will increase your understanding. Actors have created their different interpretations of the play over the centuries. Similarly, you are encouraged to make up your own mind about *Coriolanus*, rather than having someone else's interpretation handed down to you.

Cambridge School Shakespeare does not offer you a cut-down or simplified version of the play. This is Shakespeare's language, filled with imaginative possibilities. You will find on every left-hand page: a summary of the action, an explanation of unfamiliar words, and a choice of activities on Shakespeare's language, characters and stories.

Between each act and in the pages at the end of the play, you will find notes, illustrations and activities. These will help to increase your understanding of the whole play.

There are a large number of activities to give you the widest choice to suit your own particular needs. Please don't think you have to do every one. Choose the activities that help you most.

This edition will be of value to you whether you are studying for an examination, reading for pleasure, or thinking of putting on the play to entertain others. You can work on the activities on your own or in groups. Many of the activities suggest a particular group size, but don't be afraid to make up smaller or larger groups to suit your own purposes.

Although you are invited to treat *Coriolanus* as a play, you don't need special dramatic or theatrical skills to do the activities. By choosing your activities, and by exploring and experimenting, you can make your own interpretations of Shakespeare's language, characters and stories. Whatever you do, remember that Shakespeare wrote his plays to be acted, watched and enjoyed.

Rex Gibson

This edition of *Coriolanus* uses the text of the play established by Lee Bliss in *The New Cambridge Shakespeare*.

List of characters

Romans

Patricians

CAIUS MARTIUS later CORIOLANUS
VOLUMNIA his mother
VIRGILIA his wife
YOUNG MARTIUS his son
MENENIUS AGRIPPA his friend
VALERIA a noble lady
COMINIUS Consul and
   Commander-in-Chief of
   the Army
TITUS LARTIUS a general
SENATORS
NOBLES

Plebeians

SICINIUS VELUTUS ⎱ Tribunes of
JUNIUS BRUTUS ⎰ the people
CITIZENS
AEDILES
SOLDIERS

Other Romans

GENTLEWOMAN to Volumnia
NICANOR a traitor to Rome
OFFICERS
HERALD
MESSENGERS

Usher, Drummer, Trumpeter, Scout,
Captains, Lictors, Attendants

Volsces

TULLUS AUFIDIUS general of the Volsce army
LIEUTENANT to Aufidius
ADRIAN a spy
GUARDS
CITIZENS
SOLDIERS
LORDS
SENATORS
CONSPIRATORS

Attendants

The action of the play takes place in or near Rome,
Corioles and Antium

Before the play begins

The story of *Coriolanus* is Shakespeare's version of events in the early days of the Roman republic, long before Rome became a great military empire. According to legend, Rome was founded in 753 BC by Romulus who, with his brother Remus, was supposed to have been suckled by a she-wolf. It was ruled by Etruscan kings, the Tarquins, until 510 BC when the last Tarquin king was driven out, and Rome became a republic.

Shakespeare's play is set around 490 BC, shortly after the republic was established. Rome was still a small city, just one of many in Italy where warring tribes fought each other. But it was a divided city. The patricians (aristocrats) and the plebeians (citizens) had united to drive out the Tarquins, but were now locked in a bitter struggle for power.

The patricians were the ruling class of Rome. They owned most of the property, and wielded all the power. They alone held the right to become senators and make laws. From their ranks came the consuls, two of whom served for one year only with full executive powers as joint heads of the civil state and the army. Plebeians were the workers: servants, artisans, small traders and farmers, beggars. In the evolving republic, there was always smouldering resentment between the haves and the have-nots.

Republican Rome claimed that all the people had a part in affairs of state: making laws, declaring war, electing magistrates. But in practice the plebeians had little or no influence over political decisions, and they were economically exploited by the patrician class. Hard labour and military service were their daily conditions of life. Famine was an ever-present threat.

The play opens with the plebeians focussing their anger on Caius Martius, the patrician war-lord who later, because of his bravery in battle at the city of Corioles, becomes known as Coriolanus. The plebeians accuse him of hoarding corn, causing them to starve.

Coriolanus' Rome was neither a monarchy nor a democracy, but a republic ruled by an aristocracy – the patricians. Some brief definitions follow, and you will find further help with the political structure of Rome throughout the play and on pages 242–3.

Patricians the ruling elite; wealthy aristocrats; the law-makers.

Plebeians citizens and workers; neither patricians nor slaves.

Tribunes spokesmen of the plebeians, defenders of their rights.

Aediles officers of the tribunes, carrying out their orders.

The senate: the law-making body; Rome's seat of government.

Senators patricians who sat in the senate.

The Capitol the meeting house of the senate.

Consul each year the senate nominated two consuls, to serve jointly for one year only, as commanders-in-chief of the army and heads of state. The plebeians were expected to ratify the appointment in a show of general assent. Their rejection of Coriolanus as consul leads to his banishment.

Roman and Volsce territory about 490 BC, the time of Shakespeare's *Coriolanus*. Corioles was a small city, 25 miles to the south-east of Rome. Its exact location is now lost, but it was near the modern town of Velletri. Antium was the modern Anzio. After the defeat of the Volsces it became a Roman colony, a favoured retreat for Roman patricians.

The Citizens resolve to rebel, and to kill Caius Martius. The First Citizen claims that the patricians' greed causes the plebeians to starve. The Second Citizen seems to defend Caius Martius.

1 Stage the opening (in large groups)

The play explodes into action with the threat of a food riot. Talk together about the following questions, then stage the opening moments to greatest dramatic effect:

a Do the citizens enter all together, or does the stage gradually fill?

b How are they dressed? How do they handle their weapons?

c How does the First Citizen gain the attention of the crowd?

d How can you help the audience to understand the citizens' main grievance that the patricians have hoarded corn, causing starvation among the common people? (One production began with the citizens angrily watching a golden shower of corn fall into a pit on stage).

2 First impressions of Coriolanus

Caius Martius will be given the name Coriolanus at the end of Act 1. Identify the three descriptions of him in lines 5–6, 21 and 25. You will find many more views of his character as you read on.

3 Conflict: poverty versus wealth

Coriolanus is a play of conflicts, and Shakespeare's language style expresses those conflicts. For example, the First Citizen's lines 12–19 are full of antitheses (words or phrases set against each other, see page 238): 'poor'/'good', 'citizens'/'patricians' and so on. Speak the lines using physical actions to bring out the oppositions.

---

staves wooden staffs
famish go hungry
accounted reckoned
authority the patricians
surfeits over-feeds, gluttons
superfluity surplus (of corn)
humanely compassionately

leanness starvation
an inventory … abundance a list giving a detailed reminder of their wealth
pikes pitch-forks
commonalty common people, plebeians

The Tragedy of Coriolanus

ACT 1   SCENE 1
Rome: a public place

Enter a company of mutinous citizens with staves, clubs, and other weapons

FIRST CITIZEN Before we proceed any further, hear me speak.

ALL Speak, speak.

FIRST CITIZEN You are all resolved rather to die than to famish?

ALL Resolved, resolved.

FIRST CITIZEN First, you know Caius Martius is chief enemy to the 5
people.

ALL We know't, we know't.

FIRST CITIZEN Let us kill him, and we'll have corn at our own price.
Is't a verdict?

ALL No more talking on't. Let it be done. Away, away! 10

SECOND CITIZEN One word, good citizens.

FIRST CITIZEN We are accounted poor citizens, the patricians good.
What authority surfeits on would relieve us. If they would yield us
but the superfluity while it were wholesome, we might guess they
relieved us humanely. But they think we are too dear. The leanness 15
that afflicts us, the object of our misery, is as an inventory to
particularise their abundance; our sufferance is a gain to them. Let
us revenge this with our pikes, ere we become rakes; for the gods
know, I speak this in hunger for bread, not in thirst for revenge.

SECOND CITIZEN Would you proceed especially against Caius Martius? 20

ALL Against him first. He's a very dog to the commonalty.

SECOND CITIZEN Consider you what services he has done for his
country?

FIRST CITIZEN Very well, and could be content to give him good report
for't, but that he pays himself with being proud. 25

SECOND CITIZEN Nay, but speak not maliciously.

The First Citizen makes more criticisms of Caius Martius. Menenius attempts to calm the mob, and claims that the patricians care for the people and that the gods have caused the famine.

1 More impressions of Coriolanus

The First Citizen claims that Caius Martius (Coriolanus) seeks fame out of pride and a desire to please his mother. His pride is as great as his valour ('virtue'). The Second Citizen seems to defend Coriolanus, saying that he is not greedy for wealth ('covetous'). You may find it helpful to compile a 'character book' as you read on, noting down what other characters say about Coriolanus.

2 Iron hand in a velvet glove? (in pairs)

When the First Citizen cries 'To th'Capitol', he may be trying to incite the citizens to storm the senate. So Menenius, the first patrician to appear in the play, faces a mob of mutinous plebeians.

a Pick out the descriptions of the citizens in lines 42, 48 and 51. Why do you think Menenius uses such terms?

b Match the following summary to the appropriate lines:
* the patricians love you;
* you are powerless against the Roman state;
* the famine is caused by the gods, so pray to them;
* there's danger ahead
  ('transported by calamity' = made frantic by disaster);
* you wrongly criticise the patricians, who love you
  ('helms' = helmsmen who steer the ship of state).

c Step into role as Menenius and speak lines 51–64 as persuasively as you can. Explore different tones for each of his four sentences: for example, kindly and friendly, or coldly and threatening.

---

soft-conscienced unthinking, easy-going
even to the altitude … virtue to match his valour
prating foolishly talking
Soft wait a moment
bats cudgels

inkling suspicion, hint
suitors beggars
dearth famine
curbs restraints
asunder apart
impediment attempt to stop progress

FIRST CITIZEN I say unto you, what he hath done famously, he did it to that end. Though soft-conscienced men can be content to say it was for his country, he did it to please his mother and to be partly proud, which he is, even to the altitude of his virtue.   30

SECOND CITIZEN What he cannot help in his nature you account a vice in him. You must in no way say he is covetous.

FIRST CITIZEN If I must not, I need not be barren of accusations. He hath faults, with surplus, to tire in repetition.

Shouts within

What shouts are these? The other side o'th'city is risen. Why stay   35
we prating here? To th'Capitol!

ALL Come, come!

FIRST CITIZEN Soft, who comes here?

Enter MENENIUS AGRIPPA

SECOND CITIZEN Worthy Menenius Agrippa, one that hath always loved the people.   40

FIRST CITIZEN He's one honest enough. Would all the rest were so!

MENENIUS What work's, my countrymen, in hand? Where go you
    With bats and clubs? The matter, speak, I pray you.

SECOND CITIZEN Our business is not unknown to th'senate. They have had inkling this fortnight what we intend to do, which now we'll   45
show 'em in deeds. They say poor suitors have strong breaths; they shall know we have strong arms too.

MENENIUS Why, masters, my good friends, mine honest neighbours,
    Will you undo yourselves?

SECOND CITIZEN We cannot, sir; we are undone already.   50

MENENIUS I tell you, friends, most charitable care
    Have the patricians of you. For your wants,
    Your suffering in this dearth, you may as well
    Strike at the heaven with your staves as lift them
    Against the Roman state, whose course will on   55
    The way it takes, cracking ten thousand curbs
    Of more strong link asunder than can ever
    Appear in your impediment. For the dearth,
    The gods, not the patricians, make it, and
    Your knees to them, not arms, must help. Alack,   60
    You are transported by calamity
    Thither where more attends you, and you slander
    The helms o'th'state, who care for you like fathers,
    When you curse them as enemies.

The Second Citizen details how the working people of Rome are exploited. Menenius criticises him, then begins to tell a parable which compares the stomach in the body to the patricians in the state.

1 The Citizen's complaints (in pairs)

In lines 65–70, the Second Citizen denies Menenius' claim that the patricians care for Rome's ordinary people. Instead, they cause starvation by hoarding corn, supporting moneylenders ('usurers') who charge high rates of interest ('usury'), and using the law to aid the rich and oppress the poor.

Take turns to speak the lines, and invent a sequence of gestures the Second Citizen might use to emphasise the grievances he lists.

2 The tale of the belly (in pairs)

In response to the Second Citizen's list of injustices, Menenius proposes to tell a 'pretty tale' (apt story or fable). Take parts as Menenius and the Second Citizen and speak lines 71–146, using the activities below and on pages 10 and 12 to help you.

a Menenius says that the parable of the belly 'serves my purpose' (line 75), but the Second Citizen suspects that Menenius might be using the fable to 'fob off our disgrace' (dismiss with a trick our suffering and grievances). What do you think is Menenius' purpose in telling the fable of the belly?

b Try different story-telling styles for Menenius: as a fairy story to a group of children; or patronising and contemptuously; or as a seriously spoken parable, and so on. Is Menenius confident, or is he desperate and anxious, not sure if he will succeed?

c In some productions, the actor belches at 'even thus' (line 91). How does your Menenius behave here?

---

edicts laws, orders
piercing statutes harsh laws
scale't attempt it
gulf whirlpool, bottomless pit
Still always
cupboarding the viand hoarding the food

instruments body parts
mutually participate working together
his receipt what it received
muniments defences
petty small
fabric body

SECOND CITIZEN Care for us? True indeed, they ne'er cared for us yet.   65
    Suffer us to famish, and their storehouses crammed with grain;
    make edicts for usury, to support usurers; repeal daily any
    wholesome act established against the rich, and provide more
    piercing statutes daily to chain up and restrain the poor. If the
    wars eat us not up, they will; and there's all the love they bear us.   70
MENENIUS Either you must
    Confess yourselves wondrous malicious,
    Or be accused of folly. I shall tell you
    A pretty tale. It may be you have heard it,
    But since it serves my purpose, I will venture   75
    To scale't a little more.
SECOND CITIZEN Well, I'll hear it, sir; yet you must not think to fob off
    our disgrace with a tale. But, and't please you, deliver.
MENENIUS There was a time when all the body's members
    Rebelled against the belly, thus accused it: 80
    That only like a gulf it did remain
    I'th'midst o'th'body, idle and unactive,
    Still cupboarding the viand, never bearing
    Like labour with the rest, where th'other instruments
    Did see and hear, devise, instruct, walk, feel,   85
    And, mutually participate, did minister
    Unto the appetite and affection common
    Of the whole body. The belly answered –
SECOND CITIZEN Well, sir, what answer made the belly?
MENENIUS Sir, I shall tell you. With a kind of smile,   90
    Which ne'er came from the lungs, but even thus –
    For look you, I may make the belly smile
    As well as speak – it tauntingly replied
    To th'discontented members, the mutinous parts
    That envied his receipt; even so most fitly   95
    As you malign our senators for that
    They are not such as you.
SECOND CITIZEN   Your belly's answer – What?
    The kingly crownèd head, the vigilant eye,
    The counsellor heart, the arm our soldier,
    Our steed the leg, the tongue our trumpeter,   100
    With other muniments and petty helps
    In this our fabric, if that they –

Menenius explains how the belly sends food to all parts of the body, and is left only with waste. He claims that the senators represent the belly, and the plebeians are the other body parts.

1 True or false? (in small groups)

Menenius' tale of the belly uses a comparison familiar to Shakespeare's audience – society as a human body. Such comparisons were intended to show that society is naturally hierarchical, with aristocrats deserving their elite status at the top. For Menenius the belly is the patrician class, the source of all 'public benefit' in the state.

Tell each other what you think about the truth or otherwise of Menenius' claim that rich rulers serve the poor and get nothing for their pains. Is it just propaganda? If you were staging the play, would the plebeians be calmed by Menenius' fable, or more enraged?

2 Keep them interested (in pairs)

Politicians know that style (how something is said) is just as important as substance (what is said). In Shakespeare's time, as in ancient Rome, public speakers learned the rules of rhetoric (the art of speaking well, so as to persuade the hearers). The plebeians listening to Menenius' fable of the belly have empty bellies, and they are angry that the patricians are hoarding corn. But Menenius intends his tale to defuse the riot.

One quality of successful story-telling is how the narrator uses all kinds of delaying devices (pauses, distractions, added detail, and so on) to stretch out the tale and make the listeners keen to hear more. Identify several ways in which Menenius avoids telling his fable simply and directly, in order to keep the interest of the plebeians. For example, in line 138 Menenius uses humour ('the great toe') to deflect attention from the truth of his story.

'Fore me upon my word
cormorant greedy, ravenous
sink sewer
incorporate united in one body
cranks and offices winding
  passages and workrooms (arteries
  and organs)

natural competency proper
  resources
audit balance sheet, account
digest understand
Touching relating to
weal o'th'common
  commonwealth, welfare of everyone

MENENIUS   What then?
         'Fore me, this fellow speaks! What then? What then?
SECOND CITIZEN Should by the cormorant belly be restrained,
         Who is the sink o'th'body –
MENENIUS   Well, what then?·   105
SECOND CITIZEN The former agents, if they did complain,
         What could the belly answer?
MENENIUS   I will tell you.
         If you'll bestow a small – of what you have little –
         Patience awhile, you'st hear the belly's answer.
SECOND CITIZEN You're long about it.
MENENIUS   Note me this, good friend: 110
         Your most grave belly was deliberate,
         Not rash like his accusers, and thus answered:
         'True is it, my incorporate friends', quoth he,
         'That I receive the general food at first
         Which you do live upon; and fit it is,   115
         Because I am the storehouse and the shop
         Of the whole body. But, if you do remember,
         I send it through the rivers of your blood
         Even to the court, the heart, to th'seat o'th'brain;
         And, through the cranks and offices of man,   120
         The strongest nerves and small inferior veins
         From me receive that natural competency
         Whereby they live. And though that all at once' –
         You, my good friends, this says the belly, mark me –
SECOND CITIZEN Ay, sir, well, well.
MENENIUS   'Though all at once cannot   125
         See what I do deliver out to each,
         Yet I can make my audit up that all
         From me do back receive the flour of all
         And leave me but the bran.' What say you to't?
SECOND CITIZEN It was an answer. How apply you this?   130
MENENIUS The senators of Rome are this good belly
         And you the mutinous members. For examine
         Their counsels and their cares, digest things rightly
         Touching the weal o'th'common, you shall find
         No public benefit which you receive   135
         But it proceeds or comes from them to you
         And no way from yourselves. What do you think?
         You, the great toe of this assembly?

Menenius mocks the Second Citizen, then prophesies a civil war, patricians versus plebeians. Caius Martius delivers a stream of invective against the plebeians, accusing them of cowardice and inconsistency.

1 A change of tone

Menenius' apparently friendly tone towards the plebeians now changes. He began by calling them 'my countrymen', 'my good friends', and told them the tale of the belly. He now directly insults them as 'rats' who will soon be at war with Rome (the patricians).

Why does Menenius' tone change in lines 144–6? Has he seen Caius Martius approaching? Make your own suggestion and advise Menenius how to speak the three lines. For example, might they be spoken as an aside, unheard by the plebeians?

2 Coriolanus: 'choleric and impatient'
(in small groups)

Shakespeare found the story of Coriolanus (Caius Martius) in the writings of the Roman historian, Plutarch (see page 245). There, he read that Caius Martius 'was so choleric (full of anger) and impatient that he would yield to no living creature, which made him churlish, uncivil, and altogether unfit for any man's conversation'.

Shakespeare provides Martius with language to match Plutarch's description. Lines 147–71 are a tirade of scornful abuse against the plebeians. To gain an impression of Martius' character, take turns to speak the lines. Emphasise every insulting word, and try to bring out the swaying rhythm of the many antitheses (opposing words or phrases): peace/war, affrights/proud, lions/hares, and so on. You can find more on page 238 about how Shakespeare uses antithesis to intensify dramatic effect.

---

rascal ... vantage low-bred dog, leading the pack for gain
have bale be destroyed
dissentious revolting
abhorring repugnance, hatred
curs worthless dogs

offence subdues him wrongdoing is punished
affections desires
hews cuts, chops
rushes grass-like plants
garland hero
rates price

SECOND CITIZEN I the great toe? Why the great toe?
MENENIUS For that being one o'th'lowest, basest, poorest   140
    Of this most wise rebellion, thou goest foremost.
    Thou rascal, that art worst in blood to run,
    Lead'st first to win some vantage.
    But make you ready your stiff bats and clubs.
    Rome and her rats are at the point of battle;   145
    The one side must have bale.

             Enter CAIUS MARTIUS

                Hail, noble Martius!
MARTIUS Thanks. What's the matter, you dissentious rogues,
    That, rubbing the poor itch of your opinion,
    Make yourselves scabs?
SECOND CITIZEN   We have ever your good word.
MARTIUS He that will give good words to thee will flatter   150
    Beneath abhorring. What would you have, you curs,
    That like nor peace nor war? The one affrights you,
    The other makes you proud. He that trusts to you,
    Where he should find you lions finds you hares,
    Where foxes, geese you are – no surer, no,   155
    Than is the coal of fire upon the ice,
    Or hailstone in the sun. Your virtue is
    To make him worthy whose offence subdues him
    And curse that justice did it. Who deserves greatness
    Deserves your hate, and your affections are   160
    A sick man's appetite, who desires most that
    Which would increase his evil. He that depends
    Upon your favours swims with fins of lead
    And hews down oaks with rushes. Hang ye! Trust ye?
    With every minute you do change a mind   165
    And call him noble that was now your hate,
    Him vile that was your garland. What's the matter,
    That in these several places of the city
    You cry against the noble senate, who,
    Under the gods, keep you in awe, which else   170
    Would feed on one another? [*To Menenius*] What's their
      seeking?
MENENIUS For corn at their own rates, whereof they say
    The city is well stored.

Martius expresses contempt for the plebeians and wishes he could slaughter them. He is angered that they have been granted official representatives, and predicts that civil strife will result.

1 Expressing contempt

To help you speak all Martius' lines, use the following comments by an actor who played Coriolanus:

'Martius (Coriolanus) sees his class privilege under attack, and is so choked by his fury that he often struggles to find the right word to express his raging contempt. I paused before certain words ("cobbled", "shreds", "vulgar wisdoms", "fragments"), as if I were searching for a suitably offensive word. And I suggest certain tones of voice:

lines 173–9: Martius is disgusted that the plebeians dare to discuss affairs of state. [A disdainful sing-song style as you list each element.]

lines 180–3: Martius wishes he could kill the plebeians.
[A tone of savage anger.]

lines 187–92: Martius ridicules the proverbs used by the plebeians. To him, they are only childish slogans. [A sneering tone.]

lines 192–7: Martius is outraged that the plebeians have been granted tribunes. He thinks this concession will finally kill off the nobility ('break the heart of generosity') because it is a step towards democracy.
[Use a tone of amazement at the very thought of the plebeians' petition being granted, together with scorn for their joy.]

lines 198–200: Martius probably names Junius Brutus and Sicinius Velutus with great distaste, and he disdains to remember the names of the other tribunes. [A tone of dismissive ridicule.]

lines 201–4: Martius would rather see Rome destroyed ('unroofed the city') than grant any degree of democracy. He sees trouble ahead as the plebeians further undermine the patricians' power. [A tone of menace.]

---

side factions take sides with political groups
Conjectural marriages supposed alliances
ruth pity
quarry heap of slaughtered deer
quartered chopped-up

passing exceedingly
shreds feeble proverbs, soundbites
emulation triumph
'Sdeath God's death (an oath)
Win upon gain more
insurrection's arguing rebels to debate

MARTIUS   Hang 'em! They say?
        They'll sit by th'fire and presume to know
        What's done i'th'Capitol, who's like to rise,   175
        Who thrives and who declines; side factions and give out
        Conjectural marriages, making parties strong
        And feebling such as stand not in their liking
        Below their cobbled shoes. They say there's grain enough!
        Would the nobility lay aside their ruth   180
        And let me use my sword, I'd make a quarry
        With thousands of these quartered slaves as high
        As I could pitch my lance.
MENENIUS Nay, these are almost thoroughly persuaded,
        For though abundantly they lack discretion,   185
        Yet are they passing cowardly. But I beseech you,
        What says the other troop?
MARTIUS   They are dissolved. Hang 'em!
        They said they were an-hungry, sighed forth proverbs –
        That hunger broke stone walls, that dogs must eat,
        That meat was made for mouths, that the gods sent not   190
        Corn for the rich men only. With these shreds
        They vented their complainings, which being answered
        And a petition granted them – a strange one,
        To break the heart of generosity
        And make bold power look pale – they threw their caps   195
        As they would hang them on the horns o'th'moon,
        Shouting their emulation.
MENENIUS   What is granted them?
MARTIUS Five tribunes to defend their vulgar wisdoms,
        Of their own choice. One's Junius Brutus,
        Sicinius Velutus, and I know not. 'Sdeath,   200
        The rabble should have first unroofed the city
        Ere so prevailed with me! It will in time
        Win upon power and throw forth greater themes
        For insurrection's arguing.
MENENIUS This is strange.   205
MARTIUS [*To the Citizens*] Go get you home, you fragments.

                    Enter a MESSENGER *hastily*

MESSENGER Where's Caius Martius?
MARTIUS   Here. What's the matter?

15

Martius rejoices at the prospect of war with the Volsces. He praises their leader, Aufidius, and looks forward to fighting him. He is appointed second-in-command to Cominius.

1 Blood-letting (in pairs)

Martius' image in lines 209–10 – 'we shall ha' means to vent our musty superfluity' – literally means 'we will have ways of getting rid of the surplus of our old rotten corn'. But Martius is thinking of the rebellious citizens of Rome, and expressing the belief that war is like a medicine that cleanses society, killing off the excess population.

The image echoes a popular medical practice in Shakespeare's time: blood-letting. Doctors drained blood from a sick person, believing that an excess of blood caused the illness. Invent some actions with which Martius can accompany his words to show that he thinks the blood of the plebeians must be shed to purge the Roman state.

2 Irony?

Consider Martius' probable attitude to each named character who enters at line 210. Decide if he speaks 'See, our best elders' ironically.

3 Titus Lartius, a willing soldier?

In some productions, Lartius is played as physically disabled. Suggest other ways of portraying him that would justify Martius' line 225.

4 'Hence to your homes, begone'

Lines 232 and 206 echo similar commands in Act 1 Scene 1 of *Julius Caesar*. There, too, patricians order away an unruly crowd of Roman citizens. But what have the crowd been doing during the exchange between Martius and his fellow nobles? Advise the citizens how to behave during lines 210–32.

Volsces (usually pronounced 'Volskis')
vent get rid of
best elders chief statesmen
put you to't test your bravery

by th'ears locked in battle
Stand'st out? will you not come?
true bred natural fighter
priority deserve to lead

MESSENGER The news is, sir, the Volsces are in arms.
MARTIUS I am glad on't; then we shall ha' means to vent
    Our musty superfluity.

Enter SICINIUS VELUTUS, JUNIUS BRUTUS, COMINIUS,
    TITUS LARTIUS, *with other* SENATORS

              See, our best elders.   210
FIRST SENATOR Martius, 'tis true that you have lately told us:
    The Volsces are in arms.
MARTIUS   They have a leader,
    Tullus Aufidius, that will put you to't.
    I sin in envying his nobility,
    And were I any thing but what I am,   215
    I would wish me only he.
COMINIUS   You have fought together!
MARTIUS Were half to half the world by th'ears and he
    Upon my party, I'd revolt to make
    Only my wars with him. He is a lion
    That I am proud to hunt.
FIRST SENATOR   Then, worthy Martius,   220
    Attend upon Cominius to these wars.
COMINIUS It is your former promise.
MARTIUS   Sir, it is,
    And I am constant. Titus Lartius, thou
    Shalt see me once more strike at Tullus' face.
    What, art thou stiff? Stand'st out?
LARTIUS   No, Caius Martius.   225
    I'll lean upon one crutch and fight with t'other
    Ere stay behind this business.
MENENIUS   O true bred!
A SENATOR Your company to th'Capitol, where I know
    Our greatest friends attend us.
LARTIUS [*To Cominius*]   Lead you on.
    [*To Martius*] Follow Cominius. We must follow you,   230
    Right worthy you priority.
COMINIUS   Noble Martius!
A SENATOR [*To the Citizens*]
    Hence to your homes, begone.

Martius sneers at the citizens' cowardice. He departs for the war.
The two tribunes comment on Martius' pride and how the war will boost
his reputation over that of Cominius.

1 Yet more contempt (in pairs)

Martius once again insults the citizens. Identify a word or phrase in
each of lines 232–5 that he can load with heavy irony or contempt, then
take turns to speak the lines.

2 'Citizens steal away'

At the stage direction (line 235), just how do the citizens 'steal away'?
Step into role as director and write one or two paragraphs for the actors
playing the citizens, advising how and why they might leave the stage
(remember that they know that they must fight in the forthcoming
war).

3 Lip, eyes, taunts (in pairs)

Use line 239 to help you demonstrate to your partner just what Martius
did and said when Sicinius and Brutus were made tribunes to represent
the citizens' rights.

4 First impressions of the tribunes (in pairs)

The two tribunes say that whether Cominius succeeds or fails in the
war, the result will improve Coriolanus' reputation and honour. Some
critics have described the tribunes as devious politicians, whose words
are not to be trusted, but there are other views of them (see page 235).

To gain a first impression of Sicinius and Brutus, take parts and
experiment with different ways of speaking lines 236–63.

---

gnaw their garners eat the
Volsces' corn stores
spare to gird refrain from
sneering at
Tickled flattered, stirred up
brook bear, submit
miscarries goes wrong

th'utmost the highest achievement
giddy censure fickle public opinion
Opinion public opinion
aught anything
dispatch preparations and
departure for war
singularity usual pride

MARTIUS   Nay, let them follow.
        The Volsces have much corn; take these rats thither
        To gnaw their garners. Worshipful mutineers,
        Your valour puts well forth. Pray follow.   235

        Citizens steal away. [Exeunt all but] Sicinius and Brutus

SICINIUS Was ever man so proud as is this Martius?
BRUTUS He has no equal.
SICINIUS When we were chosen tribunes for the people –
BRUTUS Marked you his lip and eyes?
SICINIUS   Nay, but his taunts.
BRUTUS Being moved, he will not spare to gird the gods.   240
SICINIUS Bemock the modest moon.
BRUTUS The present wars devour him! He is grown
        Too proud to be so valiant.
SICINIUS   Such a nature,
        Tickled with good success, disdains the shadow
        Which he treads on at noon. But I do wonder   245
        His insolence can brook to be commanded
        Under Cominius.
BRUTUS   Fame, at the which he aims,
        In whom already he's well graced, cannot
        Better be held nor more attained than by
        A place below the first; for what miscarries   250
        Shall be the general's fault, though he perform
        To th'utmost of a man, and giddy censure
        Will then cry out of Martius 'O, if he
        Had borne the business!'
SICINIUS   Besides, if things go well,
        Opinion, that so sticks on Martius, shall   255
        Of his demerits rob Cominius.
BRUTUS   Come,
        Half all Cominius' honours are to Martius,
        Though Martius earned them not; and all his faults
        To Martius shall be honours, though indeed
        In aught he merit not.
SICINIUS   Let's hence, and hear   260
        How the dispatch is made and in what fashion,
        More than his singularity, he goes
        Upon this present action.
BRUTUS   Let's along.   *Exeunt*

19

Aufidius is convinced that Rome has spies among the Volsces. His own spy reports in a letter that the Roman army is advancing on Corioles. He is appointed general of the Volsce army.

1 Stage the scene (in small groups)

Scene 2 has only 41 lines. Work out how to stage the scene to greatest dramatic effect. In some productions the Volsces enter and leave in a ritual procession, and Aufidius is appointed general of the army ('Take your commission', line 26) with elaborate ceremony.

2 Costume and set design (in pairs)

Design costumes and set for the scene. Some productions portray the Volsces in the traditional image of Romans, with togas, and so on. But one production showed them like Aztec warriors, dressed in elaborate feathered costumes, who held their meetings around a blazing fire (see page 251).

3 Campaign map

Use lines 12–33 and the map on page 3 to help you draw a map that shows the planned military campaigns of the Volsces and the Romans.

4 A back-up letter from a spy

Spying is a recurring feature of the play. The first 24 lines show that both the Romans and the Volsces have spies, reporting on their opponents' military preparations. For example, 'are entered in our counsels' (line 2) means 'have spies here'.

In lines 9–17, Aufidius reads the letter from his spy. Sometimes spies write a second ('back-up') letter, giving the same information but using different words. Step into role as Aufidius' spy and write your 'back-up' letter.

---

circumvention knowledge of how to prevent
pressed a power recruited an army
dearth famine
Whither 'tis bent wherever it is going
in the field ready for battle
great pretences major plans
hatching preparing
take in capture
afoot moving
hie you … bands go swiftly to your troops
set down before's besiege us
remove raising of the siege

ACT 1 SCENE 2
Corioles: the Senate House

Enter TULLUS AUFIDIUS with SENATORS of Corioles

FIRST SENATOR So, your opinion is, Aufidius,
    That they of Rome are entered in our counsels
    And know how we proceed.
AUFIDIUS   Is it not yours?
    What ever have been thought on in this state
    That could be brought to bodily act ere Rome   5
    Had circumvention? 'Tis not four days gone
    Since I heard thence. These are the words – I think
    I have the letter here; yes, here it is:
    [*Reads*] 'They have pressed a power, but it is not known
    Whether for east or west. The dearth is great,   10
    The people mutinous. And it is rumoured
    Cominius, Martius your old enemy,
    Who is of Rome worse hated than of you,
    And Titus Lartius, a most valiant Roman,
    These three lead on this preparation   15
    Whither 'tis bent. Most likely 'tis for you.
    Consider of it.'
FIRST SENATOR   Our army's in the field.
    We never yet made doubt but Rome was ready
    To answer us.
AUFIDIUS   Nor did you think it folly
    To keep your great pretences veiled till when   20
    They needs must show themselves, which in the hatching,
    It seemed, appeared to Rome. By the discovery
    We shall be shortened in our aim, which was
    To take in many towns ere, almost, Rome
    Should know we were afoot.
FIRST SENATOR   Noble Aufidius,   25
    Take your commission; hie you to your bands.
    Let us alone to guard Corioles.
    If they set down before's, for the remove
    Bring up your army; but, I think, you'll find
    They've not prepared for us.

Aufidius vows to fight with Martius to the death. In Scene 3, Volumnia wishes that Virgilia would be more cheerful, and tells how happily she sent Martius to battle when he was very young.

1 What are Aufidius' feelings about Martius?

Scene 2 makes clear the political and military antagonism of the Volsces and the Romans, and the personal rivalry of Aufidius and Martius (Coriolanus). Identify all the references to Martius in the scene and advise the actor playing Aufidius about how he might express his attitude to Martius (is it bitter, heart-felt enmity, or ...?).

2 Volumnia: a Roman mother (in pairs)

In contrast to the exclusively male atmosphere of Scenes 1 and 2, so much concerned with conflict, Scene 3 presents the women of the play in a domestic setting. Coriolanus' mother and wife sit, sewing.

What view of Volumnia do you gain from her first speech? Try speaking lines 1–14 calmly and quietly, then passionately and emphatically. To help you understand what qualities she values most highly, think especially how she might emphasise 'honour' (lines 3 and 8), 'love' (line 4), 'cruel war' (line 11), 'man' (line 14).

3 Coriolanus' childhood (in small groups)

Volumnia's story of how she brought up her son can help you understand why Martius is like he is. In lines 9–10 ('that it ... stir') she says that such boys as her son should not hang 'picture-like' (a mere ornament), but should be moved to action to gain honour and fame. So, 'to a cruel war I sent him'. As you read on, you will find other clues suggesting how Coriolanus' upbringing has shaped his character.

Talk together about your own views on how childhood experiences influences adult personality. Try to give modern examples that support your viewpoint.

---

parcels advance units
only hitherward towards us here
comfortable sort cheerful manner
comeliness beauty
plucked all gaze attracted everyone's eyes
entreaties begging

become such a person adorn his beauty
renown ... stir it was not moved to action by fame
bound with oak encircled with oak-leaves (the reward for saving a Roman's life in battle)

AUFIDIUS   O, doubt not that;   30
        I speak from certainties. Nay, more,
        Some parcels of their power are forth already,
        And only hitherward. I leave your honours.
        If we and Caius Martius chance to meet,
        'Tis sworn between us we shall ever strike   35
        Till one can do no more.
ALL SENATORS The gods assist you!
AUFIDIUS And keep your honours safe.
FIRST SENATOR Farewell.
SECOND SENATOR Farewell.   40
ALL Farewell.

            Exeunt [Aufidius at one door, Senators at another door]

ACT 1   SCENE 3
Rome: the house of Volumnia

Enter VOLUMNIA *and* VIRGILIA, *mother and wife to Martius.*
They set them down on two low stools and sew.

VOLUMNIA I pray you, daughter, sing, or express yourself in a more
    comfortable sort. If my son were my husband, I should freelier
    rejoice in that absence wherein he won honour than in the
    embracements of his bed where he would show most love. When
    yet he was but tender-bodied and the only son of my womb, when   5
    youth with comeliness plucked all gaze his way, when for a day of
    kings' entreaties a mother should not sell him an hour from her
    beholding, I, considering how honour would become such a
    person – that it was no better than picture-like to hang by th'wall, if
    renown made it not stir – was pleased to let him seek danger where   10
    he was like to find fame. To a cruel war I sent him, from whence he
    returned, his brows bound with oak. I tell thee, daughter, I sprang
    not more in joy at first hearing he was a man-child than now in first
    seeing he had proved himself a man.
VIRGILIA But had he died in the business, madam, how then?   15

Volumnia says she would prefer to have many sons killed in battle than one to live in sensual luxury. She imagines Martius killing Volsces and conquering Aufidius. Valeria asks after Virgilia's son.

1 Like mother, like son?

Volumnia's language provides many clues to what she and her son are like. Identify how the following lines express the shared values of Volumnia and Martius (Coriolanus):

line 16: concern for honour

line 20: disgust at idle pleasure and self-indulgence

lines 25–6: joy in bravery in battle

lines 27–9: contempt for plebeian soldiers

lines 30–2: glory in destruction and death (the image is of a harvestman who must mow an entire field or lose his wages)

lines 34–8: pride in wounds received in battle (her image is from Greek mythology: Hecuba was the Queen of Troy. Her son, Hector, was killed in the siege of Troy.)

Keep these values in mind as you work through the play, to find how each of them influences what happens to Volumnia and Coriolanus.

2 Does she hesitate? (in pairs)

Is Volumnia callous, totally without a mother's feelings at the prospect of her son's death? Explore different ways of speaking her lines. You might begin by speaking without any hesitation in a 'stiff upper lip' style. Then try putting in pauses to suggest that she searches for words to cover feelings she does not wish to show.

---

issue children
voluptuously surfeit over-indulge in bodily pleasure
shunning fleeing from
got conceived
Jupiter (in Roman mythology) king of the gods

gilt his trophy cover his monument with gold
contemning contemptuously
fell cruel
manifest housekeepers obvious stay-at-homes
spot embroidered pattern

VOLUMNIA Then his good report should have been my son. I therein
would have found issue. Hear me profess sincerely: had I a dozen
sons each in my love alike, and none less dear than thine and my
good Martius, I had rather had eleven die nobly for their country
than one voluptuously surfeit out of action.   20

Enter a GENTLEWOMAN

GENTLEWOMAN Madam, the Lady Valeria is come to visit you.
VIRGILIA Beseech you, give me leave to retire myself.
VOLUMNIA Indeed you shall not.
    Methinks I hear hither your husband's drum;
    See him pluck Aufidius down by th'hair;   25
    As children from a bear, the Volsces shunning him.
    Methinks I see him stamp thus, and call thus:
    'Come on, you cowards! You were got in fear,
    Though you were born in Rome.' His bloody brow
    With his mailed hand then wiping, forth he goes,   30
    Like to a harvestman that's tasked to mow
    Or all or lose his hire.
VIRGILIA His bloody brow? O Jupiter, no blood!
VOLUMNIA Away, you fool! It more becomes a man
    Than gilt his trophy. The breasts of Hecuba,   35
    When she did suckle Hector, looked not lovelier
    Than Hector's forehead when it spit forth blood
    At Grecian sword, contemning. [*To the Gentlewoman*] Tell
      Valeria
    We are fit to bid her welcome.

Exit Gent [lewoman]

VIRGILIA Heavens bless my lord from fell Aufidius!   40
VOLUMNIA He'll beat Aufidius' head below his knee
    And tread upon his neck

Enter VALERIA *with an Usher, and a Gentlewoman*

VALERIA My ladies both, good day to you.
VOLUMNIA Sweet madam.
VIRGILIA I am glad to see your ladyship.   45
VALERIA How do you both? You are manifest housekeepers. What are
you sewing here? A fine spot, in good faith. How does your little
son?
VIRGILIA I thank your ladyship; well, good madam.

Volumnia and Valeria reveal that young Martius shares his father's liking for war and destruction. Virgilia refuses all entreaties to go visiting. Valeria has news of Martius.

1 Young Martius: like father, like son (in small groups)

Valeria's tale of how young Martius savagely destroyed a butterfly confirms her claim that the boy is 'the father's son', a chip off the old block. Imagine you are directing the play, and have decided to have young Martius on stage throughout this scene. Talk together about how you think he should behave and how he might be dressed. Use lines 50–8 as an indication of his character.

2 Valeria: a fashionable gossip? Or …? (in pairs)

In many productions Valeria is played as a light-hearted gossip who uses the affected speech style of a fashionable lady, for example, in her use of 'la' in lines 60 and 80. Later in the play you will discover that Coriolanus describes her very differently (see page 234).

Experiment with different ways of speaking Valeria's lines to discover your own preferred style of presenting her character.

3 'Another Penelope'

In lines 75–6, Valeria uses an image from Greek mythology. She compares Virgilia (who has sworn not to leave the house until Martius returns) to Penelope, the faithful wife of Ulysses. He left his home in Ithaca for the Trojan wars. During his absence, she refused to marry any of her many suitors ('moths' = parasites) until she had finished weaving a shroud. Each night she unpicked her weaving to ensure that she would never finish. Her name became the symbol of the faithful wife.

Keep Penelope in mind as you think about Virgilia's character. Why is she so determined to refuse Valeria's invitation?

O'my troth on my truth (honestly)
confirmed countenance
 determined look
mammocked tore to shreds

crack young rascal
lies in expects a baby
cambric fine linen

VOLUMNIA He had rather see the swords and hear a drum than look   50
upon his schoolmaster.
VALERIA O'my word, the father's son! I'll swear 'tis a very pretty boy.
O'my troth, I looked upon him o'Wednesday half an hour together.
'Has such a confirmed countenance! I saw him run after a gilded
butterfly, and when he caught it, he let it go again, and after it   55
again, and over and over he comes, and up again, catched it again.
Or whether his fall enraged him, or how 'twas, he did so set his
teeth and tear it. O, I warrant, how he mammocked it!
VOLUMNIA One on's father's moods.
VALERIA Indeed, la, 'tis a noble child.   60
VIRGILIA A crack, madam.
VALERIA Come, lay aside your stitchery. I must have you play the idle
huswife with me this afternoon.
VIRGILIA No, good madam, I will not out of doors.
VALERIA Not out of doors?   65
VOLUMNIA She shall, she shall.
VIRGILIA Indeed, no, by your patience. I'll not over the threshold till
my lord return from the wars.
VALERIA Fie, you confine yourself most unreasonably. Come, you
must go visit the good lady that lies in.   70
VIRGILIA I will wish her speedy strength and visit her with my prayers,
but I cannot go thither.
VOLUMNIA Why, I pray you?
VIRGILIA 'Tis not to save labour, nor that I want love.
VALERIA You would be another Penelope. Yet they say all the yarn she   75
spun in Ulysses' absence did but fill Ithaca full of moths. Come,
I would your cambric were sensible as your finger, that you might
leave pricking it for pity. Come, you shall go with us.
VIRGILIA No, good madam, pardon me; indeed I will not forth.
VALERIA In truth, la, go with me, and I'll tell you excellent news of   80
your husband.
VIRGILIA O, good madam, there can be none yet.
VALERIA Verily, I do not jest with you. There came news from him last
night.
VIRGILIA Indeed, madam?   85

Valeria reports that Martius is besieging Corioles and expects an early victory. Virgilia resists another invitation to leave the house. Martius and Lartius bet on whether Cominius has fought with the Volsces.

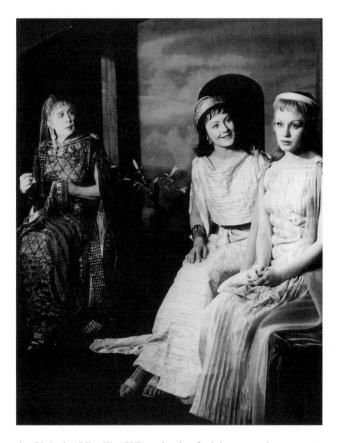

Volumnia, Valeria, Virgilia. What do the facial expressions suggest about the different personalities of the three women? How closely does this portrayal match the impression of the characters you have formed from reading the script?

power army
set down before besieging
nothing doubt prevailing are confident of victory
disease our better mirth spoil our pleasure
troth truth

at a word briefly, once and for all
Colours flags
wager bet
they have met Cominius has fought the Volsces
Summon blow a trumpet call to alert (see line 13)

VALERIA In earnest, it's true. I heard a senator speak it. Thus it is: the Volsces have an army forth, against whom Cominius the general is gone with one part of our Roman power. Your lord and Titus Lartius are set down before their city Corioles. They nothing doubt prevailing and to make it brief wars. This is true, on mine honour, and so, I pray, go with us. 90

VIRGILIA Give me excuse, good madam. I will obey you in everything hereafter.

VOLUMNIA Let her alone, lady. As she is now, she will but disease our better mirth. 95

VALERIA In troth, I think she would. Fare you well, then. Come, good sweet lady. Prithee, Virgilia, turn thy solemnness out o'door and go along with us.

VIRGILIA No, at a word, madam. Indeed, I must not. I wish you much mirth. 100

VALERIA Well then, farewell.

Exeunt

ACT 1 SCENE 4
Corioles: before the gates

Enter MARTIUS, TITUS LARTIUS, with Drummer, Trumpeter, and Colours, with Captains and Soldiers

A MESSENGER approaches

MARTIUS Yonder comes news. A wager they have met.
LARTIUS My horse to yours, no.
MARTIUS   'Tis done.
LARTIUS   Agreed.
MARTIUS Say, has our general met the enemy?
MESSENGER They lie in view, but have not spoke as yet.
LARTIUS So, the good horse is mine.
MARTIUS   I'll buy him of you. 5
LARTIUS No, I'll nor sell nor give him. Lend you him I will
          For half a hundred years. [*To the Trumpeter*] Summon the
          town.

Martius prays to Mars for quick success in the battle. The Volsce Senator defies and taunts Martius and the Romans. Martius orders an advance, but the Volsces drive the Romans back.

1 Staging the battle (in large groups)

Scenes 4–10 portray the war between Rome and the Volsces. As Valeria reported at the end of Scene 3, the Romans have divided into two armies. One, under Cominius, fights the Volsces at a place about a mile and a half from Corioles (reported by the Messenger in line 9, and heard in lines 16 and 20). The other Roman army, commanded by Martius and Lartius, is on stage, facing the walls of the city of Corioles.

Every modern production of the play tries to stage the battle action as thrillingly as possible, even with few actors, limited stage space, and lack of resources to create a realistic set. Work out how you would stage the action of Scene 4 (if you have time, include the other battle scenes). Remember, your audience must be able to hear what is said and understand what is happening. Use the following to help you.

- Design the set to show the gates of Corioles.
- How will you show the fighting: realistically or symbolically (slow motion, as tableaux, and so on)? Remember that safety is the first rule of stage combat.
- How can you represent an army with only a few actors?
- *Alarum* can mean trumpet calls or the noise of battles and skirmishes. What sound effects can you use?
- Consider each stage direction in turn, and work out how you might stage it.
- Add your own stage directions (for example, in Martius' lines 24–30 you might perform different actions at the end of each sentence).

Mars (in Roman mythology) the god of war
smoking blood-stained
fielded friends allies in the other battlefield
parley trumpet-call to negotiation
pound us up enclose us (as in a cattle pound)

pinned with rushes locked only with grass
List listen to
cloven divided
our instruction be a lesson to us
proof strong, impenetrable
mine edge my sword

MARTIUS How far off lie these armies?

MESSENGER Within this mile and half.

MARTIUS Then shall we hear their 'larum, and they ours.   10
　　　　Now, Mars, I prithee make us quick in work,
　　　　That we with smoking swords may march from hence
　　　　To help our fielded friends! Come, blow thy blast.

They sound a parley.
Enter two SENATORS *with others on the walls of Corioles*

　　　　Tullus Aufidius, is he within your walls?

FIRST SENATOR No, nor a man that fears you less than he: 15
　　　　That's lesser than a little.

Drum afar off

　　　　　　　　Hark, our drums
　　　　Are bringing forth our youth. We'll break our walls
　　　　Rather than they shall pound us up. Our gates,
　　　　Which yet seem shut, we have but pinned with rushes;
　　　　They'll open of themselves.

Alarum far off

　　　　　　　　　　Hark you, far off!   20
　　　　There is Aufidius. List what work he makes
　　　　Amongst your cloven army.

MARTIUS   O, they are at it!

LARTIUS Their noise be our instruction. Ladders, ho!

Enter the army of the Volsces [from the gates]

MARTIUS They fear us not, but issue forth their city.
　　　　Now put your shields before your hearts and fight   25
　　　　With hearts more proof than shields. Advance, brave Titus.
　　　　They do disdain us much beyond our thoughts,
　　　　Which makes me sweat with wrath. Come on, my fellows!
　　　　He that retires, I'll take him for a Volsce,
　　　　And he shall feel mine edge.   30

Alarum. The Romans are beat back to their trenches

Enter MARTIUS, *cursing*

Martius curses his soldiers for their cowardice. He enters Corioles alone and is shut in. The soldiers comment sardonically on his fate. Lartius praises Martius' bravery.

1 How to motivate soldiers? (in small groups)

Martius wants to rally his retreating soldiers, and to motivate them to attack the Volsces once more. Another of Shakespeare's 'heroes', King Henry V, found himself in the same situation, trying to encourage his troops to attack a besieged town once again.

Take turns to speak Martius' lines 31–46 and the extracts from King Henry's lines below. Then prepare a presentation of the two speeches to bring out the ways in which they differ from each other and the effects they would have on you if you were soldiers in either army.

> Once more unto the breach, dear friends, once more,
> Or close the wall up with our English dead!
> In peace there's nothing so becomes a man
> As modest stillness and humility,
> But when the blast of war blows in our ears
> Then imitate the action of the tiger:
> Stiffen the sinews, conjure up the blood,
> Disguise fair nature with hard-favoured rage.
> … I see you stand like greyhounds in the slips,
> Straining upon the start. The game's afoot.
> Follow your spirit, and upon this charge
> Cry 'God for Harry, England and Saint George!'

2 *Martius is shut in*

The soldiers think that Martius will be killed because he is now trapped inside Corioles. 'To th'pot' means 'to the cooking pot' (he's in the soup, his goose is cooked). Work out how you would stage Martius being 'shut in' at line 48.

---

south south wind
 (thought to bring plagues)
Pluto (in Greek mythology) the god
 of Hades (hell)
agued fear shivering in fright
Mend and charge home turn
 round and attack

seconds supporters, followers
fliers retreating soldiers
sensibly courageously
carbuncle entire perfect
 blood-coloured precious stone
Cato (historian who praised
 traditional Roman virtues)

MARTIUS All the contagion of the south light on you,
You shames of Rome! You herd of – boils and plagues
Plaster you o're, that you may be abhorred
Farther than seen, and one infect another
Against the wind a mile! You souls of geese   35
That bear the shapes of men, how have you run
From slaves that apes would beat! Pluto and hell!
All hurt behind: backs red, and faces pale
With flight and agued fear! Mend and charge home,
Or by the fires of heaven, I'll leave the foe   40
And make my wars on you! Look to't. Come on!
If you'll stand fast, we'll beat them to their wives,
As they us to our trenches. Follow!
Another alarum. [The Volsces fly,] and Martius follows them
to [the] gates
So, now the gates are ope. Now prove good seconds!
'Tis for the followers fortune widens them,   45
Not for the fliers. Mark me, and do the like.

Enters the gates

FIRST SOLDIER Foolhardiness! Not I.
SECOND SOLDIER Nor I.
            [Martius] is shut in. Alarum continues
FIRST SOLDIER See, they have shut him in.
ALL To th'pot, I warrant him.   50

Enter TITUS LARTIUS

LARTIUS What is become of Martius?
ALL SOLDIERS Slain, sir, doubtless.
FIRST SOLDIER Following the fliers at the very heels,
With them he enters, who upon the sudden
Clapped to their gates. He is himself alone,   55
To answer all the city.
LARTIUS   O noble fellow!
Who sensibly outdares his senseless sword
And, when it bows, stand'st up. Thou art lost, Martius.
A carbuncle entire, as big as thou art,
Were not so rich a jewel. Thou wast a soldier   60
Even to Cato's wish, not fierce and terrible
Only in strokes, but with thy grim looks and
The thunder-like percussion of thy sounds

33

Martius reappears, wounded but still fighting. The Romans follow him into Corioles. In Scene 5, Martius is disgusted by the soldiers' looting. He orders Lartius to guard the city while he goes to help Cominius.

1 A funeral oration?

Lartius thinks Martius is dead, and praises his military qualities. Speak lines 56–65 then advise the actor how they might be delivered on stage (to the audience? very formally, or …?)

2 Single-handed! (in groups of any size)

Martius' reappearance, apparently from the dead, makes an intensely exciting moment of theatre and is usually staged with great spectacle. In one production he appeared drenched from head to foot in blood. In another, he appeared at the top of the walls, forcing apart the huge gates of the city. In a modern dress production, he clung to the hook of a giant crane which lifted him over the walls. He fired his rifle at the Volsces and threw grenades, blasting a breach in the city walls through which the Roman army charged.

Work out how you would stage the stage directions at lines 65 and 68. There are all kinds of technical problems to resolve. For example, how does he manage to open the city gates, yet still fight with the Volsces ('assaulted by the enemy')?

3 Looting: a dramatic contrast (in small groups)

After Martius' heroics in Scene 4, Scene 5 opens with Roman soldiers emerging from Corioles carrying off their loot. Martius is contemptuous of the looters, saying they steal worthless things. His words echo a practice common in Shakespeare's time: the hangman was entitled to keep the clothes of the person he executed.

Brainstorm a number of reasons why Shakespeare chose to open Scene 5 in this way.

---

fetch him off rescue him
make remain alike share his fate
spoils loot, plunder
murrain on't plague on it
movers removers (looters)
prize their hours value their time
cracked drachma worthless coin

Irons of a doit weapons of little value
doublets jackets
Convenient sufficient
make good secure
the spirit courage

Thou mad'st thine enemies shake, as if the world
Were feverous and did tremble.   65

Enter MARTIUS, *bleeding, assaulted by the enemy*

FIRST SOLDIER Look, sir.
LARTIUS O! 'tis Martius!
       Let's fetch him off, or make remain alike.
They fight, and all enter the city

ACT 1   SCENE 5
Corioles: before the gates

Enter certain ROMANS, *with spoils*

FIRST ROMAN This will I carry to Rome.
SECOND ROMAN And I this.
THIRD ROMAN A murrain on't! I took this for silver.
       Alarum continues still afar off

Enter MARTIUS, *and* TITUS [LARTIUS] *with a Trumpet[er]*

Exeunt [looters]

MARTIUS See here these movers that do prize their hours
       At a cracked drachma! Cushions, leaden spoons,   5
       Irons of a doit, doublets that hangmen would
       Bury with those that wore them, these base slaves,
       Ere yet the fight be done, pack up. Down with them!
            [Alarum continues]
       And hark, what noise the general makes! To him!
       There is the man of my soul's hate, Aufidius,   10
       Piercing our Romans. Then, valiant Titus, take
       Convenient numbers to make good the city,
       Whilst I with those that have the spirit will haste
       To help Cominius.
LARTIUS   Worthy sir, thou bleed'st.
       Thy exercise hath been too violent   15
       For a second course of fight.

Martius claims that fighting has refreshed, not tired him. He leaves to join Cominius' battle against Aufidius. In Scene 6, Cominius rallies his men and prays for the success of both Roman armies.

1 Change of scene (in small groups)

Scene 5 ends with Martius leaving Corioles. Scene 6 opens at a place just over one mile away, where Cominius and his troops are taking a brief rest in their fiercely fought battle. Work out how you would manage the scene change on a stage of your own design.

2 Motivating the troops: a contrast (in pairs)

First, remind yourselves of how Martius 'motivated' his soldiers in Scene 4 lines 31–43. Then one person speaks Cominius' lines 1–9, pausing after each sentence or short section. In the pause, the other person speaks what Coriolanus might have said in the same circumstances (for example, 'Breathe you, my friends' might become Coriolanus', 'What! Are you tired, you rats?').

3 Motivating the troops: your own response (in pairs)

Would Cominius' words motivate you to fight again? One person steps into role as a Roman soldier, the other as Cominius. As Cominius speaks lines 1–9, a short section at a time, the soldier speaks a response to each short section.

4 Three Roman generals: Cominius, Martius, Lartius

Use only what is said on the opposite page to suggest two or three words for each Roman commander which you feel describes each man's personality.

---

physical medicinal, health-giving
Prosperity success
page servant
retire retreat
Breathe you take a rest
stands defence

By interims and conveying gusts by occasional noises borne on the wind
smiling fronts good success
issued counter-attacked

MARTIUS   Sir, praise me not.
    My work hath yet not warmed me. Fare you well.
    The blood I drop is rather physical
    Than dangerous to me. To Aufidius thus
    I will appear and fight.
LARTIUS   Now the fair goddess Fortune   20
    Fall deep in love with thee, and her great charms
    Misguide thy opposers' swords! Bold gentleman,
    Prosperity be thy page!
MARTIUS   Thy friend no less
    Than those she placeth highest. So, farewell.
LARTIUS Thou worthiest Martius!   25

                         [*Exit Martius*]
    Go sound thy trumpet in the market-place.
    Call thither all the officers o'th'town,
    Where they shall know our mind. Away!

                                Exeunt

ACT 1   SCENE 6
The battlefield near Corioles

Enter COMINIUS, *as it were in retire, with Soldiers*

COMINIUS Breathe you, my friends. Well fought! We are come off
    Like Romans, neither foolish in our stands,
    Nor cowardly in retire. Believe me, sirs,
    We shall be charged again. Whiles we have struck,
    By interims and conveying gusts we have heard   5
    The charges of our friends. The Roman gods
    Lead their successes as we wish our own,
    That both our powers, with smiling fronts encountering,
    May give you thankful sacrifice!

              Enter a MESSENGER

                  Thy news?
MESSENGER The citizens of Corioles have issued   10
    And given to Lartius and to Martius battle.
    I saw our party to their trenches driven,
    And then I came away.

Cominius questions why the Messenger took so long to bring his bad news. But then Martius appears, drenched in blood. He recounts how Titus Lartius is imposing military law on Corioles

1 What really happened?

Is the Messenger telling the truth about his behaviour? Cominius is suspicious of him, and asks why he took so long to cover a fairly short distance from Corioles. Messengers in Shakespeare's plays often get badly treated. In one production, Cominius was about to strike the Messenger, but stopped when Martius appeared.

Step into role as the Messenger and speak lines 18–21 in such a way as to reveal whether or not what you are saying is the truth.

2 *Enter* Martius, *bloody* (in small groups)

Martius' entrance is another highly dramatic moment in the play. Cominius at first does not recognise him, and says that he looks as if he has been skinned alive ('flayed'). One production had Martius so drenched with blood that the audience sometimes laughed at his appearance. What audience response would you wish to evoke at this moment?

3 Imagery

Suggest why you think Shakespeare gave Martius the two following images:

lines 29–32: Greeting a fellow warrior with the same emotions he felt on his wedding night

lines 37–9: Comparing the captured city of Corioles to a fawning greyhound (flattering dog)

---

confound waste
wheel twist and turn
stamp bearing, genuine appearance
knows not thunder ...
  tabor cannot more easily
  distinguish thunder from a small
  drum

mantled clothed, covered
clip ye embrace you
nuptial wedding
tapers candles
decrees commands, orders
let him slip release him

COMINIUS   Though thou speak'st truth,
            Methinks thou speak'st not well. How long is't since?
MESSENGER Above an hour, my lord.   15
COMINIUS 'Tis not a mile; briefly we heard their drums.
            How couldst thou in a mile confound an hour
            And bring thy news so late?
MESSENGER   Spies of the Volsces
            Held me in chase, that I was forced to wheel
            Three or four miles about; else had I, sir,   20
            Half an hour since brought my report.

                    Enter MARTIUS, *bloody*

COMINIUS   Who's yonder,
            That does appear as he were flayed? O gods!
            He has the stamp of Martius, and I have
            Before-time seen him thus.
MARTIUS   Come I too late?
COMINIUS The shepherd knows not thunder from a tabor   25
            More than I know the sound of Martius' tongue
            From every meaner man.
MARTIUS   Come I too late?
COMINIUS Ay, if you come not in the blood of others
            But mantled in your own.
MARTIUS   O! Let me clip ye
            In arms as sound as when I wooed, in heart   30
            As merry as when our nuptial day was done
            And tapers burned to bedward.
                    [*They embrace*]
COMINIUS Flower of warriors! How is't with Titus Lartius?
MARTIUS As with a man busied about decrees:
            Condemning some to death and some to exile,   35
            Ransoming him or pitying, threatening th'other;
            Holding Corioles in the name of Rome
            Even like a fawning greyhound in the leash,
            To let him slip at will.
COMINIUS   Where is that slave
            Which told me they had beat you to your trenches?   40
            Where is he? Call him hither.

Martius expresses contempt for the plebeian Roman soldiers.
He begs to be sent immediately into battle against Aufidius and calls
for volunteers to join him.

1 'Gentlemen'

Who are the 'gentlemen' Martius has in mind at line 42? Are they the
soldiers who dared to follow him into Corioles at the end of Scene 4?
Or are they the Roman soldiers who refused to follow him at line 46 in
Scene 4? Or ...?

Speak 'gentlemen' in a tone of voice that shows who Martius is
thinking of.

2 Who's in charge?

Do Martius' lines 46–8 sound like a second-in-command speaking to
his commanding officer? Use your answer to suggest how Cominius
replies in lines 49–50. Then advise Martius how he might speak lines
55–62, in which he implores Cominius to let him fight Aufidius.

3 Motivating the troops: a change of style

Cominius grants Martius' request and invites him to choose the
soldiers to accompany him against Aufidius. Martius' call for volunteers
in lines 66–75 is very different from the abusive language he used
against his retreating troops in Scene 4 lines 31–41.

Identify the three appeals that Martius makes (each begins with 'if').
Express the three appeals in your own language ('painting' = blood,
'person' = body, 'ill report' = reputation). Then, before you turn the
page, make a guess as to how the soldiers will respond.

---

common file ordinary infantry
  ('rank and file')
budge fly
lords o'th'field victors of the
  battlefield
men of trust crack troops
bands i'th'vaward units in the
  vanguard

Antiates soldiers from Antium
  (Aufidius' home city)
heart of hope inspiration
darts lances, arrows
prove put to the test
balms soothing lotions
disposition determination to fight

MARTIUS   Let him alone;
          He did inform the truth. But for our gentlemen,
          The common file – a plague! Tribunes for them! –
          The mouse ne'er shunned the cat as they did budge
          From rascals worse than they.
COMINIUS   But how prevailed you?   45
MARTIUS Will the time serve to tell? I do not think.
          Where is the enemy? Are you lords o'th'field?
          If not, why cease you till you are so?
COMINIUS Martius, we have at disadvantage fought
          And did retire to win our purpose.   50
MARTIUS How lies their battle? Know you on which side
          They have placed their men of trust?
COMINIUS   As I guess, Martius,
          Their bands i'th'vaward are the Antiates
          Of their best trust; o'er them Aufidius,
          Their very heart of hope.
MARTIUS   I do beseech you,   55
          By all the battles wherein we have fought,
          By th'blood we have shed together, by th'vows we have
               made
          To endure friends, that you directly set me
          Against Aufidius and his Antiates,
          And that you not delay the present, but,   60
          Filling the air with swords advanced and darts,
          We prove this very hour.
COMINIUS   Though I could wish
          You were conducted to a gentle bath
          And balms applied to you, yet dare I never
          Deny your asking. Take your choice of those   65
          That best can aid your action.
MARTIUS   Those are they
          That most are willing. If any such be here,
          As it were sin to doubt, that love this painting
          Wherein you see me smeared; if any fear
          Lesser his person than an ill report;   70
          If any think brave death outweighs bad life,
          And that his country's dearer than himself,
          Let him alone, or so many so minded,
          Wave thus [*Waving his sword*] to express his disposition,
          And follow Martius.   75

Martius welcomes the support of the soldiers, and praises them.
He resolves to select the numbers he needs. In Scene 7, Titus Lartius
leaves Corioles to support Cominius in the coming battle.

'Make you a sword of me?' Shakespeare does not specify what words
'*They all shout*'. Suggest some appropriate language for the soldiers to
shout as they respond enthusiastically to Coriolanus' call for volunteers
to fight Aufidius' Volsces.

outward insincere, mere
 appearance
As cause will be obeyed
 as occasion demands
ostentation display of enthusiasm

Divide in all share the honour and
 booty
ports gates
centuries companies of 100 soldiers
short holding brief occupation
field battle

They all shout and wave their swords, take him up in their arms,
and cast up their caps

O'me alone! Make you a sword of me?
If these shows be not outward, which of you
But is four Volsces? None of you but is
Able to bear against the great Aufidius
A shield as hard as his. A certain number,   80
Though thanks to all, must I select from all.
The rest shall bear the business in some other fight
As cause will be obeyed. Please you to march,
And I shall quickly draw out my command
Which men are best inclined.
COMINIUS   March on, my fellows.   85
Make good this ostentation, and you shall
Divide in all with us.

Exeunt

ACT 1   SCENE 7
Corioles: before the gates

TITUS LARTIUS, having set a guard upon Corioles, going with
Drummer and Trumpeter toward Cominius and Caius Martius,
enters with a LIEUTENANT, other Soldiers, and a Scout

LARTIUS So, let the ports be guarded. Keep your duties
As I have set them down. If I do send, dispatch
Those centuries to our aid; the rest will serve
For a short holding. If we lose the field,
We cannot keep the town.
LIEUTENANT   Fear not our care, sir.   5
LARTIUS Hence, and shut your gates upon's.
[*To the Scout*] Our guider, come; to th'Roman camp
conduct us.

[*Exeunt*]

Martius and Aufidius exchange insults, and Martius boasts of his single-handed victory in Corioles. Martius gets the better of Aufidius who resents being rescued by Volsce soldiers.

1 Staging the scene (in small groups)

Martius and Aufidius at last meet in face-to-face combat, and Scene 8 shows Martius' supremacy in battle. In dramatic contrast to Martius' victory at Corioles ('Alone I fought'), Aufidius needs other soldiers to help him survive.

Work out how you would stage their encounter to greatest dramatic effect. Remember that the first rule of all stage fighting is safety first. When professional actors fight, the action may seem dangerous and spontaneous, but in reality it is all very carefully planned and rehearsed to avoid injury. Use the following points to help your preparation:

- How do Martius and Aufidius enter? Do they exchange blows as they speak their opening insults?
- How can you show that Martius is clearly winning the fight at line 13, and that the Volces rescue Aufidius? How does Martius manage to fight both Aufidius and his Volsce rescuers?
- Suggest how to stage the combat in a modern dress production.
- Draw a stage plan, showing how the fight develops.

2 Insults

Martius and Aufidius compete with each other in trading insults. Aufidius' taunt in lines 11–12 is based on Greek legend. Hector was the 'whip' (chief warrior) of the Trojan army. Another Trojan warrior was Aeneas, the legendary founder of Rome, and therefore one of the ancestors of whom Martius may have boasted ('your bragged progeny').

Afric Africa (in Shakespeare's time, legendary for snakes)
budger yielder, runaway
Hollo hunt me with shouts
hare timid creature

Wert thou Even if you were
Officious meddling, interfering
condemnèd seconds damnable support

ACT 1 SCENE 8
The battlefield near Corioles

Alarum, as in battle. Enter MARTIUS *and* AUFIDIUS

MARTIUS I'll fight with none but thee, for I do hate thee
　　　　Worse than a promise-breaker.
AUFIDIUS　　　　　　　　　　　　We hate alike.
　　　　Not Afric owns a serpent I abhor
　　　　More than thy fame and envy. Fix thy foot.
MARTIUS Let the first budger die the other's slave,　　　　　　5
　　　　And the gods doom him after!
AUFIDIUS　　　　　　　　　　　　If I fly, Martius,
　　　　Hollo me like a hare.
MARTIUS　　　　　　　　　Within these three hours, Tullus,
　　　　Alone I fought in your Corioles' walls
　　　　And made what work I pleased. 'Tis not my blood
　　　　Wherein thou seest me masked. For thy revenge　　　10
　　　　Wrench up thy power to th'highest.
AUFIDIUS　　　　　　　　　　　　　Wert thou the Hector
　　　　That was the whip of your bragged progeny,
　　　　Thou shouldst not 'scape me here.

Here they fight, and certain Volsces come in the aid of Aufidius

　　　　Officious and not valiant, you have shamed me
　　　　In your condemnèd seconds.　　　　　　　　　　　15

Martius fights till they be driven in breathless. [Exeunt]

45

Cominius promises that everyone in Rome will admire Martius when they hear the story of his brave deeds. Martius wants no praise, but Cominius insists that his heroic actions must be proclaimed.

1 Reporting great deeds (in small groups)

The opening stage direction shows that the battle is over. After some sounds of fighting (Alarum), a trumpet call orders the pursuit of the fleeing enemy to be ended (retreat). Another trumpet call (Flourish) announces victory. Martius appears with his arm in a sling (scarf). His wounds will play an important part in the play. Cominius begins a speech in praise of Martius, but Martius acknowledges that other soldiers have played their part.

Speak lines 1–9 and lines 15–19 ('I have done ... act') then the following lines from *King Henry V* (Act 4 Scene 3, lines 56–67) spoken by King Henry to his troops before the battle of Agincourt on Saint Crispin's Day. What similarities can you find between the three speeches?

This story shall the good man teach his son,
And Crispin Crispian shall ne'er go by
From this day to the ending of the world
But we in it shall be remembered.
We few, we happy few, we band of brothers –
For he today that sheds his blood with me
Shall be my brother; be he ne'er so vile
This day shall gentle his condition –
And gentlemen in England, now abed,
Shall think themselves accursed they were not here,
And hold their manhoods cheap while any speaks
That fought with us upon Saint Crispin's day.

---

shrug express disbelief
gladly quaked pleasurably frightened
fusty mouldy smelling
morsel ... feast small part of this battle
caparison harness, trappings

charter to extol her blood right to praise her children
induced motivated
effected ... will achieved his good intentions
traducement slander, criticism
vouched proclaimed

ACT 1 SCENE 9
The Roman camp near Corioles

Alarum. A retreat is sounded. Flourish. Enter COMINIUS
with the ROMANS; *then* MARTIUS, *with his arm in a scarf*

COMINIUS If I should tell thee o'er this thy day's work,
    Thou't not believe thy deeds. But I'll report it
    Where senators shall mingle tears with smiles;
    Where great patricians shall attend and shrug,
    I'th'end admire; where ladies shall be frighted   5
    And, gladly quaked, hear more; where the dull tribunes,
    That with the fusty plebeians hate thine honours,
    Shall say against their hearts, 'We thank the gods
    Our Rome hath such a soldier.'
    Yet cam'st thou to a morsel of this feast,   10
    Having fully dined before.

Enter TITUS LARTIUS *with his power, from the pursuit*

LARTIUS   O general,
    Here is the steed, we the caparison.
    Hadst thou beheld –
MARTIUS   Pray now, no more. My mother,
    Who has a charter to extol her blood,
    When she does praise me grieves me. I have done   15
    As you have done, that's what I can; induced
    As you have been, that's for my country.
    He that has but effected his good will
    Hath overta'en mine act.
COMINIUS   You shall not be
    The grave of your deserving. Rome must know   20
    The value of her own. 'Twere a concealment
    Worse than a theft, no less than a traducement,
    To hide your doings and to silence that
    Which, to the spire and top of praises vouched,
    Would seem but modest. Therefore, I beseech you –   25
    In sign of what you are, not to reward
    What you have done – before our army hear me.
MARTIUS I have some wounds upon me, and they smart
    To hear themselves remembered.

Martius rejects Cominius' offer of one-tenth of the captured booty.
He also contemptuously rejects the applause that greets his decision.
Cominius awards him the name of Coriolanus.

1 'Fester 'gainst ingratitude'

Lines 29–31 are Cominius' response to Martius' claim that his wounds
would ache to hear praise. Many audience members find the imagery
that Cominius uses difficult to understand. Use the following
interpretation, or one of your own, to advise Cominius about how to
deliver the lines:

'If your wounds did not ache, they would become corrupt in the face of
lack of public gratitude, and cure themselves with death.'

2 Rejecting loot, rejecting praise (in pairs)

Martius refuses the offer of taking one-tenth of the captured booty
before it is shared between soldiers of the army ('common distribution').
The soldiers cheer his decision, but Martius rounds on them
passionately, calling for silence. He hates to hear the instruments of
war (the long flourish of drums and trumpets) used for flattery, or
swords ('steel') put to use other than killing. When that happens, he
says, all civilian life will be hypocritical flattery ('false-faced soothing'),
and flatterers ('parasites') become like 'An ovator': someone fit to lead
an army and to receive public praise.

Martius plays down his own achievements ('my little') as a mere
nose bleed or defeat of a feeble opponent ('foiled some debile wretch').
Many others have done the same without it being recorded ('without
note'). He rejects such over-the-top praise ('acclamations hyperbolical').

Work out, line by line, how to express Martius' disdain and how the
soldiers react to Martius' rejection of their praise.

---

fester become corrupt	**dieted** fed
tent cure (a rolled bandage to clean wounds)	**incensed** angered
	means his proper harm intends suicide
good store many	
bare .bare-headed (a mark of respect)	**garland** wreath of victory
parasite's silk flatterer's fancy clothes	**trim belonging** elaborate harness

48

COMINIUS   Should they not,
   Well might they fester 'gainst ingratitude   30
   And tent themselves with death. Of all the horses –
   Whereof we have ta'en good, and good store – of all
   The treasure in this field achieved and city,
   We render you the tenth, to be ta'en forth
   Before the common distribution, at   35
   Your only choice.
MARTIUS   I thank you, general,
   But cannot make my heart consent to take
   A bribe to pay my sword. I do refuse it,
   And stand upon my common part with those
   That have beheld the doing.   40
  A long flourish. They all cry, 'Martius! Martius!', cast up
  their caps and lances. Cominius and Lartius stand bare
   May these same instruments which you profane
   Never sound more! When drums and trumpets shall
   I'th'field prove flatterers, let courts and cities be
   Made all of false-faced soothing. When steel grows
   Soft as the parasite's silk, let him be made   45
   An ovator for th'wars. No more, I say!
   For that I have not washed my nose that bled,
   Or foiled some debile wretch, which without note
   Here's many else have done, you shout me forth
   In acclamations hyperbolical,   50
   As if I loved my little should be dieted
   In praises sauced with lies.
COMINIUS   Too modest are you,
   More cruel to your good report than grateful
   To us that give you truly. By your patience,
   If 'gainst yourself you be incensed, we'll put you,   55
   Like one that means his proper harm, in manacles,
   Then reason safely with you. Therefore be it known,
   As to us, to all the world, that Caius Martius
   Wears this war's garland, in token of the which
   My noble steed, known to the camp, I give him   60
   With all his trim belonging; and from this time,
   For what he did before Corioles, call him,
   With all th'applause and clamour of the host,
   Martius Caius Coriolanus.
   Bear th'addition nobly ever!   65

Martius, now Coriolanus, thanks Cominius and promises to live up to his new title. He requests that a captured Volsce, who was once his kind host, be set free. But he cannot remember the man's name.

1 Ceremony of honour (in small groups)

Caius Martius has now become Martius Caius Coriolanus. The new title ('addition') is a great honour, and signifies his heroism at Corioles. Invent a ceremony that Cominius might perform to accompany his lines 61–5 as he confers the name of Coriolanus on Martius.

2 Questions about Coriolanus

a Coriolanus' first response to his new honour is 'I will go wash'. Why do you think Shakespeare gives him such a line?

b What impression do you gain of Coriolanus when he requests the release of a prisoner, yet cannot remember the prisoner's name?

c Why does Martius, who has refused booty and praise, now accept his new title – Coriolanus?

d What different aspects of his character does Coriolanus show in Scene 9 from those shown in preceding scenes?

3 Humour in the scene?

If you were directing the play, at what lines in Scene 9 would you wish to make the audience laugh or smile?

4 Who is the real leader? (in small groups)

Coriolanus acknowledges that Cominius is in command at lines 79–80 ('beg/Of my lord general'). But who leads the Romans off at the end of the scene? Stage the final *Exeunt* stage direction to show your view of power relationships in the Roman army.

Howbeit however
stride your steed ride your horse
undercrest live up to (see page 236, Activity 1d)
addition new title
fairness exact measure, utmost

best chief citizens
articulate negotiate
lay lodged
visage face
Cornets musical instruments like horns

Flourish. Trumpets sound, and drums

ALL SOLDIERS Martius Caius Coriolanus!
CORIOLANUS I will go wash,
    And when my face is fair you shall perceive
    Whether I blush or no. Howbeit, I thank you.
    I mean to stride your steed, and at all times   70
    To undercrest your good addition
    To th'fairness of my power.
COMINIUS   So, to our tent,
    Where ere we do repose us, we will write
    To Rome of our success. You, Titus Lartius,
    Must to Corioles back. Send us to Rome   75
    The best, with whom we may articulate
    For their own good and ours.
LARTIUS   I shall, my lord.
CORIOLANUS The gods begin to mock me. I, that now
    Refused most princely gifts, am bound to beg
    Of my lord general.
COMINIUS   Take't, 'tis yours. What is't?   80
CORIOLANUS I sometime lay here in Corioles
    At a poor man's house. He used me kindly.
    He cried to me; I saw him prisoner,
    But then Aufidius was within my view,
    And wrath o'erwhelmed my pity. I request you   85
    To give my poor host freedom.
COMINIUS   O, well begged!
    Were he the butcher of my son, he should
    Be free as is the wind. Deliver him, Titus.
LARTIUS Martius, his name.
CORIOLANUS   By Jupiter, forgot!
    I am weary; yea, my memory is tired.   90
    Have we no wine here?
COMINIUS   Go we to our tent.
    The blood upon your visage dries; 'tis time
    It should be looked to. Come.

                        [A flourish. Cornets.] Exeunt

Aufidius, defeated, feels disgrace at the capture of Corioles. He abandons chivalry, and swears nothing will protect Coriolanus against his revenge. He determines to beat Coriolanus using any form of trickery.

1 Abandoning chivalry (in pairs)

In Scene 9, Martius took on a new Roman identity as Coriolanus. In contrast, in Scene 10, Aufidius regrets that in defeat he has lost his Volsce identity ('I cannot … be that I am'). In his anger and desire for revenge, he swears by earth, air, fire and water ('By th'elements') to end the personal rivalry by the death of himself or Coriolanus.

In one production Aufidius slowly removed the plumes in his helmet, one by one, to signify that he was prepared to behave dishonourably. Invent a different ritual for Aufidius to perform as he speaks lines 8–27, vowing to use any deceit to enable him to kill Coriolanus.

2 No protection

Identify in lines 19–21 the eight examples of 'privilege and custom' that Aufidius vows will not protect Coriolanus from his hate.

3 'To the pace of it'

In lines 32–3, Aufidius resolves that he will adjust to circumstances ('the pace' of 'the world'). As you read on, keep in mind that this is precisely what Coriolanus refuses to do: he will not be flexible.

---

ta'en taken, captured
condition terms (lines 2–3), identity (line 5), quality (line 6)
part that is at mercy defeated side
emulation rivalry, concern to equal
potch stab

wrath or craft anger or deceit
stain disgrace
fane shrine, temple
Embarquements restraints, embargoes
hospitable canon laws of hospitality

ACT 1 SCENE 10
A road near Corioles

Enter TULLUS AUFIDIUS, bloody, with two or three SOLDIERS

AUFIDIUS The town is ta'en.

A SOLDIER 'Twill be delivered back on good condition.

AUFIDIUS Condition!
      I would I were a Roman, for I cannot,
      Being a Volsce, be that I am. Condition? 5
      What good condition can a treaty find
      I'th'part that is at mercy? Five times, Martius,
      I have fought with thee; so often hast thou beat me,
      And wouldst do so, I think, should we encounter
      As often as we eat. By th'elements, 10
      If e'er again I meet him beard to beard,
      He's mine or I am his. Mine emulation
      Hath not that honour in't it had, for where
      I thought to crush him in an equal force,
      True sword to sword, I'll potch at him some way. 15
      Or wrath or craft may get him.

A SOLDIER   He's the devil.

AUFIDIUS Bolder, though not so subtle. My valour's poisoned
      With only suffering stain by him, for him
      Shall fly out of itself. Nor sleep nor sanctuary,
      Being naked, sick, nor fane nor Capitol, 20
      The prayers of priests, nor times of sacrifice –
      Embarquements all of fury – shall lift up
      Their rotten privilege and custom 'gainst
      My hate to Martius. Where I find him, were it
      At home, upon my brother's guard, even there 25
      Against the hospitable canon, would I
      Wash my fierce hand in's heart. Go you to th'city.
      Learn how 'tis held, and what they are that must
      Be hostages for Rome.

A SOLDIER   Will not you go?

AUFIDIUS I am attended at the cypress grove. I pray you – 30
      'Tis south the city mills – bring me word thither
      How the world goes, that to the pace of it
      I may spur on my journey.

A SOLDIER   I shall, sir.   [*Exeunt*]

Looking back at Act I
Activities for groups or individuals

1 Perspectives on Coriolanus

Shakespeare provides three kinds of evidence on Coriolanus' character: what he says, what he does, and what other people say about him.

a From each scene in which he appears in Act 1, select two examples of Coriolanus' language which reveal different aspects of his personality. For example, can you find lines that suggest he can be modest and generous?

b Make a list of all Coriolanus' actions in Act 1. Why do you think he rejects both material reward and praise in Scene 9?

c Step into role as each of the following and state what you think of Coriolanus:
  • a plebeian;
  • Aufidius;
  • Volumnia;
  • Virgilia;
  • Cominius.

2 The citizen's tale

The citizens or plebeians are the ordinary people of Rome. They are conscripted to fight the war against the Volsces, but they are led by the Roman patrician who they accuse of hoarding corn, and so threatening them with starvation. Imagine you are a plebeian who has taken part in all the events of Act 1. Tell your story, including your thoughts on why the Volsces and the Romans are at war (Shakespeare does not reveal the causes in the play).

3 The fable of the belly

The fable of the belly that Menenius tells in Scene 1 was a favourite story of King James I. Its picture of an elite class serving the state selflessly, without reward, has special appeal for all people at the top of a hierarchical society. Make your own brief summary of the fable then give your own view of its truthfulness.

4 Psychological shaping

Remind yourself of Volumnia's account in Scene 3 of Coriolanus'
boyhood. Then write notes for Volumnia's handbook titled 'A mother's
guide to bringing up children'.

Coriolanus proves himself a better warrior than Aufidius. Use the
inspiration of the Bayeux Tapestry to design a sequence of pictures
showing the progress of the war and Coriolanus' victory in Scenes 4–8.

Menenius and the tribunes try to gain the advantage of each other in word play. Menenius defends Coriolanus, accuses the tribunes of impatience, and promises to tell them what the patricians think of them.

1 Political opponents (in groups of three)

The factional conflict between patricians and plebeians shown in Act 1 Scene 1 is again made evident as the patrician Menenius mocks the tribunes, the representatives of the plebeians. Much of their talk is about Coriolanus' pride. All three men still think of him as Martius, because news has not yet reached Rome of his victory at Corioles.

To discover how Menenius tries to get the better of the tribunes, take parts and speak lines 1–78 using the suggestions below and on the following pages.

a The tribunes sometimes speak together (lines 13, 21, 23 and 34). Explore ways of delivering these shared lines, and suggest the impression of the tribunes such that speaking in unison is likely to create.

b What is the personal relationship of the tribunes and Menenius? They are political enemies, but are they personally friendly or do they detest each other? Or ...?

c Menenius tries to score off the tribunes, and they try to get the better of him, or to deflect his humour. Is the joking light-hearted or serious? Who comes off best in the banter?

d Different dramatic effects can be obtained by leaving no pauses between speakers or by delaying a response to the previous line. Experiment with pauses (for example, the tribunes or Menenius may be seen searching for a reply) to find a style you feel is appropriate.

---

augurer soothsayer, religious official who forecast the future
enormity vice, wickedness
censured criticised, judged
us o'th'right-hand file we right wingers (in battle patricians fought in the right-hand file)

very little thief of occasion slightest pretext
Give your dispositions the reins let your feelings guide you
your helps are many you have mobs to support you

ACT 2   SCENE 1
Rome: the city gates

Enter MENENIUS, with the two tribunes of the people,
SICINIUS and BRUTUS

MENENIUS The augurer tells me we shall have news tonight.

BRUTUS Good or bad?

MENENIUS Not according to the prayer of the people, for they love not
Martius.

SICINIUS Nature teaches beasts to know their friends.   5

MENENIUS Pray you, who does the wolf love?

SICINIUS The lamb.

MENENIUS Ay, to devour him, as the hungry plebeians would the noble
Martius.

BRUTUS He's a lamb indeed, that baas like a bear.   10

MENENIUS He's a bear indeed, that lives like a lamb. You two are old men.
Tell me one thing that I shall ask you.

BOTH TRIBUNES Well, sir.

MENENIUS In what enormity is Martius poor in that you two have not in
abundance?   15

BRUTUS He's poor in no one fault, but stored with all.

SICINIUS Especially in pride.

BRUTUS And topping all others in boasting.

MENENIUS This is strange now. Do you two know how you are censured
here in the city, I mean of us o'th'right-hand file? Do you?   20

BOTH TRIBUNES Why? How are we censured?

MENENIUS Because you talk of pride now – will you not be angry?

BOTH TRIBUNES Well, well, sir, well.

MENENIUS Why, 'tis no great matter. For a very little thief of occasion will
rob you of a great deal of patience. Give your dispositions the reins   25
and be angry at your pleasures – at the least, if you take it as a pleasure
to you in being so. You blame Martius for being proud.

BRUTUS We do it not alone, sir.

MENENIUS I know you can do very little alone, for your helps are many,
or else your actions would grow wondrous single. Your abilities are   30
too infant-like for doing much alone. You talk of pride. O that you
could turn your eyes toward the napes of your necks and make but an
interior survey of your good selves! O that you could!

Menenius insults the tribunes, whimsically lists his own failings, then describes the tribunes' inept performance as magistrates. Brutus says Menenius is better known as a joker than an important judge.

1 A great flow of language (in groups of three)

To help you speak Menenius' lines, use the following director's notes, together with the explanations at the foot of the page.

Menenius is trying to out-manoeuvre the tribunes, to put them down and make them feel small. All three men are political officials whose duties included judging legal cases. It is up to you as actors whether you play Menenius as teasing the tribunes, joking at their expense, or making a savage attack on them. But there is a major theme of the play here: Menenius is parodying the disorder that will happen if the tribunes and plebeians gain political control.

The key is to speak it fast, and not worry if you and the audience can't make sense of every word. Menenius wants to make the tribunes feel inferior, so he blinds them with science by making up phrases like 'bisson conspectuities', which means something like 'bleary-eyed sight'. Here's an outline of what he says in lines 38–75:

lines 38–52: I like my liquor undiluted, I judge in favour of the first speaker in a case, I love late night parties and say the first thing that comes into my head. You two are poor lawyers who give me bellyache. You mainly speak like donkeys, and people lie who say you are honest. What faults can your blurred vision find in me?

lines 54–63: You are totally ignorant, wanting people to bow and scrape to you. You spend a very long time judging a trivial case, and all your face-pulling and shouting make it even more muddled, and you simply blame both parties in the case.

lines 66–75: You are a laughing-stock, who talk nonsense and are without honour. Martius is better than all your ancestors put together.

---

allaying Tiber diluting water
tinder-like quick to explode
trivial motion small matter
wealsmen common politicians
Lycurgus famous Greek lawyer
map ... microcosm my face
caps and legs bowing
faucet tap for wine-barrels

rejourn the controversy adjourn the case
mummers mime actors
set up ... flag declare war upon
giber joker
necessary bencher good judge
botcher mender of old clothes

BOTH TRIBUNES What then, sir?

MENENIUS Why, then you should discover a brace of unmeriting, proud,   35
violent, testy magistrates, alias fools, as any in Rome.

SICINIUS Menenius, you are known well enough too.

MENENIUS I am known to be a humorous patrician, and one that loves a
cup of hot wine with not a drop of allaying Tiber in't; said, to be
something imperfect in favouring the first complaint, hasty and   40
tinder-like upon too trivial motion; one that converses more with the
buttock of the night than with the forehead of the morning. What I
think, I utter, and spend my malice in my breath. Meeting two such
wealsmen as you are – I cannot call you Lycurguses – if the drink you
give me touch my palate adversely, I make a crooked face at it. I   45
cannot say your worships have delivered the matter well, when I find
the ass in compound with the major part of your syllables. And
though I must be content to bear with those that say you are reverend
grave men, yet they lie deadly that tell you have good faces. If you see
this in the map of my microcosm, follows it that I am known well   50
enough too? What harm can your bisson conspectuities glean out of
this character, if I be known well enough too?

BRUTUS Come, sir, come. We know you well enough.

MENENIUS You know neither me, yourselves, nor anything. You are
ambitious for poor knaves' caps and legs. You wear out a good   55
wholesome forenoon in hearing a cause between an orange-wife and
a faucet-seller, and then rejourn the controversy of threepence to a
second day of audience. When you are hearing a matter between
party and party, if you chance to be pinched with the colic, you make
faces like mummers, set up the bloody flag against all patience, and,   60
in roaring for a chamber-pot, dismiss the controversy bleeding, the
more entangled by your hearing. All the peace you make in their
cause is calling both the parties knaves. You are a pair of strange ones.

BRUTUS Come, come, you are well understood to be a perfecter giber for
the table than a necessary bencher in the Capitol.   65

MENENIUS Our very priests must become mockers if they shall encounter such ridiculous subjects as you are. When you speak best unto
the purpose, it is not worth the wagging of your beards, and your
beards deserve not so honourable a grave as to stuff a botcher's
cushion, or to be entombed in an ass's pack-saddle. Yet you must be   70

Menenius, after further insults to the tribunes, greets the three women.
He rejoices at news that Coriolanus is returning to Rome, and joins
Volumnia in hoping her son is wounded.

1 A change of tone? (in groups of four)

Menenius continues to insult the tribunes, saying that they come from
generations of worthless ancestors. He dismisses them, using an image
of the plebeians as cattle. His language undergoes a sudden change
when the three Roman ladies enter. His mocking of the tribunes
changes to courteous greeting ('as fair as noble ladies'), emphasising
the social distance between the plebeians and the patricians.

   Talking with the ladies, Menenius continues to display his pleasure
in showing off his knowledge and his delight in witty images. Galen
was a famous Greek doctor, and 'empericutic' (line 91) and 'fidiussed'
(line 104) are made-up words. They probably mean 'false medicine'
and 'Aufidiussed' (a pun on Aufidius' name, implying 'thrashed').

   To gain an impression of the change in language and atmosphere,
take parts as Menenius and the three ladies and speak lines 76–130.

2 A true patrician?

As you read on, keep adding to your impression of what Menenius is
like. Some commentators say that in his love of vivid language and
high living, he resembles Falstaff, the pleasure-loving fat knight of
Shakespeare's *King Henry IV Parts 1* and *2*, and *The Merry Wives of
Windsor*.

3 Different responses to wounds

Coriolanus is returning home wounded, but wearing around his brows
a victory wreath of oak leaves ('the oaken garland'). His wounds will
play an important part in Acts 2 and 3. What do lines 94–5 suggest to
you about how Virgilia is unlike Volumnia?

---

cheap estimation lowest reckoning
Deucalion (in Greek mythology the
  equivalent of Noah in the Bible)
peradventure perhaps
the moon Valeria (see page 234)
Juno (see page 150)

prosperous approbation
  acclaimed success
state senate
make a lip at mock, sneer at
horse-drench medicine for horses
wont accustomed
possessed aware

saying Martius is proud, who, in a cheap estimation, is worth all your predecessors since Deucalion, though peradventure some of the best of 'em were hereditary hangmen. Good e'en to your worships. More of your conversation would infect my brain, being the herdsmen of the beastly plebeians. I will be bold to take my leave of you.   75

Brutus and Sicinius [stand] aside

Enter VOLUMNIA, VIRGILIA, *and* VALERIA

How now, my as fair as noble ladies – and the moon, were she earthly, no nobler – whither do you follow your eyes so fast?
VOLUMNIA Honourable Menenius, my boy Martius approaches. For the love of Juno, let's go.
MENENIUS Ha? Martius coming home?   80
VOLUMNIA Ay, worthy Menenius, and with most prosperous approbation.
MENENIUS [*Tosses up his cap*] Take my cap, Jupiter, and I thank thee. Hoo! Martius coming home?
VIRGILIA *and* VALERIA Nay, 'tis true.
VOLUMNIA Look, here's a letter from him. The state hath another, his   85
wife another, and I think there's one at home for you.
MENENIUS I will make my very house reel tonight. A letter for me?
VIRGILIA Yes, certain, there's a letter for you. I saw't.
MENENIUS A letter for me! It gives me an estate of seven years' health, in which time I will make a lip at the physician. The most sovereign   90
prescription in Galen is but empericutic and, to this preservative, of no better report than a horse-drench. Is he not wounded? He was wont to come home wounded.
VIRGILIA O no, no, no!
VOLUMNIA O, he is wounded; I thank the gods for't.   95
MENENIUS So do I too, if it be not too much. Brings 'a victory in his pocket? The wounds become him.
VOLUMNIA On's brows. Menenius, he comes the third time home with the oaken garland.
MENENIUS Has he disciplined Aufidius soundly?   100
VOLUMNIA Titus Lartius writes they fought together, but Aufidius got off.
MENENIUS And 'twas time for him too, I'll warrant him that. And he had stayed by him, I would not have been so fidiussed for all the chests in Corioles and the gold that's in them. Is the senate   105
possessed of this?

Volumnia and Menenius rejoice in Coriolanus' military achievements, and vie with each other in counting his wounds. Volumnia celebrates her son's death-dealing power. Coriolanus makes a triumphal entry.

'Welcome to Rome, renownèd Coriolanus!' Coriolanus went to fight under the command of Cominius, but returns as the chief hero of the war, and Volumnia raises his sword high in the air as he enters Rome in triumph. Compare this staging of Coriolanus' triumphal entry with that shown on page 249.

the general Cominius	**stand for his place** campaign to
whole name entire honour	become consul, see pages 242–3
In troth truly	**repulse of Tarquin** see page 2
true purchasing real achievements	**nervy** sinewy, muscular
Pow waw phooey!	**advanced, declines** raised, falls
cicatrices scars	*sennet* trumpet call for ceremonial
	entrance

VOLUMNIA Good ladies, let's go. – Yes, yes, yes. The senate has letters
from the general, wherein he gives my son the whole name of the
war. He hath in this action outdone his former deeds doubly.

VALERIA In troth, there's wondrous things spoke of him.   110

MENENIUS Wondrous? Ay, I warrant you, and not without his true
purchasing.

VIRGILIA The gods grant them true.

VOLUMNIA True? Pow waw.

MENENIUS True? I'll be sworn they are true. Where is he wounded? [*To*   115
the Tribunes] God save your good worships! Martius is coming
home. He has more cause to be proud. [*To Volumnia*] Where is he
wounded?

VOLUMNIA I'th'shoulder and i'th'left arm. There will be large
cicatrices to show the people when he shall stand for his place. He   120
received in the repulse of Tarquin seven hurts i'th'body.

MENENIUS One i'th'neck and two i'th'thigh – there's nine that I know.

VOLUMNIA He had, before this last expedition, twenty-five wounds
upon him.

MENENIUS Now it's twenty-seven. Every gash was an enemy's grave.   125

A shout and flourish

Hark, the trumpets.

VOLUMNIA These are the ushers of Martius. Before him
He carries noise, and behind him he leaves tears.
Death, that dark spirit, in's nervy arm doth lie,
Which being advanced, declines, and then men die.   130

A sennet. Enter [in state] COMINIUS *the general and* TITUS LARTIUS;
between them CORIOLANUS, *crowned with an oaken garland; with Captains
and Soldiers and a* HERALD. *Trumpets sound*

HERALD Know, Rome, that all alone Martius did fight
Within Corioles' gates, where he hath won,
With fame, a name to Martius Caius; these
In honour follows 'Coriolanus'.
Welcome to Rome, renownèd Coriolanus!   135

Flourish

ALL Welcome to Rome, renownèd Coriolanus!

CORIOLANUS No more of this, it does offend my heart.
Pray now, no more.

Volumnia welcomes Coriolanus. He tells Virgilia she looks as sad as the widows of the men he has slain. Menenius welcomes him and insults the tribunes. Volumnia hopes Coriolanus will become consul.

1 Family reunion (in small groups)

This is the first time in the play that Coriolanus is seen with his family. How does he greet his mother, his wife and their friend Valeria? Is he poised and confident, or awkward and unsure? Does he display tenderness? Stage lines 139–51 to show your view of the relationships. Think particularly about:

- Why does he kneel to his mother?
- Why and how does Volumnia say 'But, O, thy wife!'? (line 145)
- Coriolanus greets Virgilia as 'My gracious silence'. Why doesn't she speak?
- Is there any physical contact?

2 A sense of humour?

Some productions of the play try to evoke audience laughter throughout the lines opposite. For example, in one production Volumnia smiled and showed she was unsure how to pronounce her son's new name, saying line 144 with amusement as she experimented with both 'Cor-ee-olanus' and 'Cor-eye-olanus'. Identify other lines which the actors could use to comic effect.

3 'One thing wanting'

In lines 169–73, Volumnia sees fulfilled her wishes and imaginings ('inherited … buildings of my fancy'). But she still finds one thing lacking ('wanting'): for Coriolanus to become consul (one of the two most powerful political officials in Rome). Before you turn the page, make a guess as to how Coriolanus will respond to his mother's hope.

---

prosperity success
light and heavy happy and sad
on's (line 155) of his (does
  Menenius look at the tribunes?)
crabtrees sour people (the tribunes)

grafted to your relish altered to
  welcome you
Ere before
cast upon thee bestow on you

COMINIUS   Look, sir, your mother.
CORIOLANUS   O!
    You have, I know, petitioned all the gods   140
    For my prosperity. *Kneels*
VOLUMNIA   Nay, my good soldier, up,
    [*Coriolanus rises*]
    My gentle Martius, worthy Caius, and
    By deed-achieving honour newly named –
    What is it? 'Coriolanus' must I call thee? –
    But, O, thy wife!
CORIOLANUS   My gracious silence, hail!   145
    Wouldst thou have laughed had I come coffined home,
    That weep'st to see me triumph? Ah, my dear,
    Such eyes the widows in Corioles wear,
    And mothers that lack sons.
MENENIUS   Now the gods crown thee!
CORIOLANUS And live you yet? [*To Valeria*] O my sweet lady, pardon.   150
VOLUMNIA I know not where to turn. O welcome home!
    And welcome, general, and you're welcome all.
MENENIUS A hundred thousand welcomes! I could weep
    And I could laugh; I am light and heavy. Welcome.
    A curse begin at very root on's heart   155
    That is not glad to see thee! You are three
    That Rome should dote on; yet, by the faith of men,
    We have some old crabtrees here at home that will not
    Be grafted to your relish. Yet welcome, warriors!
    We call a nettle but a nettle, and   160
    The faults of fools but folly.
COMINIUS Ever right.
CORIOLANUS Menenius, ever, ever.
HERALD Give way there, and go on.
CORIOLANUS [*To Volumnia and Virgilia*] Your hand, and yours.   165
    Ere in our own house I do shade my head
    The good patricians must be visited,
    From whom I have received not only greetings,
    But with them change of honours.
VOLUMNIA   I have lived
    To see inherited my very wishes   170
    And the buildings of my fancy. Only
    There's one thing wanting, which I doubt not but
    Our Rome will cast upon thee.

Brutus describes how everybody wished to see Coriolanus' entry into Rome. The tribunes fear they will lose power if Coriolanus is made consul, but predict that his anger and pride will cause his downfall.

1 I'll do it my way (in pairs)

Coriolanus expresses his contempt for the plebeians, saying that he would rather be their servant and retain his true nature ('my way'), than rule over ('sway with') them and change his nature. Work out some stage business to show how Coriolanus' inflexibility predicts the conflicts that lie ahead: for example how Volumnia reacts to his words; whether he points to the tribunes on 'their' and 'theirs'.

2 See the conquering hero (in pairs)

a Step into role as a newspaper reporter and use Brutus' lines 176–92 to write your account of Coriolanus' triumphal entry into Rome. You can include on-the-spot interviews with some of the people Brutus mentions. You might also use the Messenger's description in lines 231–9. The following notes and those at the foot of the page can help you:

'blearèd sights' – blurred eyes
'variable complexions' – all kinds of people
'Seld-shown flamens' – rarely seen priests
'vulgar station' – place among the plebeian crowds
'Commit the war … kisses' – risk suntans (which were unfashionable in Shakespeare's time)
'wanton spoil' – ruin, wrecking
'Phoebus' – (in Greek mythology) Apollo, the sun god

b What attitude do the lines suggest that Brutus holds towards the people he represents? See also line 207 'stinking breaths'.

---

rapture fit
chats gossips about
kitchen malkin foul kitchen-maid
lockram coarse linen
reechy greasy, dirty
Stalls, bulks sales counters
leads roofs (made of lead)

ridges horsed roof ridges sat upon
pother commotion
temperately … honours behave reasonably as a war hero
Upon their ancient malice because of their long-standing hatred

CORIOLANUS   Know, good mother,
        I had rather be their servant in my way
        Than sway with them in theirs.
COMINIUS   On, to the Capitol.   175

            Flourish [of] cornets. Exeunt in state, as before
            Brutus and Sicinius [come forward]

BRUTUS All tongues speak of him, and the blearèd sights
        Are spectacled to see him. Your prattling nurse
        Into a rapture lets her baby cry
        While she chats him. The kitchen malkin pins
        Her richest lockram 'bout her reechy neck,   180
        Clambering the walls to eye him. Stalls, bulks, windows
        Are smothered up, leads filled, and ridges horsed
        With variable complexions, all agreeing
        In earnestness to see him. Seld-shown flamens
        Do press among the popular throngs and puff   185
        To win a vulgar station. Our veiled dames
        Commit the war of white and damask in
        Their nicely guarded cheeks to th'wanton spoil
        Of Phoebus' burning kisses. Such a pother
        As if that whatsoever god who leads him   190
        Were slily crept into his human powers
        And gave him graceful posture.
SICINIUS   On the sudden,
        I warrant him consul.
BRUTUS   Then our office may,
        During his power, go sleep.
SICINIUS He cannot temperately transport his honours   195
        From where he should begin and end, but will
        Lose those he hath won.
BRUTUS   In that there's comfort.
SICINIUS   Doubt not
        The commoners, for whom we stand, but they
        Upon their ancient malice will forget
        With the least cause these his new honours, which   200
        That he will give them make I as little question
        As he is proud to do't.

The tribunes say that Coriolanus will refuse to beg humbly for the citizens' support of him as consul, and that will cause his downfall. They plan to inflame the plebeians' anger against Coriolanus.

1 Politicians at work (in pairs)

In lines 192–230, the tribunes, recognising that Coriolanus will remove their power if he becomes consul, plot how they can bring about his ruin. They know that his short temper will prevent him from gaining more honours, and will result in losing those he has, because he will provoke his old enemy, the common people (lines 195–202).

To become consul, Coriolanus must follow the customary practice of standing in the market-place wearing a simple toga, showing his wounds, and begging for the citizens' approval. The tribunes know that he hates the practice, because it means he must submit to his despised enemy, the plebeians.

To experience how the tribunes plot to ensure Coriolanus' overthrow, take parts, put your heads close together like conspirators, and speak lines 192–230.

2 Are the tribunes right?

Give your own view on whether you think the tribunes are accurate in their judgements and predictions:

a that Coriolanus hates the plebeians

b that Coriolanus sees the ordinary people of Rome as mules and camels, simply to be used in Rome's wars

c that Coriolanus has 'soaring insolence'

d that it will be easy to provoke Coriolanus' anger

e that his 'fire' will inflame the people to reject him (the image in lines 228–30 is of a field set alight after it has been harvested: 'kindle their dry stubble').

---

napless vesture coarse garment, simple toga
suit of the gentry ... nobles pleas of the patricians
as our good wills as our benefit demands
fall out happen

suggest tell
pleaders representatives (tribunes)
Dispropertied taken away
provand food (provender)
teach lecture, rebuke
want lack
put upon't provoked

BRUTUS   I heard him swear,
          Were he to stand for consul, never would he
          Appear i'th'market-place nor on him put
          The napless vesture of humility,   205
          Nor showing, as the manner is, his wounds
          To th'people, beg their stinking breaths.
SICINIUS   'Tis right.
BRUTUS It was his word. O, he would miss it rather
          Than carry it but by the suit of the gentry to him
          And the desire of the nobles.
SICINIUS   I wish no better   210
          Than have him hold that purpose and to put it
          In execution.
BRUTUS   'Tis most like he will.
SICINIUS It shall be to him then as our good wills,
          A sure destruction.
BRUTUS   So it must fall out
          To him, or our authority's for an end.   215
          We must suggest the people in what hatred
          He still hath held them; that to's power he would
          Have made them mules, silenced their pleaders, and
          Dispropertied their freedoms, holding them
          In human action and capacity   220
          Of no more soul nor fitness for the world
          Than camels in their war, who have their provand
          Only for bearing burdens and sore blows
          For sinking under them.
SICINIUS   This, as you say, suggested
          At some time when his soaring insolence   225
          Shall teach the people – which time shall not want
          If he be put upon't, and that's as easy
          As to set dogs on sheep – will be his fire
          To kindle their dry stubble, and their blaze
          Shall darken him for ever.

                         Enter a MESSENGER

BRUTUS   What's the matter?   230

The Messenger describes Coriolanus' rapturous reception by every social class of Rome. The tribunes will watch, firm in their plan to secure his downfall. Two senate officials discuss Coriolanus' dislike of the people.

1 The Messenger: character or function? (in pairs)

This is the Messenger's only appearance in the play. Take turns to speak his lines, then talk together about how you would play him on stage. Would you want him to appear as a fully-rounded character, with beliefs and emotions, passionately interested in what he is reporting?

Or do you see him as simply carrying out a dramatic function? Here he might be an unmemorable character whose role is only to confirm that Coriolanus is now the best-regarded person in Rome. In your discussion, think about the dramatic effect of each style of playing.

2 'He's vengeance proud' (in pairs)

As the two officers lay cushions for the senators to sit on, they provide further perspectives on Coriolanus and the political climate of Rome. The Second Officer comments on the unreliability of the plebeians' love for their leaders, and says that Coriolanus knows this well and so is indifferent to what they think of him. Such 'noble carelessness' or aristocratic aloofness was cultivated by noblemen in Shakespeare's own time. In reply, the First Officer says that Coriolanus actively seeks the hate of the people, and lets them know it, which is just as bad as those (the tribunes?) who flatter the people to gain their love.

Take parts and speak lines 1–30. Afterwards talk together about whether you think the officers favour Coriolanus, and why you think Shakespeare wrote lines 1–30 (that is, what is the dramatic purpose of this episode?).

bended bowed	**vengeance** horribly
Jove (in Roman mythology)	**ground** reason
Jupiter, king of the gods	**manifests** makes clear, shows
commons plebeians	**disposition** nature, mood
carry with us ... event listen and	**waved indifferently** wavered
watch, but be determined to carry	without bias
out our plot	**affect** desire

MESSENGER You are sent for to the Capitol. 'Tis thought
               That Martius shall be consul. I have seen
               The dumb men throng to see him and the blind
               To hear him speak. Matrons flung gloves,
               Ladies and maids their scarfs and handkerchiefs,   235
               Upon him as he passed. The nobles bended
               As to Jove's statue, and the commons made
               A shower and thunder with their caps and shouts.
               I never saw the like.
BRUTUS   Let's to the Capitol,
               And carry with us ears and eyes for th'time,   240
               But hearts for the event.
SICINIUS   Have with you.

Exeunt

ACT 2   SCENE 2
Rome: the Capitol

Enter two OFFICERS, *to lay cushions*

FIRST OFFICER Come, come, they are almost here. How many stand for
  consulships?
SECOND OFFICER Three, they say, but 'tis thought of everyone Coriolanus
  will carry it.
FIRST OFFICER That's a brave fellow, but he's vengeance proud and loves   5
  not the common people.
SECOND OFFICER Faith, there hath been many great men that have
  flattered the people who ne'er loved them, and there be many that
  they have loved they know not wherefore; so that if they love they
  know not why, they hate upon no better a ground. Therefore, for   10
  Coriolanus neither to care whether they love or hate him manifests
  the true knowledge he has in their disposition, and out of his noble
  carelessness lets them plainly see't.
FIRST OFFICER If he did not care whether he had their love or no, he
  waved indifferently 'twixt doing them neither good nor harm; but   15
  he seeks their hate with greater devotion than they can render it him
  and leaves nothing undone that may fully discover him their opposite. Now to seem to affect the malice and displeasure of the people
  is as bad as that which he dislikes, to flatter them for their love.

The Second Officer says that Coriolanus fully deserves high status, unlike those who have done little to earn it. Menenius and the Senator propose that Coriolanus' deeds be reported and honoured.

1 Who?

Who might the Second Officer have in mind when he talks about those who achieve fame and high status through flattery and compliments ('supple and courteous'), but who do no deeds other than doffing their caps ('bonneted') to deserve their high esteem and fame ('estimation and report')? Imagine that he is thinking of the tribunes, and invent some stage business to make that interpretation clear to the audience as he speaks. You might wish to use 'bonneted' as the basis of your 'business'.

2 Stage the entry (in groups)

Work out how you would present the stage direction at line 30 to display power and social relationships in Rome. 'Sicinius and Brutus take their places by themselves' is a sign that the tribunes have less power than the patricians. As representatives of the plebeians they are intermediaries between senatorial decisions and the people. Think about why and how Coriolanus 'stands'.

3 Make two guesses

The patricians have come from a meeting of the senate in which they have 'determined of the Volsces' (decided about their defeated enemy). Now they are about to have an 'after-meeting' to honour Coriolanus. In lines 45–8, the First Senator hopes that the tribunes will advise the plebeians ('the common body') to agree to ('yield') what will now be decided. What decision do you think the Senator has in mind? Do you think that the tribunes will agree?

---

sennet ceremonial trumpet call
lictors attendants on Roman
  magistrates
determined of decided about
gratify reward

well-found successes victory at
  Corioles
Rather our state's … requital
  Rome is unable to provide a reward
  that we would wish
loving motion recommendation

SECOND OFFICER He hath deserved worthily of his country, and his   20
ascent is not by such easy degrees as those who, having been supple
and courteous to the people, bonneted, without any further deed to
have them at all into their estimation and report. But he hath so
planted his honours in their eyes and his actions in their hearts that
for their tongues to be silent and not confess so much were a kind of   25
ingrateful injury. To report otherwise were a malice that, giving
itself the lie, would pluck reproof and rebuke from every ear that
heard it.

FIRST OFFICER No more of him; he's a worthy man. Make way, they are
coming.   30

A sennet. Enter the PATRICIANS *and the tribunes of the people, lictors
before them;* CORIOLANUS, MENENIUS, COMINIUS *the consul.*
[*The Senators take their places and sit.*] SICINIUS *and* BRUTUS *take their
places by themselves.* CORIOLANUS *stands*

MENENIUS Having determined of the Volsces and
    To send for Titus Lartius, it remains
    As the main point of this our after-meeting
    To gratify his noble service that
    Hath thus stood for his country. Therefore please you,   35
    Most reverend and grave elders, to desire
    The present consul and last general
    In our well-found successes to report
    A little of that worthy work performed
    By Martius Caius Coriolanus, whom   40
    We meet here both to thank and to remember
    With honours like himself.

[*Coriolanus sits*]

FIRST SENATOR   Speak, good Cominius.
    Leave nothing out for length, and make us think
    Rather our state's defective for requital
    Than we to stretch it out. [*To the Tribunes*] Masters
      o'th'people,   45
    We do request your kindest ears and, after,
    Your loving motion toward the common body
    To yield what passes here.

Brutus criticises Coriolanus' contempt of the people and is rebuked by Menenius. Coriolanus does not wish to hear his deeds told, and leaves. Menenius scorns the plebeians and praises Coriolanus.

1 Courteous or insincere?

One critic described Sicinius' lines 48–51 as 'moderate and courteous'. Another critic said 'his oily words are a lie'. Speak the lines and make your own decision about whether Sicinius is sincere or insincere.

2 Why does he leave? (in pairs)

Coriolanus denies that Brutus' words have unsettled him, but he leaves, not wishing to hear praise of his feats in battle. Some critics see Coriolanus' decision to leave as admirable, but is it? Brainstorm as many reasons as you can why Coriolanus cannot bear to hear his bravery praised, then give your own views of his action in leaving.

3 'My nothings monstered' (in small groups)

'My nothings monstered' means 'my little deeds turned into exaggerated marvels'. Discuss what tone of voice Coriolanus uses for 'monstered', and whether you think that he is speaking truthfully, or that his behaviour is false modesty.

4 An insulting image (in pairs)

Tell each other what picture is called up in your mind by Menenius' description of the people as 'multiplying spawn' (line 72).

---

convented met, convened
pleasing treaty pleasant matter for negotiation
That's off That's out of order
pertinent relevant
disbenched unseated, unsettled

as they weigh according to their value
multiplying spawn mere child-breeders
venture … ears to hear it lose every limb for battle honours, than one ear to hear his deeds praised

SICINIUS   We are convented
         Upon a pleasing treaty, and have hearts
         Inclinable to honour and advance   50
         The theme of our assembly.
BRUTUS   Which the rather
         We shall be blessed to do if he remember
         A kinder value of the people than
         He hath hereto prized them at.
MENENIUS   That's off, that's off.
         I would you rather had been silent. Please you   55
         To hear Cominius speak?
BRUTUS   Most willingly;
         But yet my caution was more pertinent
         Than the rebuke you give it.
MENENIUS   He loves your people,
         But tie him not to be their bedfellow.
         Worthy Cominius, speak.

         Coriolanus rises and offers to go away

                              Nay, keep your place.   60
A SENATOR Sit, Coriolanus. Never shame to hear
         What you have nobly done.
CORIOLANUS   Your honours' pardon.
         I had rather have my wounds to heal again
         Than hear say how I got them.
BRUTUS   Sir, I hope
         My words disbenched you not?
CORIOLANUS   No, sir. Yet oft   65
         When blows have made me stay I fled from words.
         You soothed not, therefore hurt not. But your people,
         I love them as they weigh –
MENENIUS   Pray now, sit down.
CORIOLANUS I had rather have one scratch my head i'th'sun
         When the alarum were struck than idly sit   70
         To hear my nothings monstered.   *Exit*
MENENIUS   Masters of the people,
         Your multiplying spawn how can he flatter –
         That's thousand to one good one – when you now see
         He had rather venture all his limbs for honour
         Than one on's ears to hear it? Proceed, Cominius.   75

Cominius describes Coriolanus' brave deeds as a young man, his later battles, his single-handed attack on Corioles, and his death-dealing feats in the following battle.

1 'He was a thing of blood' (in small groups)

Cominius' speech is an exercise in rhetoric (the art of persuasion) to convince the hearers of Coriolanus' bravery and to win their support for him. The theme of bravery is declared in lines 77–9: 'It is held/ That valour is the chiefest virtue and/Most dignifies the haver'. Cominius describes Coriolanus' feats as a sixteen-year-old in his first battle against the tyrant Tarquin who had 'made a head for Rome' (recruited an army against Rome (lines 81–92)), his seventeen later battles (lines 92–5), and his superhuman deeds at Corioles (lines 95–116). Work on some of the activities below or on page 229 to help you discover what the speech tells you about Roman values.

a Share the speech, each person taking turns to speak a sentence (or up to a semi-colon). After each sentence, the speaker gives a version in their own language.

b As one person speaks, all the others echo a key word or phrase in each line.

c Trace the images through the speech, for example, 'Amazonian chin' (beardless), 'painted with shunless destiny' (covered in blood as its unavoidable fate), 'struck Corioles like a planet' (thunderbolt), 'perpetual spoil' (endless slaughter), and so on. Do they become increasingly inhuman?

d At lines 83–4 'Our then dictator', Cominius might mean Aulus (who does not appear in the play). Is his statue on stage? Make your suggestion as to whom Cominius points at.

---

haver owner
singly counterpoised matched by
 any other man
bristled lips bearded soldiers
meed reward
brow-bound with the
 oak awarded an oak-wreath

waxèd grew
brunt attack, assault
lurched robbed
speak him home tell it fully
took killed
'gan began to
fatigate fatigued, weary

COMINIUS I shall lack voice; the deeds of Coriolanus
          Should not be uttered feebly. It is held
          That valour is the chiefest virtue and
          Most dignifies the haver. If it be,
          The man I speak of cannot in the world   80
          Be singly counterpoised. At sixteen years,
          When Tarquin made a head for Rome, he fought
          Beyond the mark of others. Our then dictator,
          Whom with all praise I point at, saw him fight
          When with his Amazonian chin he drove   85
          The bristled lips before him. He bestrid
          An o'erpressed Roman, and i'th'consul's view
          Slew three opposers. Tarquin's self he met
          And struck him on his knee. In that day's feats,
          When he might act the woman in the scene,   90
          He proved best man i'th'field, and for his meed
          Was brow-bound with the oak. His pupil age
          Man-entered thus, he waxèd like a sea,
          And in the brunt of seventeen battles since
          He lurched all swords of the garland. For this last,   95
          Before and in Corioles, let me say
          I cannot speak him home. He stopped the fliers,
          And by his rare example made the coward
          Turn terror into sport. As weeds before
          A vessel under sail, so men obeyed   100
          And fell below his stem. His sword, death's stamp,
          Where it did mark, it took; from face to foot
          He was a thing of blood, whose every motion
          Was timed with dying cries. Alone he entered
          The mortal gate of th'city, which he painted   105
          With shunless destiny; aidless came off,
          And with a sudden reinforcement struck
          Corioles like a planet. Now all's his,
          When by and by the din of war 'gan pierce
          His ready sense; then straight his doubled spirit   110
          Requickened what in flesh was fatigate,
          And to the battle came he, where he did
          Run reeking o'er the lives of men as if
          'Twere a perpetual spoil; and till we called
          Both field and city ours, he never stood   115
          To ease his breast with panting.

Cominius praises Coriolanus' contempt for material gain, and his dedication to action. Coriolanus is offered the consulship, but detests the thought of having to beg the approval of the people.

1 'Speak to the people' (in small groups)

Menenius tells of the offer of the consulship, but then adds the requirement that to gain approval Coriolanus must speak to the people. He must obey the tradition of Rome and appear before them in the market-place, unarmed ('naked') and dressed only in a simple gown, show the people his wounds, and ask for their approval ('suffrage', 'voices').

Coriolanus is filled with horror at the thought of having to follow this tradition. He hates the thought of the part he must play (you will find many images of acting and role playing as you read on). To help you understand the emotional significance of what is going on, consider the following:

a Does Menenius hesitate, or show some emotion, when he reminds Coriolanus that to become consul he must 'speak to the people' (lines 129–30)?

b Does Coriolanus pause at line 130 before saying 'I do beseech you', or does he immediately respond?

c In what tone does Brutus speak 'Mark you that' at line 141 as he hears Coriolanus wish that the people's right to approve the consul might be taken away? Triumphantly? Very quietly? or …?

d Does Coriolanus intend that everything he says should be heard by everyone, or are some of his lines intended only for Menenius' ears?

with measure fully and gracefully	**still** always
spoils booty, loot	**o'erleap** omit
covets desires	**pass** leave out
misery extreme poverty	**bate** lessen, reduce
to end it to that purpose	**Put them not to't** don't provoke them

MENENIUS   Worthy man!

A SENATOR He cannot but with measure fit the honours
      Which we devise him.

COMINIUS   Our spoils he kicked at
      And looked upon things precious as they were
      The common muck of the world. He covets less   120
      Than misery itself would give, rewards
      His deeds with doing them, and is content
      To spend the time to end it.

MENENIUS   He's right noble.
      Let him be called for.

A SENATOR Call Coriolanus.   125

OFFICER He doth appear.

Enter CORIOLANUS

MENENIUS The senate, Coriolanus, are well pleased
      To make thee consul.

CORIOLANUS   I do owe them still
      My life and services.

MENENIUS   It then remains
      That you do speak to the people.

CORIOLANUS   I do beseech you,   130
      Let me o'erleap that custom, for I cannot
      Put on the gown, stand naked, and entreat them
      For my wounds' sake to give their suffrage. Please you
      That I may pass this doing.

SICINIUS   Sir, the people
      Must have their voices, neither will they bate   135
      One jot of ceremony.

MENENIUS   Put them not to't.
      Pray you, go fit you to the custom and
      Take to you, as your predecessors have,
      Your honour with your form.

CORIOLANUS   It is a part
      That I shall blush in acting, and might well   140
      Be taken from the people.

BRUTUS [*To Sicinius*]   Mark you that.

CORIOLANUS To brag unto them 'Thus I did, and thus',
      Show them th'unaching scars, which I should hide,
      As if I had received them for the hire
      Of their breath only!

Menenius urges Coriolanus not to be obstinate about the plebeians' voting rights. The senators honour Coriolanus, but the tribunes plan trouble. In Scene 3, the citizens discuss whether they will support Coriolanus.

1 Speaking together (in small groups)

All the senators acclaim Coriolanus at line 149. On stage, when a large group speaks together, the audience can have difficulty hearing just what is said. Some productions, to express the unity of the patricians in praise of their hero, have used the line as a repeated chant to accompany a formal procession in which everyone except the tribunes leave the stage.

Explore ways of speaking line 149 and enacting the stage direction. Find a style by which your audience can hear every word (see page 96 for an activity on ceremonial entrances and exits).

2 What will the tribunes say? (in pairs)

Once again the two tribunes remain behind at the end of a scene to discuss Coriolanus. Sicinius predicts that Coriolanus, even as he canvasses the plebeians' support, will show his contempt for their right to participate in his appointment as consul. Brutus intends to tell the plebeians what has happened. Before you read on, step into role as the tribunes and devise the first sentence that each will say to the people.

3 The citizens (in groups of three)

The First and Third Citizens seem to feel that they must follow custom and give their approval ('voices') to Coriolanus. Take parts and speak lines 1–41, then talk together about what impression of the citizens you think Shakespeare is creating here.

---

stand upon't make an issue of it (spoken quietly to Coriolanus alone?)
require them ask their approval, beg their approval
contemn despise

we are to put our tongues ... them we must approve him as consul
stuck not did not hesitate
abram auburn, blond

MENENIUS   Do not stand upon't. –   145
    We recommend to you, tribunes of the people,
    Our purpose to them, and to our noble consul
    Wish we all joy and honour.
SENATORS To Coriolanus come all joy and honour!

    Flourish [of] cornets. Exeunt [all but] Sicinius and Brutus

BRUTUS You see how he intends to use the people.   150
SICINIUS May they perceive's intent! He will require them
    As if he did contemn what he requested
    Should be in them to give.
BRUTUS   Come, we'll inform them
    Of our proceedings here. On th'market-place
    I know they do attend us.   155

                                      [Exeunt]

ACT 2   SCENE 3
Rome: the market-place

Enter seven or eight CITIZENS

FIRST CITIZEN Once if he do require our voices, we ought not to deny
    him.
SECOND CITIZEN We may, sir, if we will.
THIRD CITIZEN We have power in ourselves to do it, but it is a power
    that we have no power to do. For if he show us his wounds and tell   5
    us his deeds, we are to put our tongues into those wounds and speak
    for them; so if he tell us his noble deeds, we must also tell him our
    noble acceptance of them. Ingratitude is monstrous, and for the
    multitude to be ingrateful were to make a monster of the multitude,
    of the which we, being members, should bring ourselves to be   10
    monstrous members.
FIRST CITIZEN And to make us no better thought of, a little help will
    serve; for once we stood up about the corn, he himself stuck not to
    call us the many-headed multitude.
THIRD CITIZEN We have been called so of many, not that our heads are   15
    some brown, some black, some abram, some bald, but that our wits
    are so diversely coloured. And truly I think if all our wits were to

The Third Citizen's jokes imply that the Second Citizen is stupid.
The citizens resolve to speak to Coriolanus individually or in twos or
threes. Coriolanus is enraged at having to speak to the people.

1 What's the joke?

No one today really understands what the joke is in lines 28–9 ('the
fourth … wife'). Make your own guess, then suggest how you could
bring out the humour on stage. There may be a clue in the Second
Citizen's 'You may, you may', which is probably the equivalent of
today's sarcastically spoken 'Ha, ha, very funny'.

2 'The greater part carries it'

The Third Citizen seems to be saying in line 33 that the plebeians can
approve Coriolanus as consul by a majority vote ('the greater part').
But what was happening in ancient Rome was quite unlike voting in
elections in a modern democracy. Shakespeare does not make clear just
how the citizens are to approve Coriolanus, and historians are still
divided over the precise details of the part the citizens played in
selecting a consul. But it does seem that the citizens had the opportunity
to give general approval, perhaps by a shout of acclamation, to the
candidate the patricians had already chosen (see pages 88, 243).
As you read on, look for clues to what power the plebeians actually
possess.

3 The voice of contempt

In lines 44–8, Coriolanus parodies what he might say to the plebeians
as he begs for their approval of him as consul. Speak his lines putting
as much mockery as you can into your voice to express the whining,
pleading tone he probably uses.

---

issue burst
consent of agreement on
incline to side with
gown of humility simple robe
 (see page 84)
by particulars to each individual
 citizen

pace style
like the virtues … by 'em just as
 the plebeians forget the virtues that
 priests waste their breath on
 preaching to them

issue out of one skull, they would fly east, west, north, south, and
their consent of one direct way should be at once to all the points
o'th'compass.   20

SECOND CITIZEN Think you so? Which way do you judge my wit would
    fly?

THIRD CITIZEN Nay, your wit will not so soon out as another man's will;
    'tis strongly wedged up in a blockhead. But if it were at liberty,
    'twould sure southward.   25

SECOND CITIZEN Why that way?

THIRD CITIZEN To lose itself in a fog where, being three parts melted
    away with rotten dews, the fourth would return for conscience' sake
    to help to get thee a wife.

SECOND CITIZEN You are never without your tricks. You may, you   30
    may.

THIRD CITIZEN Are you all resolved to give your voices? But that's no
    matter, the greater part carries it. I say, if he would incline to the
    people, there was never a worthier man.

Enter CORIOLANUS *in a gown of humility* [*and a hat*], *with* MENENIUS

Here he comes, and in the gown of humility. Mark his behaviour.   35
We are not to stay all together, but to come by him where he stands,
by ones, by twos, and by threes. He's to make his requests by
particulars, wherein every one of us has a single honour in giving
him our own voices with our own tongues. Therefore follow me,
and I'll direct you how you shall go by him.   40

ALL Content, content.   [*Exeunt Citizens*]

MENENIUS O sir, you are not right. Have you not known
    The worthiest men have done't?

CORIOLANUS   What must I say?
    'I pray, sir'? Plague upon't, I cannot bring
    My tongue to such a pace. 'Look, sir, my wounds.   45
    I got them in my country's service, when
    Some certain of your brethren roared and ran
    From th'noise of our own drums.'

MENENIUS   O me, the gods!
    You must not speak of that. You must desire them
    To think upon you.

CORIOLANUS   Think upon me? Hang 'em!   50
    I would they would forget me, like the virtues
    Which our divines lose by 'em.

83

Coriolanus makes clear that he has no wish to be begging for the citizens' approval. The First Citizen wishes he would ask without arrogance, and the Fourth Citizen reminds him of his hate for the people.

Coriolanus (right) in his gown of humility speaks to the citizens.
Which line makes a suitable caption for this picture?

1 Begging for 'voices' (in small groups)

Take parts as Coriolanus and the citizens and act out the 'election' episode in lines 55–122. There are opportunities for both comic and serious moments, and Coriolanus probably uses a number of different styles of speaking. Like all directors, you will need to think about how the episode is similar to and different from modern electoral procedures.

mar all spoil everything	**ha't** have it
wholesome helpful	**alms** charity (gift to beggar)
brace pair	**enigma** riddle
desert deserving, merit	**scourge** whip
kindly humanely, in a friendly manner	**rod** instrument of punishment

MENENIUS   You'll mar all.
　　I'll leave you. Pray you speak to 'em, I pray you,
　　In wholesome manner.

Enter three of the CITIZENS

CORIOLANUS   Bid them wash their faces
　　And keep their teeth clean. So, here comes a brace. –   55
　　You know the cause, sir, of my standing here.
THIRD CITIZEN We do, sir. Tell us what hath brought you to't.
CORIOLANUS Mine own desert.
SECOND CITIZEN Your own desert?
CORIOLANUS Ay, but not mine own desire.   60
THIRD CITIZEN How not your own desire?
CORIOLANUS No, sir, 'twas never my desire yet to trouble the poor
　　with begging.
THIRD CITIZEN You must think, if we give you anything, we hope to
　　gain by you.   65
CORIOLANUS Well then, I pray, your price o'th'consulship?
FIRST CITIZEN The price is to ask it kindly.
CORIOLANUS Kindly, sir, I pray let me ha't. I have wounds to show
　　you, which shall be yours in private. [*To Second Citizen*] Your good
　　voice, sir. What say you?   70
SECOND CITIZEN You shall ha't, worthy sir.
CORIOLANUS A match, sir. There's in all two worthy voices begged. I
　　have your alms. Adieu.
THIRD CITIZEN But this is something odd.
SECOND CITIZEN And 'twere to give again – but 'tis no matter. 75

Exeunt [*Citizens*]

Enter two other CITIZENS

CORIOLANUS Pray you now, if it may stand with the tune of your voices
　　that I may be consul, I have here the customary gown.
FOURTH CITIZEN You have deserved nobly of your country, and you have
　　not deserved nobly.
CORIOLANUS Your enigma?   80
FOURTH CITIZEN You have been a scourge to her enemies; you have
　　been a rod to her friends. You have not indeed loved the common
　　people.

Coriolanus says that the people love flattery, so he will flatter them. He refuses to show his wounds. He condemns the custom that requires him to beg the plebeians' approval, but resolves to see it through.

1 Playing a part (in small groups)

Coriolanus hates the thought that he must act out a part, concealing his true nature, in order to gain the people's approval as consul. He tells the citizens as much in lines 87–91, saying that since the people want the appearance rather than reality ('my hat than my heart'), he will act courteously, doffing his hat ('be off to them') and so imitate the flattery of an insincere politician ('counterfeit the bewitchment of some popular man').

Experiment with ways of speaking the lines directed to the citizens to discover how much irony, sarcasm or contempt he puts into what he says at particular moments (for example, in lines 111–17, the seven repetitions of 'voices'). Do the citizens know or suspect that he is insincere?

2 Empty ritual

Coriolanus' soliloquy, lines 98–110, condemns the tradition ('custom') that demands he must beg for the approval of the common people (the 'voices' of 'Hob and Dick'). Such empty rituals obscure the truth, making him put on a hypocritical act ('fool it so'). But Coriolanus resolves to continue to beg, even though he thinks it an empty charade.

Give reasons for how Coriolanus speaks his soliloquy (for example, angrily, resignedly, mockingly, and so on) and to whom (for example, to himself or the audience), and whether or not he emphasises the rhymes (the soliloquy is in rhyming couplets). You can find an activity on the imagery of lines 103–7 on page 96.

---

dearer estimation of higher reputation from
account gentle expect from gentlemen
insinuating nod gesture that gains me favour
seal confirm

crave the hire wish for the reward
wolvish toge deceitful robe (like a wolf in sheep's clothing)
needless vouches unnecessary approval
o'erpeer be seen, see over
Watched kept guard

CORIOLANUS You should account me the more virtuous that I have not
    been common in my love. I will, sir, flatter my sworn brother, the   85
    people, to earn a dearer estimation of them; 'tis a condition they
    account gentle. And since the wisdom of their choice is rather to
    have my hat than my heart, I will practise the insinuating nod and
    be off to them most counterfeitly. That is, sir, I will counterfeit the
    bewitchment of some popular man and give it bountiful to the   90
    desirers. Therefore, beseech you I may be consul.
FIFTH CITIZEN We hope to find you our friend, and therefore give you our
    voices heartily.
FOURTH CITIZEN You have received many wounds for your country.
CORIOLANUS I will not seal your knowledge with showing them. I will   95
    make much of your voices and so trouble you no farther.
BOTH CITIZENS The gods give you joy, sir, heartily! [Exeunt Citizens]
CORIOLANUS Most sweet voices!
        Better it is to die, better to starve,
        Than crave the hire which first we do deserve.   100
        Why in this wolvish toge should I stand here
        To beg of Hob and Dick that does appear
        Their needless vouches? Custom calls me to't.
        What custom wills, in all things should we do't,
        The dust on antique time would lie unswept   105
        And mountainous error be too highly heaped
        For truth to o'erpeer. Rather than fool it so,
        Let the high office and the honour go
        To one that would do thus. I am half through;
        The one part suffered, the other will I do.   110

                    Enter three CITIZENS *more*

        Here come more voices.
        Your voices! For your voices I have fought,
        Watched for your voices; for your voices bear
        Of wounds two dozen odd. Battles thrice six
        I have seen and heard of; for your voices have   115
        Done many things, some less, some more. Your voices!
        Indeed, I would be consul.
SIXTH CITIZEN He has done nobly, and cannot go without any honest
    man's voice.
SEVENTH CITIZEN Therefore let him be consul. The gods give him joy   120
    and make him good friend to the people!

Sicinius says that Coriolanus has fulfilled the requirements to be appointed consul. He now only needs approval by the senate. The plebeians report that they were mocked by Coriolanus.

1 Staging an 'election' (in small groups)

The 'voices' episode, which began at line 1, ends with the departure of the citizens at line 122. It shows how Coriolanus follows the tradition that every candidate chosen by the senate for a consulship was required to seek the approval of the ordinary people of Rome. This procedure was not like the voting practices in modern democratic states, but rather a general show of approval when the would-be consul appeared in a simple robe before the people to ask for their 'voices' – their signs of agreement.

As noted on page 82, the actual nature of the 'voices' procedure is not known for certain, and in practice the real power in deciding who should be consul lay with the patricians in the senate. But if the citizens of Rome were very strongly against a particular candidate (see lines 197–8 below), the senate would be unlikely to appoint him.

Work out how to stage lines 1–122 to show that this is a political occasion with some similarities to a modern election.

2 Successful?

It looks as if Coriolanus will now become consul. Menenius says all that is left to do, is for Coriolanus to wear the official insignia and immediately meet the senators ('Remains/That, in th'official marks … senate'). Sicinius acknowledges that 'The people do admit you', and sees confidence in Coriolanus' expression: ''Tis warm at's heart'.

But as the citizens begin to disagree, and report that Coriolanus mocked them and refused to show his wounds, it becomes clear that trouble lies ahead. Identify a line opposite where Brutus and Sicinius see their chance to cause Coriolanus' downfall.

---

limitation time required by custom

Endue endow

your approbation approval of you as consul

Repair return

humble weeds low status robes

To my … notice in my humble opinion

ALL CITIZENS   Amen, amen. God save thee, noble consul!

[Exeunt Citizens]

CORIOLANUS   Worthy voices.

Enter MENENIUS, *with* BRUTUS *and* SICINIUS

MENENIUS   You have stood your limitation, and the tribunes
    Endue you with the people's voice. Remains   125
    That, in th'official marks invested, you
    Anon do meet the senate.
CORIOLANUS   Is this done?
SICINIUS   The custom of request you have discharged.
    The people do admit you, and are summoned
    To meet anon upon your approbation.   130
CORIOLANUS   Where? At the senate-house?
SICINIUS   There, Coriolanus.
CORIOLANUS   May I change these garments?
SICINIUS   You may, sir.
CORIOLANUS   That I'll straight do and, knowing myself again,
    Repair to th'senate-house.
MENENIUS   I'll keep you company. *[To the Tribunes]* Will you along?   135
BRUTUS   We stay here for the people.
SICINIUS   Fare you well.

Exeunt Coriolanus and Menenius

    He has it now, and by his looks methinks
    'Tis warm at's heart.
BRUTUS   With a proud heart he wore
    His humble weeds. Will you dismiss the people?

Enter the PLEBEIANS

SICINIUS   How now, my masters, have you chose this man?   140
FIRST CITIZEN   He has our voices, sir.
BRUTUS   We pray the gods he may deserve your loves.
SECOND CITIZEN   Amen, sir. To my poor unworthy notice,
    He mocked us when he begged our voices.
THIRD CITIZEN   Certainly, he flouted us downright.   145
FIRST CITIZEN   No, 'tis his kind of speech. He did not mock us.
SECOND CITIZEN   Not one amongst us, save yourself, but says
    He used us scornfully. He should have showed us
    His marks of merit, wounds received for's country.
SICINIUS   Why, so he did, I am sure.   150

The Third Citizen mimics Coriolanus' scornful behaviour. Brutus and Sicinius remind the citizens of what they might have said to prevent Coriolanus gaining power over them.

1 Imitating Coriolanus (in pairs)

How accurately does the Third Citizen catch Coriolanus' tone? Practise speaking lines 152–9 to find a suitable style. Then check with what actually happened in the market-place (lines 56–122) to judge whether the Third Citizen is exaggerating or not.

2 Politicians at work (in groups of five)

Brutus and Sicinius are determined to bring about Coriolanus' downfall, but the citizens have given him their approval and it seems likely he will become consul, with 'potency and sway' (power and control). How can they prevent that happening?

Take parts as Brutus and Sicinius and the First, Second and Third Citizens and read through from line 152 to the end of the scene. Use the activities below and on the following pages to help you understand how the tribunes work on the people to achieve their purpose of denying power to Coriolanus.

a Do the tribunes reason with the citizens, rebuke them, or ...?

b Lines 163 and 177 ('lessoned', 'fore-advised' = taught earlier) show that the tribunes had previously instructed the citizens how to behave towards Coriolanus in the market-place. Summarise as briefly as you can the instructions the tribunes gave the people (lines 171–6) and the results they hoped for (lines 176–85).

c Suggest why you think the tribunes' instructions were ineffective. Begin by answering Sicinius' question in lines 160–2: were they 'ignorant' (stupid) or of 'childish friendliness'?

Agèd custom ancient tradition
charters privileges, rights
body of the weal commonwealth
Fast foe implacable enemy
plebeii plebeians
what he stood for (the consulship)
Standing being, acting as

touched tested
As cause ... up as any crisis
  occurred
galled irritated
article ... aught a condition he
  must fulfil
choler anger

ALL CITIZENS No, no. No man saw 'em.
THIRD CITIZEN He said he had wounds which he could show in private,
   And with his hat, thus waving it in scorn,
   'I would be consul', says he. 'Agèd custom,
   But by your voices, will not so permit me.   155
   Your voices therefore.' When we granted that,
   Here was 'I thank you for your voices. Thank you,
   Your most sweet voices. Now you have left your voices,
   I have no further with you.' Was not this mockery?
SICINIUS Why either were you ignorant to see't,   160
   Or, seeing it, of such childish friendliness
   To yield your voices?
BRUTUS   Could you not have told him
   As you were lessoned? When he had no power,
   But was a petty servant to the state,
   He was your enemy, ever spake against   165
   Your liberties and the charters that you bear
   I'th'body of the weal; and now, arriving
   A place of potency and sway o'th'state,
   If he should still malignantly remain
   Fast foe to th'plebeii, your voices might   170
   Be curses to yourselves. You should have said
   That as his worthy deeds did claim no less
   Than what he stood for, so his gracious nature
   Would think upon you for your voices and
   Translate his malice towards you into love,   175
   Standing your friendly lord.
SICINIUS   Thus to have said,
   As you were fore-advised, had touched his spirit
   And tried his inclination: from him plucked
   Either his gracious promise, which you might,
   As cause had called you up, have held him to;   180
   Or else it would have galled his surly nature,
   Which easily endures not article
   Tying him to aught. So putting him to rage,
   You should have ta'en th'advantage of his choler
   And passed him unelected.

The tribunes remind the citizens that Coriolanus contemptuously asked for their support. The citizens resolve to deny their approval, and the tribunes suggest that they themselves should be blamed for the error.

1 Hurtful words? (in pairs)

The tribunes continue to work on the citizens' emotions, choosing their words to provoke an angry response. Identify all the words in lines 185–94 that you think Brutus and Sicinius might emphasise in order to arouse the citizens' anger. Then speak the lines in different ways to find a style you favour. For example, sharply and reprovingly, or with an appearance of caring concern.

2 'He's not confirmed'

The Third Citizen's line 195 shows that Coriolanus' appointment as consul has yet to be ratified by approval of the senate. The other citizens vow to gather large numbers of their friends to reject Coriolanus at the meeting at the Senate House. The tribunes plan how that rejection can be done. Their speeches can be spoken as a series of direct instructions. Match the following orders with the appropriate lines opposite:

- tell your friends that Coriolanus will treat them like dogs;
- gather your friends to deny your earlier approval of Coriolanus;
- tell of Coriolanus' pride, and hatred of you;
- remind them of his contempt in begging for approval ('suit');
- tell how your regard for his bravery led you to mistake his bearing ('portance');
- Blame us, the tribunes, for making you choose him;
- Say that you really wished to reject him, but we prevented you.

---

solicit you beg your approval
free contempt undisguised scorn
heart courage
rectorship of judgement rule of
  reason
sued-for begged for

piece 'em add to them
therefor for that purpose
Enforce emphasise
apprehension understanding
gibingly mockingly
ungravely not seriously

BRUTUS	Did you perceive	185

He did solicit you in free contempt
When he did need your loves, and do you think
That his contempt shall not be bruising to you
When he hath power to crush? Why, had your bodies
No heart among you? Or had you tongues to cry   190
Against the rectorship of judgement?

SICINIUS   Have you
Ere now denied the asker, and now again,
Of him that did not ask but mock, bestow
Your sued-for tongues?

THIRD CITIZEN He's not confirmed. We may deny him yet.   195

SECOND CITIZEN And will deny him.
I'll have five hundred voices of that sound.

FIRST CITIZEN I twice five hundred, and their friends to piece 'em.

BRUTUS Get you hence instantly, and tell those friends
They have chose a consul that will from them take   200
Their liberties, make them of no more voice
Than dogs that are as often beat for barking
As therefor kept to do so.

SICINIUS   Let them assemble,
And on a safer judgement all revoke ·
Your ignorant election. Enforce his pride   205
And his old hate unto you. Besides, forget not
With what contempt he wore the humble weed,
How in his suit he scorned you; but your loves,
Thinking upon his services, took from you
Th'apprehension of his present portance,   210
Which most gibingly, ungravely, he did fashion
After the inveterate hate he bears you.

BRUTUS   Lay
A fault on us your tribunes, that we laboured,
No impediment between, but that you must
Cast your election on him.

SICINIUS   Say you chose him   215
More after our commandment than as guided
By your own true affections, and that your minds,
Preoccupied with what you rather must do
Than what you should, made you against the grain
To voice him consul. Lay the fault on us.   220

The citizens are ordered to say that the tribunes reminded them of Coriolanus' noble ancestors, but that now their own better judgement rejects Coriolanus. The tribunes plan to exploit Coriolanus' anger.

1 One long sneer? (in small groups)

Lines 221–31 present the actor playing Brutus with fascinating choices of how he should speak. The lines might be seen as praising Coriolanus' ancestry ('stock'): 'The noble house o'th'Martians' which includes kings, an important magistrate ('censor'), and public benefactors who provided Rome with clean drinking water ('brought by conduits').

But Brutus is a tribune, a representative of the people, and Rome is a republic which has only recently overthrown the rule of tyrant kings. Brutus' intention is to turn the people against Coriolanus.

Talk together about why Brutus goes into such detail about Coriolanus' ancestors, then speak his lines in what you think is the most persuasive way to ensure that the citizens will react as he hopes.

2 Director's decision

If you were directing the play, would you cut 'Almost' in line 240? Give reasons for your decision.

3 Seizing the opportunity (in pairs)

Remind yourselves of how Brutus and Sicinius talked to the citizens throughout lines 140–240, then discuss their skill as politicians. Begin by considering whether you think they swiftly and smoothly put forward their plan of how the citizens can deny Coriolanus the consulship, or whether they pause in and between their speeches, giving the impression they are thinking up the plan as they speak.

---

wrought made efforts
remembrances memories
 (to approve him)
Scaling weighing
sudden approbation
 hasty approval
Harp on that still
 always repeat that

putting on enforcing, urging
presently immediately
drawn your number assembled
 crowds
put in hazard … greater risked
 than wait for a better opportunity
vantage opportunity
goaded provoked, driven

BRUTUS Ay, spare us not. Say we read lectures to you,
How youngly he began to serve his country,
How long continued, and what stock he springs of,
The noble house o'th'Martians, from whence came
That Ancus Martius, Numa's daughter's son,   225
Who after great Hostilius here was king;
Of the same house Publius and Quintus were,
That our best water brought by conduits hither,
[And Censorinus that was so surnamed,]
And nobly naméd so, twice being censor,   230
Was his great ancestor.

SICINIUS   One thus descended,
That hath beside well in his person wrought
To be set high in place, we did commend
To your remembrances; but you have found,
Scaling his present bearing with his past,   235
That he's your fixèd enemy, and revoke
Your sudden approbation.

BRUTUS   Say you ne'er had done't –
Harp on that still – but by our putting on.
And presently, when you have drawn your number,
Repair to th'Capitol.

ALL CITIZENS   We will so. Almost all   240
Repent in their election.

                                      Exeunt Plebeians

BRUTUS   Let them go on.
This mutiny were better put in hazard
Than stay, past doubt, for greater.
If, as his nature is, he fall in rage
With their refusal, both observe and answer   245
The vantage of his anger.

SICINIUS   To th'Capitol, come.
We will be there before the stream o'th'people;
And this shall seem, as partly 'tis, their own,
Which we have goaded onward.

                                              Exeunt

Looking back at Act 2
Activities for groups and individuals

1 Triumphal entrance – and exit

In Scene 1, Coriolanus makes a triumphal entry into Rome. Nineteenth-century productions of the play staged the entrance with great ceremony, trying to evoke the spirit of an ancient Roman Triumph, in which a conquering hero rode in a procession of magnificent splendour, displaying the loot and prisoners captured in war. In Shakespeare's time, King James I made a triumphal entry into London in 1604, in a spectacular pageant that was probably recalled by the first audiences of the play. Work out your own staging of the triumphal entry (and exit), and also decide how you would perform Coriolanus' entry to the Capitol in Scene 2, where the Roman senators gather to praise him.

2 Dramatic construction

Suggest why Shakespeare ensures that at the end of each scene in Act 2 the tribunes remain alone on stage after everyone else has left. Also suggest what stage effects you might use to bring out the significance of this aspect of dramatic construction, for example a change in lighting, or a piece of music.

3 Should soldiers be involved in politics?

Coriolanus is a brilliantly successful soldier, but will he make a successful politician? In Britain, serving soldiers are prohibited from playing any part in politics, but world-wide there are many examples of military and political life being very closely intertwined. Talk together about whether you think soldiers should take part in politics. It will help your discussion to consider actual examples today or from the recent past.

4 Empty ritual?

In Scene 3, lines 103–7, Coriolanus uses a powerful image: that by observing custom, 'mountainous error' grows like unswept dust. Talk together about examples of political customs, for example the state opening of parliament in the UK, or a party convention in the USA at which a presidential candidate is nominated. Do such political customs obscure the truth? What would Coriolanus make of such gatherings?

The tribunes instruct the citizens about how to prevent Coriolanus becoming consul. Rome is a society divided against itself, and in each scene of Act 2 the tribunes plot Coriolanus' downfall. Choose a line from Scene 3 as a caption to this picture.

5 Write Coriolanus' letters

Scene 1 shows that Coriolanus has written letters to his mother, his wife, Menenius and the senate. Does he use a different style in each letter? Step into role as Coriolanus and write the four letters.

6 Coriolanus' wounds

Coriolanus' wounds play an important part in the act. Volumnia and Menenius rejoice in counting them, and in the market-place they are used as political bribes: the citizens wish to see them as the price of approving Coriolanus as consul. Symbolically, Coriolanus' wounds are like the notches on a gunfighter's revolver, or like duelling scars on the face of a Prussian officer. Design a poster advertising a production of the play which uses the wounds as its dominant image.

Coriolanus expects another invasion by the Volsces, but Cominius says they are too battle-weary. Lartius speaks of Aufidius' hatred for Coriolanus. The tribunes approach, and Coriolanus scorns them.

1 First impression (in groups of five)

The simmering conflict between Coriolanus and the people of Rome will boil over in this scene. To gain a first impression of the scene's atmosphere and events, take parts as Coriolanus, Brutus, Sicinius and Menenius. The fifth person can speak all the other parts. Read quickly through the whole scene without pausing, then choose some of the activities below and on the following pages.

2 Eager for news of Aufidius?

Coriolanus is on his way from the Capitol to the market-place. There the final approval of his election as consul should take place, as the citizens confirm their earlier vote. His first words are about his military rival, the Volscian leader, Aufidius.

How eager is Coriolanus for news of Aufidius? Advise the actor about how to speak each of his seven speeches in lines 1–20 to show his feelings about his opponent. As you prepare your advice, think about the theatrical convention that when a line is shared (for example, lines 8, 12 and 17), there is no pause between speakers. Would you follow that convention, or would you advise Coriolanus to pause before he speaks?

3 Dramatic irony

'I wish I had a cause to seek him there'. In view of what will happen in Act 3, Coriolanus' line 19 is full of dramatic irony (see page 144). He is unaware that he will very soon have a 'cause' to go to Antium to find Aufidius. Keep the line in mind as you read on to discover how Coriolanus' wish comes true in a way he does not expect.

---

all the gentry many patricians
made new head recruited a fresh army
composition peace treaty
worn exhausted
safeguard safe conduct pass

To hopeless restitution beyond hope of recovery
prank them dress themselves
Against all noble sufferance beyond the endurance of the nobility

ACT 3 SCENE 1
Rome: a street

Cornets. Enter CORIOLANUS, MENENIUS, all the gentry,
COMINIUS, TITUS LARTIUS, and other SENATORS

CORIOLANUS Tullus Aufidius then had made new head?
LARTIUS He had, my lord, and that it was which caused
  Our swifter composition.
CORIOLANUS So then the Volsces stand but as at first,
  Ready when time shall prompt them to make raid   5
  Upon's again.
COMINIUS   They are worn, lord consul, so,
  That we shall hardly in our ages see
  Their banners wave again.
CORIOLANUS   Saw you Aufidius?
LARTIUS On safeguard he came to me and did curse
  Against the Volsces for they had so vilely   10
  Yielded the town. He is retired to Antium.
CORIOLANUS Spoke he of me?
LARTIUS   He did, my lord.
CORIOLANUS   How? what?
LARTIUS How often he had met you sword to sword;
  That of all things upon the earth he hated
  Your person most; that he would pawn his fortunes 15
  To hopeless restitution, so he might
  Be called your vanquisher.
CORIOLANUS   At Antium lives he?
LARTIUS At Antium.
CORIOLANUS I wish I had a cause to seek him there,
  To oppose his hatred fully. Welcome home.   20

    Enter SICINIUS *and* BRUTUS

  Behold, these are the tribunes of the people,
  The tongues o'th'common mouth. I do despise them,
  For they do prank them in authority
  Against all noble sufferance.
SICINIUS Pass no further.   25
CORIOLANUS Ha? What is that?

The tribunes report the plebeians' anger against Coriolanus. He claims it is a plot against the patricians. After an exchange of insults, Sicinius advises Coriolanus to behave courteously.

1 The tribunes get to work

Brutus and Sicinius have planned to exploit Coriolanus' fiery temper. They want to goad him into rash speech and action, and so display his unfitness to rule. One director advised the actors playing the tribunes to think of themselves as matadors, facing a dangerous bull. Their job is to continually infuriate the bull, and to weaken him with well-placed thrusts.

Give your own advice to the tribunes as to how they should speak and behave. For example, will they be controlled and rational, or assertive and melodramatic, or …? Which words might they emphasise in order to spark off Coriolanus' anger? What does Sicinius do as he speaks 'Pass no further' (line 25)? Many actors find Brutus' line 50 difficult; it may be an insult meaning 'My political skill is better than yours'.

2 Coriolanus' feelings (in pairs)

Coriolanus is contemptuous of the plebeians and refers to them dismissively in all kinds of ways ('children', 'herd', 'tongues', 'them', and so on).

One person quietly speaks everything that Coriolanus says opposite, a sentence at a time. After each sentence, the partner also speaks the sentence, but emphasises the key words which suggest what Coriolanus is feeling at that moment.

---

disclaim their tongues deny what
 they have said
offices duties
set them on urged them to attack
 (like dogs)
purposed thing planned trick
Suffer't accept it

repined complained
Scandalled the suppliants
 slandered those who pleaded
sithence since then
stir rebel
yoke pair up

BRUTUS It will be dangerous to go on. No further.

CORIOLANUS What makes this change?

MENENIUS The matter?

COMINIUS Hath he not passed the noble and the common?   30

BRUTUS Cominius, no.

CORIOLANUS   Have I had children's voices?

FIRST SENATOR Tribunes, give way. He shall to th'market-place.

BRUTUS The people are incensed against him.

SICINIUS   Stop,
Or all will fall in broil.

CORIOLANUS   Are these your herd?
Must these have voices, that can yield them now   35
And straight disclaim their tongues? What are your offices?
You being their mouths, why rule you not their teeth?
Have you not set them on?

MENENIUS   Be calm, be calm.

CORIOLANUS It is a purposed thing, and grows by plot
To curb the will of the nobility.   40
Suffer't, and live with such as cannot rule
Nor ever will be ruled.

BRUTUS   Call't not a plot.
The people cry you mocked them; and of late,
When corn was given them gratis, you repined,
Scandalled the suppliants for the people, called them   45
Time-pleasers, flatterers, foes to nobleness.

CORIOLANUS Why this was known before.

BRUTUS   Not to them all.

CORIOLANUS Have you informed them sithence?

BRUTUS   How? I inform them?

CORIOLANUS You are like to do such business.

BRUTUS Not unlike each way to better yours.   50

CORIOLANUS Why then should I be consul? By yond clouds,
Let me deserve so ill as you, and make me
Your fellow tribune.

SICINIUS   You show too much of that
For which the people stir. If you will pass
To where you are bound, you must enquire your way,   55
Which you are out of, with a gentler spirit,
Or never be so noble as a consul,
Nor yoke with him for tribune.

Coriolanus insists on speaking. He claims that treating the plebeians kindly only produces rebellion, and he will fearlessly speak his mind. The tribunes rebuke him.

1 Accurate descriptions? (in pairs)

Coriolanus describes the people as a changeable, stinking mob ('mutable, rank-scented meinie'), and as a disease that produces scabs ('measles', 'tetter'). In response, Brutus says that Coriolanus speaks as if he were a stern god, not a man with weaknesses like other men (lines 81–3).

Coriolanus declares that his words act as a mirror, showing the people as they really are. But how true are his and Brutus' descriptions? Give your response to each, and talk together about what each suggests about the speaker.

2 Imagery

Imagine that you are directing the play, and that the actors ask you whether they might do anything in performance to make the following images meaningful to the audience:

lines 61–2: imagery from the game of bowls ('rub' is an obstacle; 'laid falsely' means a bowl deceitfully placed; 'plain way' means that the bowl runs truly, without hindrance).

lines 70–5: Coriolanus uses corn-growing imagery, calling the plebeians 'cockle' (a weed growing among the corn: see the parable of the wheat and tares in the Bible, Matthew 13:24–30).

lines 78–81: imagery of disease (see the body-politic imagery, page 239).

3 'Shall remain'

When you turn the page you will find that Sicinius' word 'shall' in line 88 provokes an outraged response from Coriolanus.

---

abused, set on deceived, incited
paltering tricky word play
Becomes not does not dignify
soothing flattering, giving in to
honoured number honourable
  rulers (patricians)

Coin create
measles diseases
tetter infect us with scabs
choler anger
Jove (in Roman mythology)
  Jupiter, king of the gods

MENENIUS   Let's be calm.

COMINIUS The people are abused, set on. This paltering
    Becomes not Rome, nor has Coriolanus   60
    Deserved this so dishonoured rub, laid falsely
    I'th'plain way of his merit.

CORIOLANUS   Tell me of corn!
    This was my speech, and I will speak't again –

MENENIUS Not now, not now.

FIRST SENATOR   Not in this heat, sir, now.

CORIOLANUS Now as I live, I will.   65
    My nobler friends, I crave their pardons. For
    The mutable, rank-scented meinie, let them
    Regard me, as I do not flatter, and
    Therein behold themselves. I say again,
    In soothing them, we nourish 'gainst our senate   70
    The cockle of rebellion, insolence, sedition,
    Which we ourselves have ploughed for, sowed, and scattered
    By mingling them with us, the honoured number,
    Who lack not virtue, no, nor power, but that
    Which they have given to beggars.

MENENIUS   Well, no more.   75

FIRST SENATOR No more words, we beseech you.

CORIOLANUS   How? no more?
    As for my country I have shed my blood,
    Not fearing outward force, so shall my lungs
    Coin words till their decay against those measles
    Which we disdain should tetter us, yet sought   80
    The very way to catch them.

BRUTUS   You speak o'th'people
    As if you were a god to punish, not
    A man of their infirmity.

SICINIUS   'Twere well
    We let the people know't.

MENENIUS   What, what? His choler?

CORIOLANUS Choler!   85
    Were I as patient as the midnight sleep,
    By Jove, 'twould be my mind.

SICINIUS   It is a mind
    That shall remain a poison where it is,
    Not poison any further.

Coriolanus is infuriated by hearing a tribune dare to give orders. He warns the senators against giving power to the people, and argues that divisions in the state lead to destruction.

1 'Triton of the minnows'

In Greek mythology, Triton was a minor sea god who blew a trumpet to announce Poseidon, the chief sea god. Coriolanus' insult means something like 'Captain of the small fry' (minnows are tiny fish). The image is echoed in line 96, picturing the tribunes as the noisy trumpeters of the people. Make up one or two modern versions of the expression 'Triton of the minnows'.

2 Coriolanus in full flow (in small groups)

Stung by hearing a tribune daring to issue an order ('shall'), Coriolanus first repeats and ridicules the word, then launches into three long speeches against what he sees as the dangers of democracy. Lines 92–113 are addressed to his fellow patricians, warning them that if they give any power to the people, they will lose all of their own.

Coriolanus uses images he knows will have a strong effect on the patricians: the people as a many-headed monster; the people stealing the patricians' power; the thought that the people will sit beside the patricians in the Senate and their 'voice' will overwhelm the patricians. He ends with a political lesson about the need for hierarchy: that if there is not a single, supreme power, then competing factions will destroy each other: 'when two authorities are up … th'other'.

The speech is an exercise in rhetoric (the art of persuasion), so take turns to speak lines 92–113 as persuasively as you can to other members of the group. Emphasise each 'shall' disdainfully. Try to bring out the pendulum-like, swinging rhythm of the speech, as Coriolanus constantly contrasts words and thoughts, setting patricians against plebeians: 'good'/'unwise', 'grave'/'reckless', 'your'/'his', and so on.

---

from the canon against the law
Given Hydra allowed this
  many-headed monster
turn your current … his
  seize your power
vail your ignorance bow down in
  stupidity

awake / Your dangerous lenity
  be aware that your mildness
  threatens you
cushions seats in the senate
palates savours of
a graver bench wiser rulers
recompense reward for service
pressed conscripted

CORIOLANUS   'Shall remain'?
          Hear you this Triton of the minnows? Mark you   90
          His absolute 'shall'?
COMINIUS   'Twas from the canon.
CORIOLANUS   'Shall'!
          O good but most unwise patricians! Why,
          You grave but reckless senators, have you thus
          Given Hydra here to choose an officer
          That with his peremptory 'shall', being but   95
          The horn and noise o'th'monster's, wants not spirit
          To say he'll turn your current in a ditch
          And make your channel his? If he have power,
          Then vail your ignorance; if none, awake
          Your dangerous lenity. If you are learned,   100
          Be not as common fools; if you are not,
          Let them have cushions by you. You are plebeians,
          If they be senators; and they are no less
          When, both your voices blended, the great'st taste
          Most palates theirs. They choose their magistrate,   105
          And such a one as he, who puts his 'shall',
          His popular 'shall', against a graver bench
          Than ever frowned in Greece. By Jove himself,
          It makes the consuls base, and my soul aches
          To know, when two authorities are up,   110
          Neither supreme, how soon confusion
          May enter 'twixt the gap of both and take
          The one by th'other.
COMINIUS   Well, on to th'market-place.
CORIOLANUS Whoever gave that counsel to give forth
          The corn o'th'storehouse gratis, as 'twas used   115
          Sometime in Greece –
MENENIUS   Well, well, no more of that.
CORIOLANUS Though there the people had more absolute power –
          I say they nourished disobedience, fed
          The ruin of the state.
BRUTUS   Why shall the people give
          One that speaks thus their voice?
CORIOLANUS   I'll give my reasons,   120
          More worthier than their voices. They know the corn
          Was not our recompense, resting well assured
          They ne'er did service for't. Being pressed to th'war,

Coriolanus accuses the plebeians of cowardice and mutiny, and says they will claim that the patricians fear them. He implores the senators to dismiss the tribunes and end moves towards democracy.

1 Who should rule? (in small groups)

Use the following summaries to help you speak Coriolanus' diatribes against the plebeians and democracy.

In lines 120–40, Coriolanus gives his reasons why he detests the plebeians and why they do not deserve free corn ('corn gratis'). At times of crisis ('when the navel of the state was touched') they would not come out fighting for Rome ('thread the gates'); as soldiers, they mutinied; they complain without reason ('All cause unborn'); and they claim that the patricians fear them because they are the majority ('greater poll'). To give in to the plebeians disgraces the patricians' right to rule in the Senate ('The nature of our seats'), allowing inferiors to attack superiors ('The crows to peck the eagles').

In lines 141–62, Coriolanus returns to his condemnation of any kind of democracy or divided authority ('double worship'). He claims that such power sharing, in which the patricians cannot rule without the approval of the mob ('general ignorance'), results in the neglect of important issues ('Real necessities') in favour of constantly changing trivialities ('unstable slightness'), with nothing worthwhile achieved.

He flatters the patricians, saying they are wise rather than cowardly ('less fearful than discreet'), they love Rome and hate to see it changed, they prefer honour before life itself, and they wish to cure Rome of its diseases even though the medicine is risky ('dangerous physic'). He begs them to rid themselves of the tribunes ('pluck out the multitudinous tongue' = the voice of the people) – who enjoy the power ('lick the sweet') which is poisonous to the state. Not to do so is dishonourable and unwise, because it removes the unity of Rome ('bereaves the state of that integrity') which dignifies it ('become't'), because the evil plebeians ('th'ill') prevent the patricians from doing good.

---

navel very centre
native ... donation origin of our generous gift
bosom multiplied mob
seats places in the senate
double worship divided authority
conclude rule, make laws

Purpose so barred objectives thus obstructed
doubt the change on't wish it changed
jump dose
become't give dignity to the state

Even when the navel of the state was touched,
They would not thread the gates. This kind of service   125
Did not deserve corn gratis. Being i'th'war,
Their mutinies and revolts, wherein they showed
Most valour, spoke not for them. Th'accusation
Which they have often made against the senate,
All cause unborn, could never be the native   130
Of our so frank donation. Well, what then?
How shall this bosom multiplied digest
The senate's courtesy? Let deeds express
What's like to be their words: 'We did request it;
We are the greater poll, and in true fear   135
They gave us our demands.' Thus we debase
The nature of our seats and make the rabble
Call our cares fears, which will in time
Break ope the locks o'th'senate and bring in
The crows to peck the eagles.

MENENIUS   Come, enough.   140
BRUTUS Enough, with over-measure.
CORIOLANUS   No, take more!
What may be sworn by, both divine and human,
Seal what I end withal! This double worship,
Where one part does disdain with cause, the other
Insult without all reason; where gentry, title, wisdom   145
Cannot conclude but by the yea and no
Of general ignorance – it must omit
Real necessities, and give way the while
To unstable slightness. Purpose so barred, it follows
Nothing is done to purpose. Therefore beseech you –   150
You that will be less fearful than discreet,
That love the fundamental part of state
More than you doubt the change on't, that prefer
A noble life before a long, and wish
To jump a body with a dangerous physic   155
That's sure of death without it – at once pluck out
The multitudinous tongue; let them not lick
The sweet which is their poison. Your dishonour
Mangles true judgement, and bereaves the state
Of that integrity which should become't,   160
Not having the power to do the good it would
For th'ill which doth control't.

Coriolanus insults the tribunes, claiming they were wrongly appointed at a time of crisis, and should now be dismissed. He resists arrest, and general confusion follows.

1 But who is a traitor?

In line 163, Sicinius once again uses 'shall', the word that so angers Coriolanus. He adds insult to injury by calling Coriolanus 'traitor'. His accusation provokes another outburst from Coriolanus, who claims that the tribunes were appointed at a time of rebellion 'When what's not meet but must be was law' – when what was right ('meet') was overwhelmed by sheer force ('must be').

But does the notion of who is a 'traitor', what is a 'rebellion', and what is 'meet' (right), depend on the point of view of the speaker? As you read on, keep in mind all three words, and think about whether their meaning changes depending on who uses the words (for example, why does Sicinius accuse Coriolanus of being a traitor, and why does Coriolanus think he is not?).

2 Bald, bearded and body odour? (in pairs)

Coriolanus calls Sicinius 'bald', 'old goat' and 'rotten thing'. Bald can mean both hairless and witless, goats are bearded, and 'rotten thing' suggests stink and bad breath. Talk together about whether you think these descriptions of Sicinius are accurate or merely untrue insults.

3 'Tribunes! Patricians! Citizens!' (in small groups)

The page opposite is filled with explicit and implicit stage directions. Work out how you would stage the episode. Will you present the '*bustle*' (stage direction, line 186) as general confusion, with everyone on stage milling around in a riot, or would you show the patricians and plebeians, squaring up to each other in two very distinct groups?

---

answer pay the penalty
despite contempt
th'greater bench the Senate
aediles officers of the tribunes
apprehended arrested

Attach arrest
innovator rebel, revolutionary
weal welfare, commonwealth
surety stand bail for

BRUTUS   He's said enough.
SICINIUS He's spoken like a traitor and shall answer
        As traitors do.
CORIOLANUS   Thou wretch, despite o'erwhelm thee!
        What should the people do with these bald tribunes,   165
        On whom depending, their obedience fails
        To th'greater bench? In a rebellion,
        When what's not meet but what must be was law,
        Then were they chosen. In a better hour
        Let what is meet be said it must be meet,   170
        And throw their power i'th'dust.
BRUTUS Manifest treason!
SICINIUS This a consul? No.
BRUTUS The aediles, ho!

                    Enter an AEDILE

                Let him be apprehended.
SICINIUS Go call the people,

                                        [*Exit Aedile*]

        [*To Coriolanus*]   in whose name myself   175
        Attach thee as a traitorous innovator,
        A foe to th'public weal. Obey, I charge thee,
        And follow to thine answer.
                    [*Lays hold on Coriolanus*]
CORIOLANUS   Hence, old goat!
ALL PATRICIANS We'll surety him.
COMINIUS   Aged sir, hands off.
CORIOLANUS Hence, rotten thing, or I shall shake thy bones   180
        Out of thy garments.
SICINIUS   Help, ye citizens!

        Enter a rabble of PLEBEIANS *with the* AEDILES

MENENIUS On both sides more respect.
SICINIUS Here's he that would take from you all your power.
BRUTUS Seize him, aediles!
ALL PLEBEIANS Down with him! Down with him!   185
SECOND SENATOR Weapons! weapons! weapons!
                They all bustle about Coriolanus
ALL Tribunes! Patricians! Citizens! What ho!
        Sicinius! Brutus! Coriolanus! Citizens!

Menenius wants the tribunes to restore order, but Sicinius accuses Coriolanus of wishing to remove the people's rights, and orders his immediate death. The crowd agrees. Menenius calls for calm.

1 What is Coriolanus doing? (in pairs)

Coriolanus is silent between lines 181–224. In one production he sat, silent and still, contemptuously watching the commotion around him. Make your own suggestions about how he might behave, particularly at the points where Sicinius calls him Martius (line 196) and orders his immediate execution (lines 214–16).

2 'What is the city but the people?' (in small groups)

a By 'the people' does Sicinius mean every person who lives in Rome, or only the plebeians? Talk together about just what you think Sicinius means by line 200.

b Which words do you think Sicinius would stress as he speaks the line?

c Give your views on whether you agree with those commentators who have claimed that line 200 is a major key to understanding the whole play.

d What is your own response to line 200? What relevance does it have today?

3 'Th'rock Tarpeian'

The Tarpeian rock is a high cliff on Rome's Capitoline Hill. Traitors were executed by being flung from the rock.

---

at point about, in danger
kindle inflame, incite a riot
quench extinguish

distinctly ranges separately stands (houses and social structure)
present immediate
redress set right, restore

AEDILES Peace, peace, peace! Stay! hold! peace!

MENENIUS What is about to be? I am out of breath.   190
       Confusion's near; I cannot speak. You, tribunes
       To th'people – Coriolanus, patience! –
       Speak, good Sicinius.

SICINIUS   Hear me, people. Peace!

ALL PLEBEIANS Let's hear our tribune. Peace! Speak, speak, speak.

SICINIUS You are at point to lose your liberties.   195
       Martius would have all from you, Martius,
       Whom late you have named for consul.

MENENIUS   Fie, fie, fie!
       This is the way to kindle, not to quench.

FIRST SENATOR To unbuild the city and to lay all flat.

SICINIUS What is the city but the people?   200

ALL PLEBEIANS True. The people are the city.

BRUTUS By the consent of all we were established
       The people's magistrates.

ALL PLEBEIANS You so remain.

MENENIUS And so are like to do.   205

COMINIUS That is the way to lay the city flat,
       To bring the roof to the foundation
       And bury all, which yet distinctly ranges,
       In heaps and piles of ruin.

SICINIUS   This deserves death.

BRUTUS Or let us stand to our authority   210
       Or let us lose it. We do here pronounce,
       Upon the part o'th'people, in whose power
       We were elected theirs, Martius is worthy
       Of present death.

SICINIUS   Therefore lay hold of him.
       Bear him to th'rock Tarpeian, and from thence   215
       Into destruction cast him.

BRUTUS   Aediles, seize him.

ALL PLEBEIANS Yield, Martius, yield!

MENENIUS   Hear me one word.
       Beseech you, tribunes, hear me but a word.

AEDILES Peace, peace!

MENENIUS Be that you seem, truly your country's friend,   220
       And temperately proceed to what you would
       Thus violently redress.

Brutus orders Coriolanus' removal to execution, but Coriolanus draws his sword and drives away all the plebeians. He speaks of them as farm animals. The patricians try to persuade Coriolanus to leave.

'The people are beat in'. This Royal Shakespeare Company production set the play in the time of the French Revolution, with Coriolanus resembling the young Napoleon. Think of the key words of the Revolution: 'Liberty, Equality, Fraternity' and speculate about how this setting can heighten the relevance and dramatic impact of the play.

cold ways calm methods	**littered** born
beat in driven off stage	**One time ... another** wait for a
naught ruin, nothing	better occasion
tent treat, cure	**brace** pair
barbarians savages (not Romans)	

BRUTUS   Sir, those cold ways,
  That seem like prudent helps, are very poisonous
  Where the disease is violent. – Lay hands upon him
  And bear him to the rock.

     Coriolanus draws his sword

CORIOLANUS   No, I'll die here.   225
  There's some among you have beheld me fighting;
  Come, try upon yourselves what you have seen me.
MENENIUS Down with that sword! Tribunes, withdraw awhile.
BRUTUS Lay hands upon him.
MENENIUS   Help Martius, help!
  You that be noble, help him, young and old!   230
ALL PLEBEIANS Down with him! Down with him!

 In this mutiny, the tribunes, the aediles, and the people are beat in

MENENIUS [*To Coriolanus*] Go, get you to your house. Be gone, away!
  All will be naught else.
SECOND SENATOR   Get you gone.
CORIOLANUS   Stand fast!
  We have as many friends as enemies.
MENENIUS Shall it be put to that?
FIRST SENATOR   The gods forbid!   235
  I prithee, noble friend, home to thy house;
  Leave us to cure this cause.
MENENIUS   For 'tis a sore upon us
  You cannot tent yourself. Begone, beseech you.
COMINIUS Come, sir, along with us.
CORIOLANUS I would they were barbarians, as they are,   240
  Though in Rome littered, not Romans, as they are not,
  Though calved i'th'porch o'th'Capitol.
MENENIUS   Begone!
  Put not your worthy rage into your tongue.
  One time will owe another.
CORIOLANUS   On fair ground
  I could beat forty of them.
MENENIUS   I could myself   245
  Take up a brace o'th'best of them, yea, the two tribunes.

Cominius urges caution, warning that the plebeians' rage will destroy all order. Coriolanus leaves, and Menenius describes his inflexible character. The plebeians return, intent on Coriolanus' instant execution.

1 Going quietly? (in small groups)

Work out different ways of playing the stage direction at line 255. Does Coriolanus go willingly, or does he have to be physically persuaded, or …?

2 Character reference: straight speaking

Menenius sums up Coriolanus' character in lines 257–62. For example, 'His heart's his mouth' means he must instantly say what he feels. Consider each of the four sentences in turn and suggest what a plebeian would say after each.

3 Imagery

All the images below may refer, in some way, to Rome. Put them in order of how powerfully they conjure up pictures in your mind that help your understanding of what the speakers mean.

line 247: ''tis odds beyond arithmetic' – it's overwhelming numbers against us

lines 248–9: 'manhood is called foolery … falling fabric' – courage is foolish when the world is collapsing about our ears

lines 251–2: 'Like interrupted waters … bear' – like a dammed up river bursting its banks.

lines 254–5: 'This must be patched with cloth of any colour' – Rome is pictured as a torn garment to be repaired in any way possible.

lines 273–4: 'mouths', 'hands' – an echo of Menenius' tale of the belly in the opening scene of the play?

---

manhood courage	**trident** spear with three prongs
fabric building	**Jove** (in Roman mythology)
tag mob, rabble	Jupiter, king of the gods (who
in request of any help	caused thunder)
marred spoiled	**breast forges** emotions dictate
Neptune (in Roman mythology)	**vent** speak
god of the sea	**speak 'em fair** flatter them

COMINIUS But now 'tis odds beyond arithmetic,
       And manhood is called foolery when it stands
       Against a falling fabric. Will you hence
       Before the tag return, whose rage doth rend   250
       Like interrupted waters, and o'erbear
       What they are used to bear?
MENENIUS   Pray you, begone.
       I'll try whether my old wit be in request
       With those that have but little. This must be patched
       With cloth of any colour.
COMINIUS   Nay, come away.   255

Exeunt Coriolanus and Cominius [and others]

A PATRICIAN This man has marred his fortune.
MENENIUS His nature is too noble for the world.
       He would not flatter Neptune for his trident
       Or Jove for's power to thunder. His heart's his mouth.
       What his breast forges, that his tongue must vent,   260
       And, being angry, does forget that ever
       He heard the name of death.
              A noise within
       Here's goodly work.
A PATRICIAN   I would they were abed.
MENENIUS I would they were in Tiber! What the vengeance,
       Could he not speak 'em fair?

Enter BRUTUS *and* SICINIUS *with the* RABBLE *again*

SICINIUS   Where is this viper   265
       That would depopulate the city and
       Be every man himself?
MENENIUS   You worthy tribunes –
SICINIUS He shall be thrown down the Tarpeian rock
       With rigorous hands. He hath resisted law,
       And therefore law shall scorn him further trial   270
       Than the severity of the public power
       Which he so sets at naught.
FIRST CITIZEN   He shall well know
       The noble tribunes are the people's mouths,
       And we their hands.
ALL PLEBEIANS He shall, sure on't.   275

Menenius tries to calm the plebeians and to defend Coriolanus.
The tribunes scorn the thought of Coriolanus as consul and are
determined to kill him. Sicinius rejects Menenius' praise of Coriolanus.

1 Menenius faces a problem

Menenius finds himself in a tight corner. Not only must he try to
protect Coriolanus, but he himself is under threat. Sicinius accuses
him of helping Coriolanus to escape ('make this rescue'). In
Shakespeare's time, 'rescue' was a legal term for assisting the escape of
a prisoner, for which the penalty could be death.

Menenius uses his skill in debating to try to placate the tribunes.
Match each of the following techniques he uses with the lines opposite,
and identify other techniques as you read on:

- flattery;
- reasoning that his hearers will lose little by listening;
- appealing to traditional authorities (gods, Rome, parents);
- countering an assertion with a reassurance;
- praising Coriolanus' service to Rome at great personal cost;
- implying that Rome is united;
- warning of shame that might come on his hearers.

2 Which image has more power to calm?

Menenius is trying to placate the plebeians' fury. In lines 295–9, he
says that if Coriolanus is killed, Rome would be like an 'unnatural dam'
(cruel mother) who eats her own children. 'Jove's own book' may be
some kind of Roll of Honour, kept in the Temple of Jupiter (Jove) on
the Capitoline Hill. It records the names of famous people in Rome's
history ('her deservèd children'). Which image ('dam' or 'book') do
you think is likely to have more influence in calming the plebeians'
anger? Why?

---

cry havoc give the order to
  slaughter
modest warrant limited licence
  to kill
rescue escape of Coriolanus
leave permission

peremptory determined
enrolled recorded
Mortal deadly
brand shameful scar
clean kam all wrong

MENENIUS Sir, sir –

SICINIUS Peace!

MENENIUS Do not cry havoc where you should but hunt
    With modest warrant.

SICINIUS   Sir, how comes't that you
    Have holp to make this rescue?

MENENIUS   Hear me speak.   280
    As I do know the consul's worthiness,
    So can I name his faults.

SICINIUS Consul? What consul?

MENENIUS The consul Coriolanus.

BRUTUS He consul?   285

ALL PLEBEIANS No, no, no, no, no!

MENENIUS If, by the tribunes' leave and yours, good people,
    I may be heard, I would crave a word or two,
    The which shall turn you to no further harm
    Than so much loss of time.

SICINIUS   Speak briefly, then,   290
    For we are peremptory to dispatch
    This viperous traitor. To eject him hence
    Were but one danger, and to keep him here
    Our certain death. Therefore it is decreed
    He dies tonight.

MENENIUS   Now the good gods forbid   295
    That our renownèd Rome, whose gratitude
    Towards her deservèd children is enrolled
    In Jove's own book, like an unnatural dam
    Should now eat up her own!

SICINIUS He's a disease that must be cut away.   300

MENENIUS O, he's a limb that has but a disease –
    Mortal to cut it off, to cure it easy.
    What has he done to Rome that's worthy death?
    Killing our enemies, the blood he hath lost –
    Which I dare vouch is more than that he hath   305
    By many an ounce – he dropped it for his country;
    And what is left, to lose it by his country
    Were to us all that do't and suffer it
    A brand to th'end o'th'world.

SICINIUS   This is clean kam.

The tribunes are determined that Coriolanus must die, but Menenius warns that civil war will result unless Coriolanus has a fair trial. The tribunes agree to a public hearing.

1 Patching up the quarrel

Earlier in the scene, Menenius said that the quarrel between Coriolanus and the plebeians 'must be patched with cloth of any colour' (lines 254–5). Now he tries to do that patching up, urging caution rather than speed, and that to avoid Roman fighting Roman they should 'Proceed by process' – by due process of law. He uses various arguments:

- be cautious;
- proceed lawfully;
- avoid civil war;
- Coriolanus was raised to be a soldier;
- he is not skilled in language;
- let him have fair trial that may result in death.

Put the six arguments in order of importance from the tribunes' point of view (for example, will the tribunes be more swayed by hearing that Coriolanus cannot use refined ('bolted') language, or by hearing that feuding factions ('parties') may reduce Rome to rubble?).

2 Advise the actors

a Should the actors use an ironic tone when they speak the word 'Noble' in lines 331 and 334?

b What gestures might Menenius use to help the audience with the animal imagery of lines 317–19, and the imagery of corn being turned to flour 'and is ... distinction' (lines 326–8)?

Merely awry absolutely wrong
gangrened fatally diseased
unscanned swiftness
  unthinking haste
leaden pounds heavy weights

process due process of law
sack devastate
smote struck, beaten
lawful form legal trial

BRUTUS   Merely awry. When he did love his country,   310
    It honoured him.
SICINIUS   The service of the foot,
    Being once gangrened, is not then respected
    For what before it was.
BRUTUS   We'll hear no more.
    Pursue him to his house and pluck him thence,
    Lest his infection, being of catching nature,   315
    Spread further.
MENENIUS   One word more, one word!
    This tiger-footed rage, when it shall find
    The harm of unscanned swiftness, will, too late,
    Tie leaden pounds to's heels. Proceed by process,
    Lest parties – as he is beloved – break out   320
    And sack great Rome with Romans.
BRUTUS   If it were so –
SICINIUS What do ye talk?
    Have we not had a taste of his obedience?
    Our aediles smote, ourselves resisted? Come.
MENENIUS Consider this: he has been bred i'th'wars   325
    Since 'a could draw a sword, and is ill-schooled
    In bolted language; meal and bran together
    He throws without distinction. Give me leave,
    I'll go to him and undertake to bring him
    Where he shall answer by a lawful form,   330
    In peace, to his utmost peril.
FIRST SENATOR   Noble tribunes,
    It is the humane way. The other course
    Will prove too bloody, and the end of it
    Unknown to the beginning.
SICINIUS   Noble Menenius,
    Be you then as the people's officer.   335
    [*To the Plebeians*]
    Masters, lay down your weapons.
BRUTUS   Go not home.
SICINIUS Meet on the market-place. [*To Menenius*] We'll attend you
    there,
    Where, if you bring not Martius, we'll proceed
    In our first way.

Menenius promises to bring Coriolanus to trial. In Scene 2, Coriolanus is determined, in spite of his mother's disapproval, to endure any punishment rather than give in to the plebeians. Volumnia rebukes her son.

1 I won't change! (in pairs)

Coriolanus refuses to change his attitude to the plebeians, whatever punishment they might inflict on him: total destruction; being tied to a wheel and having his bones broken; dragged behind wild horses; or flung over an infinitely high cliff.

Shakespeare often uses monosyllables to enable a character to intensify meaning. Take turns to speak lines 1–6, and find a way to make each one of the final eight words ('yet will I still/Be thus to them') as emphatic and absolute as you can.

2 Questions for the actors (in pairs)

Give reasons for your replies to each of the following questions:

a Does Volumnia hear what Coriolanus says in lines 8–14?

b Does Coriolanus know his mother is on stage as he speaks the lines?

c What might Volumnia do between lines 6–14?

d Why does Shakespeare bring Volumnia on stage at line 6, but not have Coriolanus speak to her until line 14?

3 Patrician views of the plebeians

In lines 8–14, Coriolanus lists six things his mother taught him about the plebeians. Each one is contemptuous. Invent an action to accompany each of the six descriptions.

---

pull all ... ears destroy everything around me
precipitation headlong fall, precipice
Below the beam of sight farther than the eye can see
muse wonder, am puzzled

was wont habitually, customarily
woollen vassals slaves in woollen tunics
groats coins of little value (four pence)
ordinance rank
Let go that's enough!

MENENIUS I'll bring him to you.
[*To the Senators*] Let me desire your company. He must
    come, 340
Or what is worst will follow.
FIRST SENATOR Pray you, let's to him.
Exeunt [tribunes and Plebeians at one door, patricians at another]

ACT 3   SCENE 2
Rome: the house of Coriolanus

Enter CORIOLANUS *with* NOBLES

CORIOLANUS Let them pull all about mine ears, present me
Death on the wheel or at wild horses' heels,
Or pile ten hills on the Tarpeian rock,
That the precipitation might down stretch
Below the beam of sight, yet will I still 5
Be thus to them.

Enter VOLUMNIA

A NOBLE You do the nobler.
CORIOLANUS I muse my mother
Does not approve me further, who was wont
To call them woollen vassals, things created 10
To buy and sell with groats, to show bare heads
In congregations, to yawn, be still, and wonder
When one but of my ordinance stood up
To speak of peace or war. [*To Volumnia*] I talk of you.
Why did you wish me milder? Would you have me 15
False to my nature? Rather say I play
The man I am.
VOLUMNIA O, sir, sir, sir,
I would have had you put your power well on
Before you had worn it out.
CORIOLANUS Let go.

Volumnia wishes that Coriolanus had disguised his true nature. She urges him to take advice in this time of crisis, and to use both honour and political trickery. Menenius supports her plea.

1 'Honour and policy'

Scene 2 is centrally concerned with whether Coriolanus should stay true to his nature. He asks his mother if she would 'have me false to my nature' rather than having him 'play the man I am' (lines 15–17). In response, Volumnia embarks on a succession of speeches each arguing that it would be better if Coriolanus did conceal what he is truly like.

As you read the scene keep in mind the paradox that Volumnia has brought up her son to be the man he is, rigidly following a strict code of military honour. But now she wishes him to dissemble, to combine 'policy' (political trickery, stratagems) with 'Honour'. To help you speak Volumnia's speeches, experiment with different styles: scornful, wheedling, bossy, maternal, and so on. You can find help with her language below and in the activities on following pages.

> Lines 20–4: If you had only disguised your true nature, you could have prevented the now powerful tribunes from thwarting you.
>
> Lines 29–32: Accept advice, I'm as stubborn as you, but I use my intelligence better.
>
> Lines 40–6: You are inflexible, a noble quality, but unhelpful when crises threaten. So combine honour with trickery in peace, just as you do in war. (But is Volumnia telling the truth? From what you have seen of Coriolanus so far, do you think that in war he used 'policy' (trickery) as well as 'honour'?).

**checkings of your
  dispositions** challenges to what
  you wanted
Cleave split
little apt stubborn, unwilling
The violent fit o'th'time today's
  madness

physic medicine
absolute inflexible,
  uncompromising
extremities speak crises threaten,
  necessities demand
unsevered inseparable

VOLUMNIA You might have been enough the man you are   20
       With striving less to be so. Lesser had been
       The checkings of your dispositions, if
       You had not showed them how ye were disposed
       Ere they lacked power to cross you.
CORIOLANUS   Let them hang!
VOLUMNIA Ay, and burn too.   25

Enter MENENIUS *with the* SENATORS

MENENIUS Come, come, you have been too rough, something too rough.
       You must return and mend it.
A SENATOR   There's no remedy,
       Unless, by not so doing, our good city
       Cleave in the midst, and perish.
VOLUMNIA   Pray be counselled.
       I have a heart as little apt as yours,   30
       But yet a brain that leads my use of anger
       To better vantage.
MENENIUS   Well said, noble woman!
       Before he should thus stoop to th'herd, but that
       The violent fit o'th'time craves it as physic
       For the whole state, I would put mine armour on,   35
       Which I can scarcely bear.
CORIOLANUS   What must I do?
MENENIUS Return to th'tribunes.
CORIOLANUS   Well, what then? What then?
MENENIUS Repent what you have spoke.
CORIOLANUS For them? I cannot do it to the gods;
       Must I then do't to them?
VOLUMNIA   You are too absolute,   40
       Though therein you can never be too noble,
       But when extremities speak. I have heard you say
       Honour and policy, like unsevered friends,
       I'th'war do grow together. Grant that, and tell me
       In peace what each of them by th'other lose   45
       That they combine not there?
CORIOLANUS   Tush, tush!
MENENIUS   A good demand.

Volumnia urges Coriolanus to be deceitful, and speak insincerely to the people, just as she or any patrician would do when necessary to support her class. She tells Coriolanus just how to behave.

1 Improvising – or well prepared?

Does Volumnia speak to her son without hesitation, as if she was delivering a long-prepared speech? Or is she making it up as she goes along, with many pauses as she works out what she might say next?

Speak Volumnia's lines, first with many pauses, then without any hesitations. Decide which style you think most appropriately fits her character.

2 Be deceitful! (in pairs)

Volumnia's advice to Coriolanus ('seem the same you are not' = use deceit), echoes that of Machiavelli (1469–1527) whose book *The Prince* was widely read in Shakespeare's time (and still is today). It is a guide for rulers and politicians, and argues that any behaviour, however deceitful, is justifiable if it keeps the ruler in power.

In lines 47–70, Volumnia uses many different expressions and examples of deceit ('seem', 'policy', 'not by your own instruction', and so on). To feel how she urges Coriolanus to be false, one person speaks her lines, pausing at each punctuation mark. In each pause, the other person whispers 'Be deceitful'.

3 'Action is eloquence'

Volumnia instructs Coriolanus in the gestures he should make when he speaks to the people. Lines 74–81 are full of implicit stage directions. Act them out as you speak her words, Her mulberry image 'Now humble ... handling' probably means 'be soft as an over-ripe fruit that falls off the tree when touched'.

---

hold companionship keep company

stands in like request is equally necessary

roted in insincerely on

Of no allowance ... truth unlike your true thoughts

take in capture

general louts common people

spend a fawn upon 'em flatter them

want lack

salve save, salvage

bussing kissing

VOLUMNIA If it be honour in your wars to seem
        The same you are not, which for your best ends
        You adopt your policy, how is it less or worse
        That it shall hold companionship in peace   50
        With honour as in war, since that to both
        It stands in like request?
CORIOLANUS   Why force you this?
VOLUMNIA Because that now it lies you on to speak
        To th'people, not by your own instruction,
        Nor by th'matter which your heart prompts you,   55
        But with such words that are but roted in
        Your tongue, though bastards and syllables
        Of no allowance to your bosom's truth.
        Now, this no more dishonours you at all
        Than to take in a town with gentle words,   60
        Which else would put you to your fortune and
        The hazard of much blood.
        I would dissemble with my nature where
        My fortunes and my friends at stake required
        I should do so in honour. I am in this   65
        Your wife, your son, these senators, the nobles;
        And you will rather show our general louts
        How you can frown, than spend a fawn upon 'em
        For the inheritance of their loves and safeguard
        Of what that want might ruin.
MENENIUS   Noble lady!   70
        [*To Coriolanus*] Come, go with us; speak fair. You may salve
          so,
        Not what is dangerous present, but the loss
        Of what is past.
VOLUMNIA   I prithee now, my son,
        Go to them, with this bonnet in thy hand,
        And thus far having stretched it – here be with them –   75
        Thy knee bussing the stones – for in such business
        Action is eloquence, and the eyes of th'ignorant
        More learnèd than the ears – waving thy head,
        Which often thus correcting thy stout heart,
        Now humble as the ripest mulberry   80
        That will not hold the handling; or say to them

Volumnia urges Coriolanus to say falsely that he will act kindly towards the plebeians in future. Cominius reports that an angry crowd awaits Coriolanus, who then agrees to follow his mother's advice.

'Prithee now, / Go' – Volumnia persuades Coriolanus to act insincerely. But does she plead with him, for example emphasising her frequent use of 'Prithee' (pray you). Or is she angry with him, using a sharp, chiding tone? As you read all that Volumnia speaks in this scene, think about the tone of voice she is likely to use from line to line.

1 How does he accept?

In lines 100–7, Coriolanus agrees to act out ('discharge') a part on behalf of the patricians, even though for himself he would rather lose his life. To help you speak his lines, pick out all the words he would speak with contempt, for example 'them' in line 100, 'base' in line 101, and so on. To whom might he point at 'You' in line 106?

---

broils wars, battles
frame alter
forsooth truthfully
fiery gulf flaming whirlpool
bower lady's chamber, delightful
  place

make strong party go with many
  supporters
unbarbed sconce bare head
  (a sign of respect)
single plot piece of earth
  (his body)
discharge act out

Thou art their soldier and, being bred in broils,
Hast not the soft way which, thou dost confess,
Were fit for thee to use, as they to claim,
In asking their good loves; but thou wilt frame   85
Thyself, forsooth, hereafter theirs so far
As thou hast power and person.
MENENIUS   This but done,
Even as she speaks, why, their hearts were yours,
For they have pardons, being asked, as free
As words to little purpose.
VOLUMNIA   Prithee now,   90
Go, and be ruled, although I know thou hadst rather
Follow thine enemy in a fiery gulf
Than flatter him in a bower.

Enter COMINIUS

                                Here is Cominius.
COMINIUS I have been i'th'market-place; and, sir, 'tis fit
You make strong party, or defend yourself   95
By calmness or by absence. All's in anger.
MENENIUS Only fair speech.
COMINIUS   I think 'twill serve, if he
Can thereto frame his spirit.
VOLUMNIA   He must, and will.
Prithee now, say you will, and go about it.
CORIOLANUS Must I go show them my unbarbed sconce? Must I   100
With my base tongue give to my noble heart
A lie that it must bear? Well, I will do't.
Yet were there but this single plot to lose,
This mould of Martius, they to dust should grind it
And throw't against the wind. To th'market-place!   105
You have put me now to such a part which never
I shall discharge to th'life.
COMINIUS   Come, come, we'll prompt you.
VOLUMNIA I prithee now, sweet son, as thou hast said
My praises made thee first a soldier, so,
To have my praise for this, perform a part   110
Thou hast not done before.

*Coriolanus agrees to put on an act, but then refuses to do so.
Volumnia accuses him of pride, and Coriolanus again agrees to act
deceitfully when he meets the people.*

1 Help from actors (in pairs)

Use the following comments by actors to help your own acting as
Coriolanus.

'Coriolanus starts the scene refusing to meet the plebeians, then he says
he will, then at line 121 he says he won't, then he changes his mind again
in lines 131–8. You must first discover his motivation: why he changes at
each point. His relationship with his mother is one very crucial reason.
Then you decide whether you want to make the audience laugh at those
moments.'

Lines 111–21: 'Coriolanus agrees to put on a false face, but he goes over
the top in the examples he gives. He says he'll become a harlot, a piping
voice, a smiling villain, a tearful schoolboy, and a lying beggar. It's all a
parody of acting deceitfully, and he adds all kinds of hammy gestures to
show his disdain for acting a part.'

Lines 122–4: 'This is the key to Coriolanus' character, and to his
personal tragedy. The lines explain why he refuses to put on an act. He's
obsessed with the sense of his own integrity: "mine own truth". That's
the guide to how to portray him on stage.'

Line 130: 'If Coriolanus silently mouths the line as his mother speaks it,
it shows he has heard it spoken by Volumnia many times before. It's an
effective comment on the mother–son relationship.'

Line 146: 'Coriolanus' final word, "mildly", can be delivered in all kinds
of different ways: contemptuously sneered, or shouted, or whispered, and
so on. You have to make it a really memorable exit line.'

---

disposition true nature
choired sung in harmony
Tent camp, appear
an alms charity
inherent baseness ingrained
 dishonour
stoutness inflexibility

list please
owe own
mountebank/Cog swindle, cheat
 (a mountebank is a dishonest,
 fast-talking trader)
trades common people
invention lies

CORIOLANUS   Well, I must do't.
    Away, my disposition, and possess me
    Some harlot's spirit! My throat of war be turned,
    Which choired with my drum, into a pipe
    Small as an eunuch or the virgin voice   115
    That babies lull asleep! The smiles of knaves
    Tent in my cheeks, and schoolboys' tears take up
    The glasses of my sight! A beggar's tongue
    Make motion through my lips, and my armed knees,
    Who bowed but in my stirrup, bend like his   120
    That hath received an alms! I will not do't,
    Lest I surcease to honour mine own truth
    And by my body's action teach my mind
    A most inherent baseness.
VOLUMNIA   At thy choice then.
    To beg of thee, it is my more dishonour   125
    Than thou of them. Come all to ruin. Let
    Thy mother rather feel thy pride than fear
    Thy dangerous stoutness, for I mock at death
    With as big heart as thou. Do as thou list.
    Thy valiantness was mine, thou suck'st it from me,   130
    But owe thy pride thyself.
CORIOLANUS   Pray be content.
    Mother, I am going to the market-place.
    Chide me no more. I'll mountebank their loves,
    Cog their hearts from them, and come home beloved
    Of all the trades in Rome. Look, I am going.   135
    Commend me to my wife. I'll return consul,
    Or never trust to what my tongue can do
    I'th'way of flattery further.
VOLUMNIA   Do your will.   *Exit*
COMINIUS Away! The tribunes do attend you. Arm yourself
    To answer mildly, for they are prepared   140
    With accusations, as I hear, more strong
    Than are upon you yet.
CORIOLANUS The word is 'mildly'. Pray you, let us go.
    Let them accuse me by invention, I
    Will answer in mine honour.
MENENIUS   Ay, but mildly.   145
CORIOLANUS Well, mildly be it then, 'mildly'.   *Exeunt*

The tribunes plan Coriolanus' rejection by the plebeians. They instruct the Aedile to bring the people to the market-place, and rehearse them in how to respond at the end of the forthcoming trial.

1 Set design for a trial

Scene 3 is set in the market-place, the Forum of Rome, where the trial of Coriolanus will take place. Sketch a design of the set, to give the audience an impression that it is to be a place of trial and judgement.

2 Three charges

Brutus lists the three accusations against Coriolanus:

- he wishes to seize absolute power;
- he hates the plebeians;
- he has not distributed the booty won in the war against the Antiates (the Volsces).

Consider each charge in turn and say how true you think it to be.

3 Giving instructions (in groups of three)

The Aedile has a list ('catalogue') showing a head count ('th'poll') of the people. It has been collected by 'tribes' (groupings somewhat like modern electoral districts), and ensures that there will be a majority against Coriolanus. Sicinius and Brutus must now ensure that the Aedile understands their instructions very accurately, so that the people will behave in the way they wish.

Take parts as the tribunes and speak lines 13–25. The third person, playing the Aedile, does not look at the script, but listens carefully. When the tribunes have finished speaking, the Aedile repeats back what he or she must do. How accurately are the instructions remembered?

---

charge him home accuse him sharply
affects desires
Enforce him press him hard
envy to hatred for
spoil war booty

procured gained, paid
presently immediately
old prerogative traditional rights
i'th'truth o'th'cause of the justice of the case
hap happen

ACT 3   SCENE 3
Rome: the market-place

Enter SICINIUS *and* BRUTUS

BRUTUS In this point charge him home, that he affects
  Tyrannical power. If he evade us there,
  Enforce him with his envy to the people,
  And that the spoil got on the Antiates
  Was ne'er distributed.

Enter an AEDILE

      What, will he come?   5
AEDILE He's coming.
BRUTUS How accompanied?
AEDILE With old Menenius and those senators
  That always favoured him.
SICINIUS   Have you a catalogue
  Of all the voices that we have procured,   10
  Set down by th'poll?
AEDILE   I have; 'tis ready.
SICINIUS Have you collected them by tribes?
AEDILE   I have.
SICINIUS Assemble presently the people hither,
  And when they hear me say 'It shall be so
  I'th'right and strength o'th'commons', be it either 15
  For death, for fine, or banishment, then let them,
  If I say 'Fine', cry 'Fine!', if 'Death', cry 'Death!',
  Insisting on the old prerogative
  And power i'th'truth o'th'cause.
AEDILE   I shall inform them.
BRUTUS And when such time they have begun to cry, 20
  Let them not cease, but with a din confused
  Enforce the present execution
  Of what we chance to sentence.
AEDILE   Very well.
SICINIUS Make them be strong, and ready for this hint
  When we shall hap to give't them.

The tribunes plot to enrage Coriolanus, making him use reckless language that will destroy him. Coriolanus enters, makes a formal greeting and agrees to accept the tribunes' judgement.

1 Emphasise the monosyllables

Brutus' final nineteen words in lines 29–31 are monosyllables. Shakespeare knew that such short words can be spoken on stage to great dramatic effect, almost like hammer blows. Speak them as you feel they might be delivered in performance.

2 Sincere or false? (in pairs)

Coriolanus' greeting or blessing at lines 35–9 ('Th'honoured gods … war!') has been described in very different ways: as 'very false', 'very sincere', and 'both false and sincere'. To find your own view of the lines, let one person speak the lines, a sentence at a time. The other person, at the end of each sentence, speaks what Coriolanus really means by what he says.

3 Entrances (in groups of any size)

Work out how to stage the entrances of the two groups (stage directions at lines 31 and 41) to greatest dramatic effect.

4 'I am content' – is he?

In lines 46–7, Coriolanus twice asks whether every charge against him will now be decided. But he does not get his questions answered. So how long does he pause at line 51 before he agrees to the demand that he accepts the legality of being judged by the people and the tribunes? What is going on in his mind before he speaks his three words?

---

choler anger
have his worth/Of
  contradiction overcome
  opposition, have his own way
chafed enraged
hostler ostler, stableman

poorest piece smallest coin
Will bear … volume will endure
  being continually called servant
all determine here all charges be
  tried here
censure judgement, sentence

BRUTUS   Go about it.   25
                                              [*Exit Aedile*]
          Put him to choler straight. He hath been used
          Ever to conquer and to have his worth
          Of contradiction. Being once chafed, he cannot
          Be reined again to temperance; then he speaks
          What's in his heart, and that is there which looks   30
          With us to break his neck.

          Enter CORIOLANUS, MENENIUS, *and* COMINIUS,
               with [SENATORS *and* PATRICIANS]

SICINIUS Well, here he comes.
MENENIUS [*To Coriolanus*] Calmly, I do beseech you.
CORIOLANUS Ay, as an hostler, that for th'poorest piece
          Will bear the knave by th'volume. [*Aloud*] Th'honoured
               gods   35
          Keep Rome in safety and the chairs of justice
          Supplied with worthy men! Plant love among's!
          Throng our large temples with the shows of peace,
          And not our streets with war!
FIRST SENATOR Amen, Amen.   40
MENENIUS A noble wish.

          Enter the AEDILE *with the* PLEBEIANS

SICINIUS Draw near, ye people.
AEDILE List to your tribunes. Audience! Peace, I say!
CORIOLANUS First, hear me speak.
BOTH TRIBUNES Well, say. – Peace, ho!   45
CORIOLANUS Shall I be charged no further than this present?
          Must all determine here?
SICINIUS   I do demand
          If you submit you to the people's voices,
          Allow their officers, and are content
          To suffer lawful censure for such faults   50
          As shall be proved upon you?
CORIOLANUS   I am content.
MENENIUS Lo, citizens, he says he is content.
          The warlike service he has done, consider. Think
          Upon the wounds his body bears, which show
          Like graves i'th'holy churchyard.

Coriolanus dismisses his war wounds as mere scratches. Menenius tries to excuse Coriolanus' harsh language, but hearing himself called 'traitor', Coriolanus reacts with fury. The people and Sicinius call for his death.

'You are a traitor to the people.' Sicinius accuses Coriolanus.

1 Losing his temper

As the tribunes hoped, Coriolanus explodes with rage at being charged as a traitor, and unleashes a torrent of abuse against the plebeians and the tribunes. Are there hints between lines 55–67 that he is already losing the struggle to maintain self control and to behave 'mildly' as he had promised? Speak all his lines before Sicinius' accusation, so as to express the emotions he is experiencing.

---

find judge
envy express hatred towards
ought so should do it
contrived plotted
seasoned office traditional
  positions (the tribunes)

wind … tyrannical deceitfully
  seize absolute power
To th'rock fling him from the
  Tarpeian rock (see page 110)
new matter fresh accusations

CORIOLANUS   Scratches with briers,   55
    Scars to move laughter only.
MENENIUS   Consider further,
    That when he speaks not like a citizen,
    You find him like a soldier. Do not take
    His rougher accents for malicious sounds,
    But, as I say, such as become a soldier   60
    Rather than envy you.
COMINIUS   Well, well, no more.
CORIOLANUS What is the matter
    That, being passed for consul with full voice,
    I am so dishonoured that the very hour
    You take it off again?   65
SICINIUS Answer to us.
CORIOLANUS Say then. 'Tis true, I ought so.
SICINIUS We charge you that you have contrived to take
    From Rome all seasoned office and to wind
    Yourself into a power tyrannical,   70
    For which you are a traitor to the people.
CORIOLANUS How? 'Traitor'?
MENENIUS   Nay, temperately! Your promise.
CORIOLANUS The fires i'th'lowest hell fold in the people!
    Call me their 'traitor', thou injurious tribune!
    Within thine eyes sat twenty thousand deaths,   75
    In thy hands clutched as many millions, in
    Thy lying tongue both numbers, I would say
    'Thou liest' unto thee with a voice as free
    As I do pray the gods.
SICINIUS Mark you this, people?   80
ALL PLEBEIANS To th'rock, to th'rock with him!
SICINIUS Peace!
    We need not put new matter to his charge.
    What you have seen him do and heard him speak –
    Beating your officers, cursing yourselves,   85
    Opposing laws with strokes, and here defying
    Those whose great power must try him – even this,
    So criminal and in such capital kind,
    Deserves th'extremest death.
BRUTUS   But since he hath
    Served well for Rome –

Coriolanus, angered by the tribunes, says he will endure any punishment rather than ask them for mercy. Sicinius pronounces the sentence of banishment. Cominius tries to intervene.

---

1 'Service' (in small groups)

Coriolanus is incensed by Brutus' talk of 'service' to Rome, and implies that Brutus has given no service to the state. Talk together about what different meanings Coriolanus and Brutus probably have in mind when they speak of 'service'. Do you think that both men have served Rome equally?

2 Which punishment? (in pairs)

Coriolanus lists four punishments he would rather endure than beg for mercy or be polite to the plebeians. But why do the tribunes sentence him to banishment rather than to death? Do they whisper together (perhaps at line 100) before Sicinius pronounces sentence?

Step into role as Brutus and Sicinius and talk together about your reasons for preferring to let Coriolanus live in exile rather than sentencing him to death. Begin by reminding yourselves of the three punishments the tribunes considered at line 16.

3 Pronouncing sentence: '... It shall be so!'

In lines 106–12, Sicinius delivers judgement 'in the name o'th'people'. Does he emphasise 'shall' at line 112? It is the word that sparked off Coriolanus' anger in Act 3 Scene 1, line 89. Speak Sicinius' lines as formally and impressively as you can, and consider whether the plebeians and Brutus echo 'shall' in their chanting at lines 113–14 and 126–7.

---

prate chatter
Vagabond exile wandering banishment
flaying flogging that removes skin
pent ... day imprisoned and starved

Inveighed against reviled
estimate reputation
womb's increase children
treasure of my loins my children
drift meaning

CORIOLANUS   What do you prate of service?   90
BRUTUS I talk of that that know it.
CORIOLANUS You?
MENENIUS Is this the promise that you made your mother?
COMINIUS Know, I pray you –
CORIOLANUS   I'll know no further.
    Let them pronounce the steep Tarpeian death,   95
    Vagabond exile, flaying, pent to linger
    But with a grain a day, I would not buy
    Their mercy at the price of one fair word,
    Nor check my courage for what they can give,
    To have't with saying 'Good morrow'.
SICINIUS   For that he has,   100
    As much as in him lies, from time to time
    Inveighed against the people, seeking means
    To pluck away their power, as now at last
    Given hostile strokes, and that not in the presence
    Of dreaded justice, but on the ministers   105
    That doth distribute it – in the name o'th'people
    And in the power of us the tribunes, we,
    Ev'n from this instant, banish him our city,
    In peril of precipitation
    From off the rock Tarpeian, never more   110
    To enter our Rome gates. I'th'people's name,
    I say it shall be so.
ALL PLEBEIANS It shall be so, it shall be so! Let him away!
    He's banished, and it shall be so!
COMINIUS Hear me, my masters and my common friends –   115
SICINIUS He's sentenced. No more hearing.
COMINIUS   Let me speak.
    I have been consul, and can show for Rome
    Her enemies' marks upon me. I do love
    My country's good with a respect more tender,
    More holy and profound, than mine own life,   120
    My dear wife's estimate, her womb's increase
    And treasure of my loins. Then if I would
    Speak that –
SICINIUS   We know your drift. Speak what?

The people cry for Coriolanus' banishment. He leaves, cursing them, and predicting that fear, defeat and enslavement lie ahead for them. Sicinius orders the plebeians to follow and torment him.

1 'You common cry of curs' (in small groups)

Coriolanus' cursing of the plebeians and his rejection of Rome is a great moment of theatre. Every production attempts to ensure that the lines are delivered to maximum dramatic effect. Actors spend much time exploring ways of speaking, particularly such phrases as 'You common cry of curs', 'I banish you' and 'There is a world elsewhere'. For example, Coriolanus' final line 143 has been whispered, shouted, accompanied with all kinds of gestures, and, in one production, spoken off stage after Coriolanus has left the stage.

Experiment with different versions of staging the episode, using some of the following suggestions to help you.

a Does the Aedile act as cheerleader, orchestrating the plebeians' responses before and after Coriolanus' speech? Are the plebeians still shouting as Coriolanus begins to speak?

b Suggest which words Coriolanus might emphasise in each line, and work out any accompanying actions. For example, what does he do at 'thus' in line 142?

c Consider what the images of rottenness in his first four lines suggest about Coriolanus' state of mind.

d Work out how you will stage his final exit. In one production he contemptuously took off his consul's robe and flung it at the crowd on his final line.

e Does Coriolanus have the support of all the patricians? Suggest how the patricians respond to Coriolanus' words, and how they leave the stage at line 143.

---

cry pack
nodding of their plumes the mere appearance of their helmets
finds not till it feels only learns by bitter experience
Making but ... yourselves leaves only you plebeians in Rome

Still your own foes your own worst enemies
abated beaten, defeated
despite contempt
vexation torment

BRUTUS   There's no more to be said, but he is banished
        As enemy to the people and his country.   125
        It shall be so.
ALL PLEBEIANS   It shall be so, it shall be so!
CORIOLANUS   You common cry of curs, whose breath I hate
        As reek o'th'rotten fens, whose loves I prize
        As the dead carcasses of unburied men   130
        That do corrupt my air, I banish you.
        And here remain with your uncertainty!
        Let every feeble rumour shake your hearts;
        Your enemies, with nodding of their plumes,
        Fan you into despair! Have the power still   135
        To banish your defenders, till at length
        Your ignorance – which finds not till it feels,
        Making but reservation of yourselves,
        Still your own foes – deliver you
        As most abated captives to some nation   140
        That won you without blows! Despising
        For you the city, thus I turn my back.
        There is a world elsewhere.

    Exeunt Coriolanus, Cominius [, Menenius, Senators, and Patricians]
        They all shout, and throw up their caps

AEDILE   The people's enemy is gone, is gone!
ALL PLEBEIANS   Our enemy is banished! He is gone! Hoo–oo!   145
SICINIUS   Go see him out at gates and follow him
        As he hath followed you, with all despite.
        Give him deserved vexation. Let a guard
        Attend us through the city.
ALL PLEBEIANS   Come, come, let's see him out at gates! Come.   150
        The gods preserve our noble tribunes! Come.

                              Exeunt

Looking back at Act 3
Activities for groups or individuals

1 Dramatic contrast

Shakespeare structures his plays so that each scene makes a dramatic contrast with its preceding and following scene. Compare the final few lines of Scene 1 with the opening lines of Scene 2, then the final few lines of Scene 2 with the opening lines of Scene 3. Suggest how 'endings' and 'beginnings' contrast with each other and how this contrast heightens dramatic effect.

2 Hierarchy or democracy?

Coriolanus' view of society is that it should be sharply hierarchical with a small elite firmly in control at the top and the great mass of the people at the bottom with no say in government. In Scene 1, between lines 21 and 171 he makes his view clear in a series of speeches that condemn plebeian interference with patrician rule, and see only disaster in challenges to that rule. Shakespeare explored the same issues of social order and hierarchy in *Troilus and Cressida*. Find a copy of that play and compare Ulysses' speech (Act 1 Scene 3, lines 78–124) with Coriolanus' speeches. Then state your own view as to whether such conceptions of society have any place in today's world.

3 Completely egocentric?

Act 3 ends with Coriolanus' banishment from Rome. What is your impression of him at this point in the play? Does he think of anyone other than himself? Keep your answer in mind as you read on, and see if you wish to alter your view in the light of what happens in Acts 4 and 5.

4 Manipulating the people

A publisher wishes to produce a handbook for politicians entitled 'How to get the people to do what you want them to do', and asks Coriolanus, Sicinius and Volumnia each to contribute a short piece of advice, with reasons why the advice will work. Step into role as each character in turn and use what you say in Act 3 to write your contribution.

5 'Policy'

Act 3 is much concerned with 'policy', the use of deceit to gain one's objectives. Volumnia urges Coriolanus to use policy, to dissemble and put on a false face when he meets the people in the market-place. Although Coriolanus agrees, he feels he cannot play a part and hide his true nature, which he sees as noble and heroic, because such hypocrisy violates his integrity: 'Must I/With my base tongue give to my noble heart/A lie that it must bear?' As a result, because he refuses to hide his true feelings behind a mask, he is banished from Rome.

a But is there a place for 'policy' in social affairs? Give examples from your own experience or knowledge, where you, or someone else, have used 'policy' to achieve a particular purpose.

b Volumnia's advice is: pretend! Think of famous public apologies in modern times, perhaps by television. Do you think the speaker was only pretending to be contrite and humble?

In this modern dress production, the cheering plebeians raise the tribunes shoulder high. Identify a moment in Act 3 when this action could have taken place.

Coriolanus, about to leave for exile, tries to cheer his mother by reminding her how she taught him to endure hardships. She curses the plebeians. Coriolanus offers more comfort to his family and friends.

1 Farewell and comfort (in groups of five)

Take parts and speak Scene 1 to gain a first impression of how Coriolanus takes farewell of his family and friends. Then discuss the following questions to help you stage the scene.

a Is Coriolanus eager or reluctant to leave Rome? anguished or calm? or …?

b Some productions stage this scene against the sound of the plebeians jeering at Coriolanus and rejoicing at his banishment. How might such sounds affect the delivery of some of the lines?

c Virgilia, Coriolanus' wife, speaks only at lines 12 and 37. Advise her how to play her part, and suggest how Coriolanus behaves towards her (is he annoyed, or sympathetic, or …?).

d What emotional atmosphere would you wish to create in your staging of the scene?

e Identify lines where the actors might evoke audience laughter. Would you wish the audience to laugh?

f How does the scene affect your feelings about Coriolanus? Do you see a different side of his character here?

2 'Precepts': are they true?

In lines 3–9, Coriolanus recalls four proverbs or maxims ('precepts') that his mother had taught him. Put them in your own words, and give your response to each: is it true? The fourth (lines 7–9) probably means 'When ill fortune strikes, aristocrats should bear its blows with nobleness'.

---

beast / With many heads
  (the plebeians)
extremities was crises were
trier tester
conned learned by heart
lacked missed, needed

were wont used
Hercules strong man of classical
  legend who had to perform twelve
  labours
fond foolish

ACT 4 SCENE 1
Rome: the city gates

Enter CORIOLANUS, VOLUMNIA, VIRGILIA, MENENIUS, COMINIUS,
with the young nobility of Rome

CORIOLANUS Come, leave your tears; a brief farewell. The beast
   With many heads butts me away. Nay, mother,
   Where is your ancient courage? You were used
   To say extremities was the trier of spirits;
   That common chances common men could bear;   5
   That when the sea was calm, all boats alike
   Showed mastership in floating; fortune's blows
   When most struck home, being gentle wounded craves
   A noble cunning. You were used to load me
   With precepts that would make invincible   10
   The heart that conned them.
VIRGILIA O heavens! O heavens!
CORIOLANUS   Nay, I prithee, woman –
VOLUMNIA Now the red pestilence strike all trades in Rome,
   And occupations perish!
CORIOLANUS   What, what, what!
   I shall be loved when I am lacked. Nay, mother,   15
   Resume that spirit when you were wont to say,
   If you had been the wife of Hercules,
   Six of his labours you'd have done and saved
   Your husband so much sweat. Cominius,
   Droop not. Adieu. Farewell, my wife, my mother.   20
   I'll do well yet. Thou old and true Menenius,
   Thy tears are salter than a younger man's
   And venomous to thine eyes. My sometime general,
   I have seen thee stern, and thou hast oft beheld
   Heart-hardening spectacles. Tell these sad women   25
   'Tis fond to wail inevitable strokes
   As 'tis to laugh at 'em.

Coriolanus continues to comfort his mother, saying he will succeed and will avoid being tricked. He refuses Cominius' offer to accompany him, and bids farewell to all.

1 A lonely dragon? (in pairs)

Coriolanus says that in his exile he will be like a lonely dragon in his fen, much talked about, but rarely seen. Talk together about how compelling you find the image to describe Coriolanus at this moment – about to go into banishment, alone. Explore whether you think he really believes in that image or whether he uses it mainly to cheer his mother, or for some other reason.

After your discussion, use the image of a lonely dragon in his fen as the basis of a design for a cover for an edition of the play.

2 Dramatic irony

Lines 32–3 and 52–4 are filled with dramatic irony (contrasting strongly with what actually happens later). Coriolanus claims he will not 'be caught/With cautelous baits and practice' (deceitful traps and tricks), and that he will never change ('aught … formerly'). You will find as you read on that both claims are proved false.

3 Stage the departure (in small groups)

To whom does Coriolanus speak his final line? Stage line 58 and the departure to show how Coriolanus relates to everyone on stage at this moment, and their feelings about him.

4 Where? What?

Does Coriolanus have any thoughts about where he might go and what he might do? Step into role and reveal your thoughts. Keep a note of what you say, to discover how well it matches what happens as the play unfolds.

---

wot know
hazards dangerous exploits
exceed the common surpass ordinary men
wild exposure to dangerous meeting with
repeal recall

advantage the opportunity
surfeits wounds, battles
rove wander
noble touch true nobility (an image from a touchstone used to test gold)
aught anything

My mother, you wot well
My hazards still have been your solace, and
Believe't not lightly – though I go alone,
Like to a lonely dragon that his fen   30
Makes feared and talked of more than seen – your son
Will or exceed the common or be caught
With cautelous baits and practice.

VOLUMNIA   My first son,
Whither will thou go? Take good Cominius
With thee a while. Determine on some course   35
More than a wild exposure to each chance
That starts i'th'way before thee.

VIRGILIA   O the gods!

COMINIUS I'll follow thee a month, devise with thee
Where thou shalt rest, that thou mayst hear of us
And we of thee. So if the time thrust forth   40
A cause for thy repeal, we shall not send
O'er the vast world to seek a single man
And lose advantage, which doth ever cool
I'th'absence of the needer.

CORIOLANUS   Fare ye well.
Thou hast years upon thee, and thou art too full   45
Of the wars' surfeits to go rove with one
That's yet unbruised. Bring me but out at gate.
Come, my sweet wife, my dearest mother, and
My friends of noble touch; when I am forth,
Bid me farewell and smile. I pray you, come.   50
While I remain above the ground you shall
Hear from me still, and never of me aught
But what is like me formerly.

MENENIUS   That's worthily
As any ear can hear. Come, let's not weep.
If I could shake off but one seven years   55
From these old arms and legs, by the good gods,
I'd with thee every foot.

CORIOLANUS Give me thy hand. Come.

Exeunt

Sicinius and Brutus give orders that the plebeians return home.
Volumnia curses the tribunes and questions their trickery in banishing
Coriolanus.

1 Success at last (in pairs)

Scene 2 closes the long period of political action, set in Rome, that began at Act 2 Scene 1, in which the tribunes plotted Coriolanus' downfall. Their plan has now succeeded and their class enemy is banished. They now propose to keep a lower profile in public ('Let us seem humbler').

Before you work through Scene 2, briefly remind each other of how the tribunes engineered Coriolanus' fall.

2 Act out the meeting (in groups of five)

Take parts and speak lines 9–46, in which Volumnia and Virgilia berate the tribunes. Invent stage business to accompany your words. For example, in one production Volumnia aimed a blow at Sicinius at line 22, provoking him to exclaim 'O blessèd heavens!'. In another production the audience laughed as the tribunes tried to sneak out, but were physically restrained by the women.

3 Another view of Virgilia

'You shall stay too' orders Virgilia at line 17, preventing the tribunes from leaving. Give your response to this line and to her lines 27–8. Do her words match your view of her character in previous scenes?

4 'Are you mankind?'

In Shakespeare's day, 'mankind' could mean 'mad'. Suggest other meanings that Sicinius might have in mind as he uses 'mankind' to describe Volumnia.

---

vexed angry
sided / In his behalf supported
 Coriolanus
Stand in their ancient strength
 have regained their traditional
 power

hoarded stored up
Requite reward, avenge
foxship low cunning

ACT 4   SCENE 2
Rome: the market-place

Enter the two tribunes, SICINIUS *and* BRUTUS, *with the* AEDILE

SICINIUS [*To the Aedile*] Bid them all home. He's gone, and we'll no
    further.
    The nobility are vexed, whom we see have sided
    In his behalf.
BRUTUS   Now we have shown our power,
    Let us seem humbler after it is done
    Than when it was a-doing.
SICINIUS [*To the Aedile*]   Bid them home.   5
    Say their great enemy is gone, and they
    Stand in their ancient strength.
BRUTUS   Dismiss them home.
                                        [*Exit Aedile*]
    Here comes his mother.

Enter VOLUMNIA, VIRGILIA, *and* MENENIUS

SICINIUS Let's not meet her.
BRUTUS Why?   10
SICINIUS They say she's mad.
BRUTUS They have ta'en note of us. Keep on your way.
VOLUMNIA O, you're well met. Th'hoarded plague o'th'gods
    Requite your love!
MENENIUS   Peace, peace; be not so loud.
VOLUMNIA If that I could for weeping, you should hear –   15
    Nay, and you shall hear some. Will you be gone?
VIRGILIA You shall stay too. I would I had the power
    To say so to my husband.
SICINIUS [*To Volumnia*]   Are you mankind?
VOLUMNIA Ay, fool, is that a shame? Note but this, fool:
    Was not a man my father? Hadst thou foxship   20
    To banish him that struck more blows for Rome
    Than thou hast spoken words?
SICINIUS   O blessèd heavens!

Volumnia wishes Coriolanus could kill the tribunes. She accuses them of stirring up the plebeians and says Coriolanus is superior to them all. She wishes she could curse the tribunes every day.

'I would he had'! Just as Coriolanus was stung by the tribunes 'shall' and echoed it back to them, so Volumnia pounces fiercely on both tribunes' 'I would he had' and repeats it back to them. What other line could make a suitable caption for this picture?

Arabia the desert, land beyond Roman law	**fitly** appropriately
posterity descendants	**baited** mocked, harassed
noble knot bond (between Coriolanus and Rome)	**wants** lacks
	told them home hit their guilty consciences
incensed whipped up the rage of	**by my troth** in truth
Cats (used contemptuously, like Coriolanus' 'curs')	**sup** dine

VOLUMNIA More noble blows than ever thou wise words,
　　　　　And for Rome's good. I'll tell thee what – yet go.
　　　　　Nay, but thou shalt stay too. I would my son　　　　　25
　　　　　Were in Arabia and thy tribe before him,
　　　　　His good sword in his hand.
SICINIUS　　　　　　　　　　　What then?
VIRGILIA　　　　　　　　　　　　　　　What then!
　　　　　He'd make an end of thy posterity.
VOLUMNIA Bastards and all.
　　　　　Good man, the wounds that he does bear for Rome!　　　30
MEMENIUS Come, come, peace.
SICINIUS I would he had continued to his country
　　　　　As he began and not unknit himself
　　　　　The noble knot he made.
BRUTUS　　　　　　　　　I would he had.
VOLUMNIA 'I would he had'! 'Twas you incensed the rabble –　　35
　　　　　Cats that can judge as fitly of his worth
　　　　　As I can of those mysteries which heaven
　　　　　Will not have earth to know.
BRUTUS [*To Sicinius*] Pray, let's go.
VOLUMNIA　　　　　　　　　Now pray, sir, get you gone.
　　　　　You have done a brave deed. Ere you go, hear this:　　40
　　　　　As far as doth the Capitol exceed
　　　　　The meanest house in Rome, so far my son –
　　　　　This lady's husband here, this, do you see? –
　　　　　Whom you have banished, does exceed you all.
BRUTUS Well, well, we'll leave you.
SICINIUS　　　　　　　　　　Why stay we to be baited　　　45
　　　　　With one that wants her wits?
　　　　　　　　　　　　　　　　　Exeunt Tribunes
VOLUMNIA　　　　　　　　　Take my prayers with you.
　　　　　I would the gods had nothing else to do
　　　　　But to confirm my curses. Could I meet 'em
　　　　　But once a day, it would unclog my heart
　　　　　Of what lies heavy to't.
MENENIUS　　　　　　　　You have told them home,　　　50
　　　　　And, by my troth, you have cause. You'll sup with me?

Volumnia is consumed with anger. She tells Virgilia to imitate her and express her grief wrathfully. In Scene 3, Nicanor, a Roman in the pay of the Volsces, reports the unrest in Rome.

1 'Anger's my meat' (in pairs)

Talk together about how accurately Volumnia's lines 52–3 describe her character. Begin by saying how far you agree with the following comment:

> 'These words are the key to Volumnia's character. Her imagery of cannibalism suggests that she is so full of anger that expressing it, or dwelling on it, will destroy her ('starve with feeding').'

2 How does Virgilia behave?

Volumnia accuses Virgilia of 'faint puling' (feeble whining or whimpering). Remind yourself of what Virgilia says in lines 17–18 and 27–8. Do her words sound like whimpers?

3 Treachery (in pairs)

Scene 3 introduces the theme of treachery that will run through the remainder of the play. Both men are spies, and Nicanor the Roman is also a traitor, a secret agent who betrays his own country by passing on information that will help the enemy. Take parts and read through the scene, then work on the activities below and on page 152.

Who is Nicanor? In one production, Nicanor was revealed as a Roman patrician who had appeared in previous scenes. In another production both spies were plebeians, and the director declared that his intention was to show the solidarity of the working class in both countries against the patrician class. Talk together about what you think about these ideas then work out how you would present the Roman spy.

Juno (in Roman mythology) chief goddess and wife of Jupiter, famous for her anger which caused the destruction of Troy
favour … tongue face matches your language

strange insurrections unnatural uprisings
blaze disturbance (an image of civil war)
in a ripe aptness ready

VOLUMNIA Anger's my meat. I sup upon myself,
    And so shall starve with feeding.
    [*To Virgilia*]   Come, let's go.
    Leave this faint puling and lament as I do,
    In anger, Juno-like. Come, come, come.   55
                    Exeunt [Volumnia and Virgilia]
MENENIUS Fie, fie, fie.   *Exit*

ACT 4   SCENE 3
A road between Rome and Antium

Enter a ROMAN and a VOLSCE

ROMAN I know you well, sir, and you know me. Your name, I think, is
    Adrian?
VOLSCE It is so, sir. Truly, I have forgot you.
ROMAN I am a Roman, and my services are, as you are, against 'em.
    Know you me yet?   5
VOLSCE Nicanor, no?
ROMAN The same, sir.
VOLSCE You had more beard when I last saw you, but your favour is well
    appeared by your tongue. What's the news in Rome? I have a note
    from the Volscian state to find you out there. You have well saved   10
    me a day's journey.
ROMAN There hath been in Rome strange insurrections: the people
    against the senators, patricians and nobles.
VOLSCE Hath been? Is it ended then? Our state thinks not so. They are in
    a most warlike preparation and hope to come upon them in the heat   15
    of their division.
ROMAN The main blaze of it is past, but a small thing would make it flame
    again, for the nobles receive so to heart the banishment of that
    worthy Coriolanus that they are in a ripe aptness to take all power
    from the people and to pluck from them their tribunes forever. This   20
    lies glowing, I can tell you, and is almost mature for the violent
    breaking out.
VOLSCE Coriolanus banished?
ROMAN Banished, sir.

Nicanor emphasises Rome's present weakness, and says how Aufidius will find success now that Coriolanus is banished. Adrian reveals that the Volsces have an army ready to attack Rome.

1 Write the spy's report

Nicanor is on his way to Antium, the capital city of the Volsces. He brings information which will immediately set the Volsces' army on the march against Rome (lines 39–40). Imagine Nicanor has already written a report telling of 'most strange things from Rome'. Write his report.

2 Imagery (in pairs)

Identify the lines in which Shakespeare uses the following images in Scene 3. Talk about how each image deepens meaning.

- civil war as a blazing fire;
- political opportunity as ripening fruit;
- sexual relationships as military action.

3 Where is the place?

No one can be absolutely sure where Shakespeare intended Scene 3 to be set, although line 11 suggests it is close to Antium (see map on page 3). How important is it to give the audience a sense of a specific location for this scene?

4 To cut or not to cut (in small groups)

Scene 3 is sometimes cut in performance. One person steps into role as William Shakespeare, the others take parts as director and actors about to perform the play. Some actors want to cut the scene, others don't. Argue your case for and against cutting, and question Shakespeare about why he wrote this scene.

---

intelligence military information
in no request of not wanted by
He cannot choose he certainly will!
centurions commanders of one hundred men
charges troops

distinctly billeted listed man by man
in th'entertainment on the payroll
on foot marching to battle
present immediate

VOLSCE You will be welcome with this intelligence, Nicanor.   25

ROMAN The day serves well for them now. I have heard it said the fittest
    time to corrupt a man's wife is when she's fallen out with her
    husband. Your noble Tullus Aufidius will appear well in these wars,
    his great opposer Coriolanus being now in no request of his country.

VOLSCE He cannot choose. I am most fortunate thus accidentally to   30
    encounter you. You have ended my business, and I will merrily
    accompany you home.

ROMAN I shall, between this and supper, tell you most strange things
    from Rome, all tending to the good of their adversaries. Have you
    an army ready, say you?   35

VOLSCE A most royal one: the centurions and their charges distinctly
    billeted, already in th'entertainment, and to be on foot at an hour's
    warning.

ROMAN I am joyful to hear of their readiness and am the man, I think, that
    shall set them in present action. So, sir, heartily well met, and most   40
    glad of your company.

VOLSCE You take my part from me, sir. I have the most cause to be glad of
    yours.

ROMAN Well, let us go together.

Exeunt

Coriolanus, knowing that his life is at risk in Antium, reflects that just as firm friends fall out over trivial matters, so too may deadly enemies become friends. He decides to meet Aufidius.

1 Coriolanus' appearance

Study the picture on page 156, then design Coriolanus' costume for this scene ('mean apparel' is poor, tattered clothing). Think about the effect you wish his appearance to have upon an audience.

2 Is it true?

In lines 12–26, Coriolanus comments on the changeable nature of the world. He argues that just as firm friends become bitter foes because of a quarrel over nothing ('dissension of a doit' – a doit is a tiny coin), so two deadly enemies, who lose sleep in their desire to kill each other, can become firm friends by chance or by a worthless action.

Is what Coriolanus says true? Give one or two actual examples, from your own experience or from any other source, that confirm or deny his claims about friends and enemies.

3 What kind of soliloquy? (in pairs)

In Shakespeare's plays, characters alone on stage often reveal their innermost thoughts in soliloquy. Coriolanus is about to transfer his allegiance to his deadliest enemy, Aufidius. But does his soliloquy reveal why he decides to hate Rome and love Antium, the capital city of the Volsces, or are his lines merely a justification of a decision he has already taken?

Speak the lines to each other several times. Then talk about whether you think his argument fits his own case: for example, is it 'some chance, Some trick not worth an egg' that has brought him to Antium?

---

fair edifices noble buildings
'fore my wars before my onslaughts
spits roasting irons
puny weak
slippery turns fickle changes
fast sworn firmly bonded

double bosoms two bodies
fellest deadliest
take the one the other destroy each other
interjoin their issues let their children intermarry

ACT 4   SCENE 4
Antium: before the house of Aufidius

Enter CORIOLANUS *in mean apparel, disguised, and muffled*

CORIOLANUS A goodly city is this Antium. City,
   'Tis I that made thy widows. Many an heir
   Of these fair edifices 'fore my wars
   Have I heard groan and drop. Then know me not,
   Lest that thy wives with spits and boys with stones   5
   In puny battle slay me.

Enter a CITIZEN

       Save you, sir.
CITIZEN And you.
CORIOLANUS   Direct me, if it be your will,
   Where great Aufidius lies. Is he in Antium?
CITIZEN He is, and feasts the nobles of the state
   At his house this night.
CORIOLANUS   Which is his house, beseech you?   10
CITIZEN This here before you.
CORIOLANUS   Thank you, sir. Farewell.

           Exit Citizen

   O world, thy slippery turns! Friends now fast sworn,
   Whose double bosoms seems to wear one heart,
   Whose hours, whose bed, whose meal and exercise
   Are still together, who twin, as 'twere, in love   15
   Unseparable, shall within this hour,
   On a dissension of a doit, break out
   To bitterest enmity. So fellest foes,
   Whose passions and whose plots have broke their sleep
   To take the one the other, by some chance,   20
   Some trick not worth an egg, shall grow dear friends
   And interjoin their issues. So with me.
   My birthplace hate I, and my love's upon
   This enemy town. I'll enter. If he slay me,
   He does fair justice; if he give me way,   25
   I'll do his country service.

           Exit

A feast is in progress offstage, and the servants bustle about.
They order Coriolanus to leave but he refuses. The First Servingman
decides to send for Aufidius.

Coriolanus is described in Scene 1 as 'in mean apparel, disguised, and muffled'. Aufidius' servants obviously find his behaviour strange, and Coriolanus himself says that he appears 'not like a guest'. What movements and gestures (if any) would add to the dramatic impact of lines 5–23?

entertainment reception
companions (the Servingman
  probably speaks the word
  ironically, to suggest it means
  beggars, or disreputable strangers)

brave insolent
anon very soon
avoid leave

ACT 4 SCENE 5
Antium: the house of Aufidius

Music plays. Enter a SERVINGMAN

FIRST SERVINGMAN Wine, wine, wine! What service is here? I think our
fellows are asleep.   [*Exit*]

Enter SECOND SERVINGMAN

SECOND SERVINGMAN Where's Cotus? My master calls for him.
Cotus!   *Exit*

Enter CORIOLANUS

CORIOLANUS A goodly house. The feast smells well, but I   5
Appear not like a guest.

Enter the FIRST SERVINGMAN

FIRST SERVINGMAN What would you have, friend? Whence are you?
Here's no place for you. Pray go to the door.
                                                          Exit
CORIOLANUS I have deserved no better entertainment
In being Coriolanus.   10

Enter SECOND SERVINGMAN

SECOND SERVINGMAN Whence are you, sir? Has the porter his eyes in
his head that he gives entrance to such companions? Pray get you
out.
CORIOLANUS Away!
SECOND SERVINGMAN Away? Get you away.   15
CORIOLANUS Now th'art troublesome.
SECOND SERVINGMAN Are you so brave? I'll have you talked with
anon.

Enter THIRD SERVINGMAN*; the* FIRST [*, entering,*] *meets him*

THIRD SERVINGMAN What fellow's this?
FIRST SERVINGMAN A strange one as ever I looked on. I cannot get him   20
out o'th'house. Prithee, call my master to him.
THIRD SERVINGMAN What have you to do here, fellow? Pray you avoid
the house.

Coriolanus rejects all the attempts of the servants to make him leave.
He beats the Third Servingman. Aufidius demands to know his name.
Coriolanus reveals his face.

1 Comedy? (in groups of four)

Take parts and speak lines 1–46. Work out how you would stage the comic aspects of this episode of Coriolanus and the servants. Also decide how severely or mildly Coriolanus beats the Third Servingman. In one production he evoked audience laughter at line 46 as he tapped the servant playfully on the head with a wooden platter.

2 'Under the canopy'

Coriolanus says he lives 'under the canopy' (sky) in the 'city of kites and crows' (birds well known as scavengers on battlefields). The Third Servingman seems baffled by Coriolanus' words and tries to make a joke of it: daws (jackdaws) were traditionally thought of as stupid birds. Coriolanus turns the joke back on the servant.

Many people find this exchange between Coriolanus and the Third Servingman puzzling. They are not sure if it gives insight into themes and characters. Give your own reasons for whether you judge it to be a revealing moment in the play.

3 'What's thy name?' (in pairs)

'Name' occurs nine times in lines 50–62. Does Aufidius make his demands to know the stranger's name with growing impatience, or with amused interest, or …? Speak the lines, emphasising each mention of 'name'. You can find an activity on names on page 237.

---

take up some other station go somewhere else
Follow your function attend to your duties

batten on cold bits grow fat on scraps of food
prat'st chatter
trencher wooden plate

CORIOLANUS Let me but stand. I will not hurt your hearth.

THIRD SERVINGMAN What are you?   25

CORIOLANUS A gentleman.

THIRD SERVINGMAN A marvellous poor one.

CORIOLANUS True, so I am.

THIRD SERVINGMAN Pray you, poor gentleman, take up some other
     station. Here's no place for you. Pray you avoid. Come.   30

CORIOLANUS Follow your function, go, and batten on cold bits.

                    Pushes him away from him

THIRD SERVINGMAN What, you will not? Prithee tell my master what a
     strange guest he has here.

SECOND SERVINGMAN And I shall.   *Exit*

THIRD SERVINGMAN Where dwell'st thou?   35

CORIOLANUS Under the canopy.

THIRD SERVINGMAN Under the canopy?

CORIOLANUS Ay.

THIRD SERVINGMAN Where's that?

CORIOLANUS I'th'city of kites and crows.   40

THIRD SERVINGMAN I'th'city of kites and crows? What an ass it is! Then
     thou dwell'st with daws too?

CORIOLANUS No, I serve not thy master.

THIRD SERVINGMAN How, sir? Do you meddle with my master?

CORIOLANUS Ay, 'tis an honester service than to meddle with thy   45
     mistress. Thou prat'st and prat'st. Serve with thy trencher. Hence!

                    Beats him away

                    [*Exit Third Servingman*]

          Enter AUFIDIUS *with the* [SECOND] SERVINGMAN

AUFIDIUS Where is this fellow?

SECOND SERVINGMAN Here, sir. I'd have beaten him like a dog but for
     disturbing the lords within.

          [*First and Second Servingmen stand aside*]

AUFIDIUS Whence com'st thou? What wouldst thou? Thy name?   50
          Why speak'st not? Speak man. What's thy name?

CORIOLANUS [*Unmuffling*]   If, Tullus,
     Not yet thou know'st me, and, seeing me, dost not
     Think me for the man I am, necessity
     Commands me name myself.

AUFIDIUS   What is thy name?

Coriolanus reveals his name. He speaks of the injuries he has inflicted on the Volsces, and how ungrateful Romans have banished him. He offers to fight for the Volsces in order to be revenged on Rome.

1 Shakespeare at work (in pairs)

At this intensely dramatic moment Coriolanus stands, unarmed, before his deadliest enemy. The vital questions in performance are: 'How does Coriolanus deliver his speech?' and 'How does Aufidius respond?'. You can find help with these on page 162. But his speech shows something of Shakespeare's working methods. The passage below is what Shakespeare read in Plutarch (see page 245), and rewrote as lines 62–85. One person speaks Plutarch's words, a short section at a time. After each section, the other person speaks the corresponding lines opposite. Afterwards, discuss why Shakespeare made the changes that he did, and whether he can be accused of plagiarism (stealing someone else's writings).

I am Caius Martius, who hath done to thy self particularly, and to all the Volsces generally, great hurt and mischief, which I cannot deny for my surname of Coriolanus that I bear. For I never had other benefit nor recompense, of all the true and painful service I have done, and the extreme dangers I have been in, but this only surname; a good memory and witness, of the malice and displeasure thou shouldst bear me. In deed the name only remaineth with me, by the sufferance of the dastardly nobility and magistrates, who have forsaken me, and let me be banished by the people. This extremity hath now driven me to come as a poor suitor, to take thy chimney hearth, not of any hope I have to save my life thereby. For if I had feared death, I would not have come hither to have put my life in hazard; but pricked forward with spite and desire I have to be revenged of them that thus have banished me, whom now I begin to be avenged on, putting my person between thy enemies. Wherefore, if thou have any heart to be wreaked of the injuries thy enemies have done thee, speed thee now, and let my misery serve thy turn ...

a command authority	**full quit of** revenged on
tackle clothes (ship's rigging)	**wreak** vengeance
vessel body	**maims/Of shame** shameful
requited rewarded	wounds
memory memorial	**cankered** diseased, corrupted
dastard nobles cowardly patricians	**spleen** anger
Whooped jeered	**under-fiends** devils in Hell

CORIOLANUS A name unmusical to the Volscians' ears   55
     And harsh in sound to thine.
AUFIDIUS   Say, what's thy name?
     Thou hast a grim appearance, and thy face
     Bears a command in't. Though thy tackle's torn,
     Thou show'st a noble vessel. What's thy name?
CORIOLANUS Prepare thy brow to frown. Know'st thou me yet?   60
AUFIDIUS I know thee not. Thy name?
CORIOLANUS My name is Caius Martius, who hath done
     To thee particularly and to all the Volsces
     Great hurt and mischief; thereto witness may
     My surname, Coriolanus. The painful service,   65
     The extreme dangers, and the drops of blood
     Shed for my thankless country are requited
     But with that surname – a good memory
     And witness of the malice and displeasure
     Which thou shouldst bear me. Only that name remains.   70
     The cruelty and envy of the people,
     Permitted by our dastard nobles, who
     Have all forsook me, hath devoured the rest
     And suffered me by th'voice of slaves to be
     Whooped out of Rome. Now this extremity   75
     Hath brought me to thy hearth; not out of hope –
     Mistake me not – to save my life, for if
     I had feared death, of all the men i'th'world
     I would have 'voided thee, but in mere spite,
     To be full quit of those my banishers,   80
     Stand I before thee here. Then if thou hast
     A heart of wreak in thee, that wilt revenge
     Thine own particular wrongs and stop those maims
     Of shame seen through thy country, speed thee straight
     And make my misery serve thy turn. So use it   85
     That my revengeful services may prove
     As benefits to thee, for I will fight
     Against my cankered country with the spleen
     Of all the under-fiends. But if so be
     Thou dar'st not this, and that to prove more fortunes   90
     Thou'rt tired, then, in a word, I also am
     Longer to live most weary and present
     My throat to thee and to thy ancient malice,

Coriolanus claims Aufidius will be shamed unless he either kills him or accepts him as an ally. Aufidius says all his hatred is gone. He rejoices to see his old enemy and offers friendship.

1 Speaking and responding (in pairs)

Lines 62–132 present challenges for the actors playing Coriolanus and Aufidius. Each has a single speech to which the other must react. Match the summaries below with the appropriate lines, then explore ways of speaking and reacting, using the questions to help you.

Coriolanus: I am Coriolanus / I have injured the Volsces / Rome has only rewarded me with the surname Coriolanus / The patricians have allowed the plebeians to drive me out of Rome / I come to Antium not to save my life, but to be revenged on Rome / To further your own revenge on Rome, invade now, I'll fight for you / Otherwise, kill me.

Aufidius: I no longer hate you / You speak truthfully / Let me lovingly embrace you, whom I fought so many times / You give me more joy than my own wedding day / I had intended to fight you again / Each night I have fought you in my dreams / Let's destroy Rome for banishing you / Now meet the Volsce senators.

- What tones of voice does Coriolanus use in different sections?
- Does Coriolanus hesitate at particular points in his speech?
- How does Aufidius react at line 62 on learning his greatest enemy now faces him?
- How does Aufidius react to each section of Coriolanus' speech?
- How long a pause before Aufidius' 'O Martius, Martius!'? (line 98)
- How genuine is Aufidius' response? Might he be affected by drink?
- How does Coriolanus react to the erotic imagery of lines 113–15 and 119–23?
- How does he respond to Aufidius' embrace?
- Aufidius' speech is rich in hyperbole (extravagant and exaggerated language). How does that affect his delivery?

---

tuns barrels
grainèd ash strong lance
clip embrace
rapt enraptured
Mars (in Roman mythology) the god of war
power on foot army prepared

hew thy target ... brawn cut your shield from your strong arm
Unbuckling helms unfastening helmets
muster recruit as soldiers
flood o'erbeat torrent overwhelm Rome

Which not to cut would show thee but a fool,
Since I have ever followed thee with hate,   95
Drawn tuns of blood out of thy country's breast,
And cannot live but to thy shame, unless
It be to do thee service.
AUFIDIUS   O Martius, Martius!
Each word thou hast spoke hath weeded from my heart
A root of ancient envy. If Jupiter   100
Should from yond cloud speak divine things
And say ''Tis true', I'd not believe them more
Than thee, all-noble Martius. Let me twine
Mine arms about that body whereagainst
My grainèd ash an hundred times hath broke   105
And scarred the moon with splinters.

[*He embraces Coriolanus*]

                              Here I clip
The anvil of my sword, and do contest
As hotly and as nobly with thy love
As ever in ambitious strength I did
Contend against thy valour. Know thou first,   110
I loved the maid I married; never man
Sighed truer breath. But that I see thee here,
Thou noble thing, more dances my rapt heart
Than when I first my wedded mistress saw
Bestride my threshold. Why, thou Mars, I tell thee,   115
We have a power on foot, and I had purpose
Once more to hew thy target from thy brawn,
Or lose mine arm for't. Thou hast beat me out
Twelve several times, and I have nightly since
Dreamt of encounters 'twixt thyself and me –   120
We have been down together in my sleep,
Unbuckling helms, fisting each other's throat –
And waked half dead with nothing. Worthy Martius,
Had we no other quarrel else to Rome but that
Thou art thence banished, we would muster all   125
From twelve to seventy and, pouring war
Into the bowels of ungrateful Rome,
Like a bold flood o'erbeat. O, come, go in,
And take our friendly senators by th'hands,

*Aufidius appoints Coriolanus to command half the Volsce army and to
decide how best to attack Rome. The two servants comment on
Coriolanus' strength. They discuss the merits of their leaders.*

1 Joining the enemy

Aufidius makes it clear that he welcomes Coriolanus as an ally to attack
Rome. In response, Coriolanus speaks only a half line 'You bless me,
gods!'. Otherwise he is silent. When Aufidius offers Coriolanus his
hand at line 144, the handshake will seal their alliance.

How does Coriolanus respond to the invitation to shake hands, and
how do the two men leave the stage? Work out how can each man show
the audience what is going on in his mind in these few moments.

2 Servants discuss their masters (in groups of three)

The servants' discussion of who is the greater soldier, Coriolanus or
Aufidius, hints at future competition between the two leaders. Take
parts as the three servants and speak from line 145 to the end of the
scene. Use the activities below and on following pages to help your
understanding of this episode.

a The servants are the Volsce equivalents of the Roman plebeians.
  On stage, what advantages might come from emphasising the
  similarities between the two groups?

b At first it is not obvious which leader, Coriolanus or Aufidius, is
  thought by the servants to be the greater soldier. Why are they
  wary of speaking clearly?

c Suggest how you might use the comic atmosphere of this episode
  to reinforce the audience's understanding of the main plot.

d Invent stage business for the servants to perform as they speak.

---

absolute incomparable, perfect	**set up a top** start a child's top
commission command, army	spinning
set down decide what to do	**term** describe
ere destroy before destroying them	**wot** know

Who now are here taking their leaves of me,   130
Who am prepared against your territories,
Though not for Rome itself.
CORIOLANUS   You bless me, gods!
AUFIDIUS Therefore, most absolute sir, if thou wilt have
The leading of thine own revenges, take
Th'one half of my commission and set down   135
As best thou art experienced, since thou know'st
Thy country's strength and weakness, thine own ways,
Whether to knock against the gates of Rome
Or rudely visit them in parts remote
To fright them ere destroy. But come in,   140
Let me commend thee first to those that shall
Say yea to thy desires. A thousand welcomes!
And more a friend than e'er an enemy;
Yet, Martius, that was much. Your hand. Most welcome!
                        Exeunt [Coriolanus and Aufidius]

            [*The two* SERVINGMEN *come forward*]

FIRST SERVINGMAN Here's a strange alteration!   145
SECOND SERVINGMAN By my hand, I had thought to have strucken
    him with a cudgel, and yet my mind gave me his clothes made a false
    report of him.
FIRST SERVINGMAN What an arm he has! He turned me about with his
    finger and his thumb as one would set up a top.   150
SECOND SERVINGMAN Nay, I knew by his face that there was some-
    thing in him. He had, sir, a kind of face, methought – I cannot tell
    how to term it.
FIRST SERVINGMAN He had so, looking as it were – would I were hanged
    but I thought there was more in him than I could think.   155
SECOND SERVINGMAN So did I, I'll be sworn. He is simply the rarest
    man i'th'world.
FIRST SERVINGMAN I think he is. But a greater soldier than he, you wot
    one.
SECOND SERVINGMAN Who, my master?   160
FIRST SERVINGMAN Nay, it's no matter for that.
SECOND SERVINGMAN Worth six on him.
FIRST SERVINGMAN Nay, not so neither. But I take him to be the
    greater soldier.
SECOND SERVINGMAN Faith, look you, one cannot tell how to say that. 165
    For the defence of a town, our general is excellent.

The servants agree that Coriolanus is a greater soldier than Aufidius. The Third Servingman tells how the Volsce nobles treat Coriolanus as a god, and that he has vowed to devastate Rome.

1 Different personalities (in groups of three)

The Servingmen do not have names, but actors on stage try to give each a distinct personality. As you work on this episode, think about ways in which you might make each servant different from the other. For example, an actor who played the Third Servingman said:

'I think of him as like Nick Bottom in *A Midsummer's Night Dream*. He's full of his own self-importance, and thinks he's more intelligent than the others. He revels in describing what he's just seen at the banquet, and he loves using big words like "directitude". It sounds impressive, it might mean "command", but it probably doesn't mean anything'.

2 Honouring Coriolanus (in small groups)

Lines 186–95 describe how Aufidius and the Volsce nobles honour Coriolanus. Aufidius treats him as a lover and as a holy relic to worship, and the nobles give him half the Volsce army. Rehearse and perform a mime or series of tableaux of the lines, showing each short section in turn, for example:

- treating Coriolanus as the son and heir of the war god, Mars;
- placing him in the most honoured seat at the feast;
- the senators removing their hats before they speak to him. In Shakespeare's time, men kept their hats on indoors. It was a mark of respect to remove your hat before speaking to someone;
- Aufidius' admiration of Coriolanus;
- the Senators granting Coriolanus command of half the Volsce army.

---

partake share	**bald** bare-headed
as lief rather	**entreaty and grant** begging and
was wont to thwack used to beat	gift
scotched slashed	**sowl** drag
a carbonado barbecued meat	**polled** shaved bare
so made on celebrated, praised,	**durst** dare
feted	**conies** rabbits

FIRST SERVINGMAN Ay, and for an assault too.

Enter the THIRD SERVINGMAN

THIRD SERVINGMAN O slaves, I can tell you news – news, you rascals!

FIRST *and* SECOND SERVINGMEN What, what, what? Let's partake.

THIRD SERVINGMAN I would not be a Roman, of all nations. I had as lief   170
be a condemned man.

FIRST *and* SECOND SERVINGMEN Wherefore? Wherefore?

THIRD SERVINGMAN Why, here's he that was wont to thwack our
general, Caius Martius.

FIRST SERVINGMAN Why do you say 'thwack our general'?   175

THIRD SERVINGMAN I do not say 'thwack our general', but he was always
good enough for him.

SECOND SERVINGMAN Come, we are fellows and friends. He was ever too
hard for him; I have heard him say so himself.

FIRST SERVINGMAN He was too hard for him directly. To say the troth   180
on't, before Corioles he scotched him and notched him like a
carbonado.

SECOND SERVINGMAN And he had been cannibally given, he might have
broiled and eaten him too.

FIRST SERVINGMAN But more of thy news.   185

THIRD SERVINGMAN Why, he is so made on here within as if he were
son and heir to Mars; set at upper end o'th'table; no question asked
him by any of the senators but they stand bald before him. Our
general himself makes a mistress of him, sanctifies himself with's
hand, and turns up the white o'th'eye to his discourse. But the   190
bottom of the news is, our general is cut i'th'middle and but one half
of what he was yesterday, for the other has half by the entreaty and
grant of the whole table. He'll go, he says, and sowl the porter of
Rome gates by th'ears. He will mow all down before him and leave
his passage polled.   195

SECOND SERVINGMAN And he's as like to do't as any man I can
imagine.

THIRD SERVINGMAN Do't? He will do't, for look you, sir, he has as
many friends as enemies; which friends, sir, as it were, durst not –
look you, sir – show themselves, as we term it, his friends whilst   200
he's in directitude.

FIRST SERVINGMAN 'Directitude'? What's that?

THIRD SERVINGMAN But when they shall see, sir, his crest up again and
the man in blood, they will out of their burrows, like conies after
rain, and revel all with him.   205

The Servingmen criticise peace and praise war. They look forward to marching against Rome. In Scene 6, Sicinius describes how banishing Coriolanus has brought tranquillity to Rome.

1 Change the characters? (in small groups)

In one production the Servingmen were played as characters who very obviously would never fight in a war. In another production (which portrayed the patrician class as warmongers and the working class as united in desiring peace), lines 210–22 in praise of war were given to Volsce Senators. Talk about what you think was the director's intention in each production.

2 War and peace

The Servingmen claim that war is a medicine that cures the corruptions of peace, and that men 'hate one another' in peace because they 'less need one another'. Copy and complete the following table, using every description in lines 211–21.

War	Peace
'sprightly walking' (puts a spring in your step)	'rust iron' (swords become rusty through lack of use)
'audible' (noisy, excitingly clear)	'increase tailors' (because men throw away armour and buy fancy clothes)

When you have completed the table, add your own appraisal of every item, showing whether or not you agree with each view of war and peace.

---

presently immediately
parcel part, outcome
vent cries, rumours, explosive
  energies
apoplexy sickness
mulled dulled
  (like wine sweetened and heated)

cuckolds deceived husbands
rising finishing the feast
His remedies are tame
  the medicine (banishment) we gave
  Coriolanus has brought peace

FIRST SERVINGMAN But when goes this forward?

THIRD SERVINGMAN Tomorrow, today, presently. You shall have the drum struck up this afternoon. 'Tis as it were a parcel of their feast, and to be executed ere they wipe their lips.

SECOND SERVINGMAN Why, then we shall have a stirring world again. This peace is nothing but to rust iron, increase tailors, and breed ballad-makers.   210

FIRST SERVINGMAN Let me have war, say I. It exceeds peace as far as day does night. It's sprightly walking, audible, and full of vent. Peace is a very apoplexy, lethargy; mulled, deaf, sleepy, insensible; a getter   215 of more bastard children than war's a destroyer of men.

SECOND SERVINGMAN 'Tis so. And as wars in some sort may be said to be a ravisher, so it cannot be denied but peace is a great maker of cuckolds.

FIRST SERVINGMAN Ay, and it makes men hate one another.   220

THIRD SERVINGMAN Reason: because they then less need one another. The wars for my money. I hope to see Romans as cheap as Volscians.

[*A sound within*]

They are rising, they are rising.

FIRST *and* SECOND SERVINGMEN In, in, in, in!

Exeunt

ACT 4   SCENE 6
Rome: the market-place

Enter the two tribunes, SICINIUS and BRUTUS

SICINIUS We hear not of him, neither need we fear him.
His remedies are tame – the present peace
And quietness of the people, which before
Were in wild hurry. Here do we make his friends
Blush that the world goes well, who rather had,   5
Though they themselves did suffer by't, behold
Dissentious numbers pestering streets than see
Our tradesmen singing in their shops and going
About their functions friendly.

Sicinius tells Menenius that only the patricians miss Coriolanus, and Rome prospers without him. The citizens offer prayers for the tribunes, who comment on Coriolanus' desire to rule alone as king.

'Your Coriolanus is not much missed'. Although Coriolanus is banished, he still remains the main topic of conversation in Rome, but Menenius (right) is not amused by Sicinius' jibe.

stood to't took a firm stand	**comely** respectable
temporised been able to compromise	**affecting one sole throne** wishing to rule alone as king
Good e'en good evening	**lamentation** grief

Enter MENENIUS

BRUTUS We stood to't in good time. Is this Menenius?   10
SICINIUS 'Tis he, 'tis he. O, he is grown most kind of late.
       Hail, sir!
MENENIUS Hail to you both.
SICINIUS Your Coriolanus is not much missed
       But with his friends. The commonwealth doth stand,   15
       And so would do were he more angry at it.
MENENIUS All's well, and might have been much better if
       He could have temporised.
SICINIUS   Where is he, hear you?
MENENIUS Nay, I hear nothing.
       His mother and his wife hear nothing from him.   20

Enter three or four CITIZENS

CITIZENS The gods preserve you both!
SICINIUS   Good e'en, our neighbours.
BRUTUS Good e'en to you all, good e'en to you all.
FIRST CITIZEN Ourselves, our wives, and children, on our knees
       Are bound to pray for you both.
SICINIUS   Live and thrive.
BRUTUS Farewell, kind neighbours.   25
       We wished Coriolanus had loved you as we did.
CITIZENS Now the gods keep you!
BOTH TRIBUNES Farewell, farewell.
                           Exeunt Citizens
SICINIUS This is a happier and more comely time
       Than when these fellows ran about the streets   30
       Crying confusion.
BRUTUS   Caius Martius was
       A worthy officer i'th'war, but insolent,
       O'ercome with pride, ambitious, past all thinking
       Self-loving.
SICINIUS   And affecting one sole throne
       Without assistance.   35
MENENIUS   I think not so.
SICINIUS We should by this, to all our lamentation,
       If he had gone forth consul found it so.
BRUTUS The gods have well prevented it, and Rome
       Sits safe and still without him.

The Aedile tells that a messenger reports that the Volsces have invaded.
The tribunes say it is not true, and order the messenger to be whipped.
But a second messenger says he has worse news.

1 Shooting the messenger (in pairs)

The messenger ('a slave', line 40) has brought bad news, but he seems
likely to be rewarded with a whipping. Messengers in other Shakespeare
plays get beaten because of the news they bring, for example in *Antony
and Cleopatra*, *Macbeth* and *King Richard III*. The long tradition of
punishing messengers who bring bad news goes back to Greek plays
written over 2,000 years ago. The modern expression 'shooting the
messenger' shows that the tradition still continues.

Why are messengers punished? Talk together about what such a
response suggests about Brutus and Sicinius, or any person who orders
punishment because they dislike the news a messenger brings.

2 Creating dramatic atmosphere (in groups of four)

In this scene, Shakespeare builds up an atmosphere of crisis by using
four 'messengers' (the Aedile, two Messengers and Cominius). He
creates a sense of growing fear as the tribunes hear more and more
reports of the impending destruction of Rome.

Speak lines 39–99, with one person reading all four 'messenger'
parts, whilst the others take on the roles of Brutus, Sicinius and
Menenius.

Afterwards talk about how Shakespeare creates a growing sense of
urgency as each messenger brings increasingly worse news. Why does
he choose to use four separate 'messengers', rather than having all the
news reported by the 'slave' who is first mentioned?

---

several powers separate armies
inshelled drawn in
  (like a snail's horns)
break break their peace treaty
record written history

turns their countenances makes
  their faces pale
raising rumour-mongering
  (spreading rumours)
seconded confirmed, supported

Enter an AEDILE

AEDILE   Worthy tribunes,
  There is a slave, whom we have put in prison,   40
  Reports the Volsces with two several powers
  Are entered in the Roman territories,
  And with the deepest malice of the war
  Destroy what lies before 'em.
MENENIUS   'Tis Aufidius,
  Who, hearing of our Martius' banishment,   45
  Thrusts forth his horns again into the world,
  Which were inshelled when Martius stood for Rome,
  And durst not once peep out.
SICINIUS Come, what talk you of Martius?
BRUTUS Go see this rumourer whipped. It cannot be   50
  The Volsces dare break with us.
MENENIUS   Cannot be?
  We have record that very well it can,
  And three examples of the like hath been
  Within my age. But reason with the fellow
  Before you punish him, where he heard this,   55
  Lest you shall chance to whip your information
  And beat the messenger who bids beware
  Of what is to be dreaded.
SICINIUS   Tell not me.
  I know this cannot be.
BRUTUS   Not possible.

Enter a MESSENGER

MESSENGER The nobles in great earnestness are going   60
  All to the senate-house. Some news is come
  That turns their countenances.
SICINIUS   'Tis this slave –
  [*To the Aedile*] Go whip him 'fore the people's eyes – his
   raising,
  Nothing but his report.
MESSENGER   Yes, worthy sir,
  The slave's report is seconded, and more,   65
  More fearful, is delivered.
SICINIUS   What more fearful?

The tribunes think the news a trick, and Menenius cannot believe that Coriolanus has united with Aufidius, but the Second Messenger and Cominius confirm the bad news that Rome is threatened with destruction.

---

1 Speaking to effect (in small groups)

Use the following to guide your speaking of the lines opposite.

a The Messenger knows that bringers of bad news are likely to be whipped for speaking it. He has to tell the tribunes to their face that Coriolanus is marching on Rome, determined on revenge. But will his news earn him a beating? Explore ways of speaking lines 67–71, bearing in mind that you may be punished for your message.

b Identify words or phrases in lines 72–6 that the tribunes and Menenius might emphasise to show their disbelief of the news that Coriolanus and Aufidius are marching on Rome.

c Experiment with different ways of speaking 'Good Martius' in line 73 (remember that Brutus has just been reviling Coriolanus).

d Speak the Second Messenger's lines 77–82 as if you have just run through all of Rome trying to find the tribunes.

e Find different ways of delivering lines 84, 88 and 91–2 in which Menenius says virtually the same thing again and again.

f Speak Cominius' lines, emphasising each 'your' or 'you' as contemptuously as possible. Decide whether such emphasis is justified in performance.

The very trick on't that's the cunning plan!
atone be reconciled (at one)
violent'st contrariety most extreme opposites
O'erborne their way overcome every obstacle in their path

holp helped
city leads … pates Rome's lead-covered roofs on your heads
franchises … stood rights on which you insisted
auger's bore tiny hole (made by an auger, a drill)

MESSENGER It is spoke freely out of many mouths –
        How probable I do not know – that Martius,
        Joined with Aufidius, leads a power 'gainst Rome
        And vows revenge as spacious as between   70
        The young'st and oldest thing.
SICINIUS   This is most likely!
BRUTUS Raised only that the weaker sort may wish
        Good Martius home again.
SICINIUS   The very trick on't.
MENENIUS This is unlikely.
        He and Aufidius can no more atone   75
        Than violent'st contrariety.

Enter [a SECOND] MESSENGER

SECOND MESSENGER You are sent for to the senate.
        A fearful army, led by Caius Martius
        Associated with Aufidius, rages
        Upon our territories and have already   80
        O'erborne their way, consumed with fire, and took
        What lay before them.

Enter COMINIUS

COMINIUS O, you have made good work!
MENENIUS What news? What news?
COMINIUS You have holp to ravish your own daughters and   85
        To melt the city leads upon your pates,
        To see your wives dishonoured to your noses –
MENENIUS What's the news? What's the news?
COMINIUS Your temples burnèd in their cement, and
        Your franchises, whereon you stood, confined   90
        Into an auger's bore.
MENENIUS   Pray now, your news –
        [*To the Tribunes*] You have made fair work, I fear me – Pray,
          your news.
        If Martius should be joined wi'th'Volscians –

Cominius describes Coriolanus as a pitiless destroyer. He and Menenius berate the tribunes and the plebeians, and say that no one can persuade Coriolanus to show mercy to Rome.

1 Expressing contempt (in pairs)

The two patricians heap a tirade of abuse on the two tribunes, and each mention of the plebeians is probably spoken with contempt ('apron-men', 'garlic-eaters', 'people', 'crafts'). Identify the lines opposite that Cominius and Menenius speak directly to the tribunes, and speak them putting as much scorn into your voices as possible (for example, Menenius' 'You have made good work' may be spoken with great sarcasm). Is there also a strong accusatory tone of 'I told you so'?

2 Four images of Coriolanus

Line 94: 'a thing'. Compare with other descriptions of Coriolanus as 'a thing' at Act 2 Scene 2 line 103, Act 5 Scene 4, lines 10 and 17.

Lines 98–9: Turn back to Act 1 Scene 3, lines 54–8 to remind yourself of the description of Coriolanus' son killing a butterfly. Cominius' lines echo an image that Shakespeare had used in *King Lear* (Act 4 Scene 1, lines 36–7):

> As flies to wanton boys are we to th'gods;
> They kill us for their sport.

Line 104 compares Coriolanus to Hercules, the classical strong man who, as one of his twelve labours, picked ripe ('mellow') golden apples from a tree in the Hesperides, the farthest limit of the world.

Lines 115–16: Is Coriolanus the wolf or the shepherd in this image?

---

deity god
brats children
apron-men workmen, plebeians, artisans, tradesmen
voice of occupation votes of the workers

smilingly revolt gladly rebel
brand firebrand, blazing torch
crafts workmen, deceits
S'incapable of so powerless to

COMINIUS   If?
  He is their god. He leads them like a thing
  Made by some other deity than Nature,   95
  That shapes man better, and they follow him
  Against us brats with no less confidence
  Than boys pursuing summer butterflies
  Or butchers killing flies.
MENENIUS [*To the Tribunes*] You have made good work,
  You and your apron-men, you that stood so much 100
  Upon the voice of occupation and
  The breath of garlic-eaters!
COMINIUS He'll shake your Rome about your ears.
MENENIUS As Hercules did shake down mellow fruit.
  You have made fair work!   105
BRUTUS But is this true, sir?
COMINIUS   Ay, and you'll look pale
  Before you find it other. All the regions
  Do smilingly revolt, and who resists
  Are mocked for valiant ignorance
  And perish constant fools. Who is't can blame him? 110
  Your enemies and his find something in him.
MENENIUS We are all undone, unless
  The noble man have mercy.
COMINIUS   Who shall ask it?
  The tribunes cannot do't for shame; the people
  Deserve such pity of him as the wolf   115
  Does of the shepherds. For his best friends, if they
  Should say 'Be good to Rome', they charged him even
  As those should do that had deserved his hate
  And therein showed like enemies.
MENENIUS   'Tis true.
  If he were putting to my house the brand   120
  That should consume it, I have not the face
  To say 'Beseech you, cease.' [*To the Tribunes*] You have
  made fair hands,
  You and your crafts! You have crafted fair!
COMINIUS   You have brought
  A trembling upon Rome such as was never
  S'incapable of help.
BOTH TRIBUNES   Say not we brought it.   125

Menenius blames the patricians for giving in to the plebeians' demand for Coriolanus' banishment. He berates the citizens, who express regret for exiling Coriolanus.

1 More contempt

Menenius and Cominius continue their scornful abuse of the tribunes. When the citizens enter, Menenius uses the same contemptuous tone towards them. Speak lines 133–43 trying to make every word count as Menenius jeers at, tries to frighten, and roundly condemns the plebeians. For example, he probably sneers 'clusters' (crowds of plebeians) and many other words or phrases.

2 Fickle and fearful? (in small groups)

Cominius comments on the changeable nature of the plebeians at line 129 'They'll roar him in again'. His judgement seems to be confirmed in lines 144–9, where the citizens are shown as having changed from the triumphant crowds that jeered Coriolanus out of Rome. Now they appear frightened, and seek to excuse their earlier behaviour in banishing Coriolanus.

Some productions have attempted to show the plebeians as having integrity and honesty. But is that possible in this episode? To find out, try out different ways of staging lines 144–9 to discover if you can portray the plebeians in a favourable light.

3 Attacking the tribunes? (in small groups)

One production of the play showed the citizens physically assaulting the tribunes, blaming them for their plight. Talk together about what you think of that staging.

---

second name of men second in fame to Coriolanus
points orders
coxcombs fools' heads

voices votes, refusal to confirm him as consul
coal piece of charcoal
cry pack of hounds
side faction (the patricians)

MENENIUS How? Was't we? We loved him, but, like beasts
    And cowardly nobles, gave way unto your clusters,
    Who did hoot him out o'th'city.
COMINIUS   But I fear
    They'll roar him in again. Tullus Aufidius,
    The second name of men, obeys his points   130
    As if he were his officer. Desperation
    Is all the policy, strength, and defence
    That Rome can make against them.

Enter a troop of CITIZENS

MENENIUS   Here come the clusters.
    And is Aufidius with him? You are they
    That made the air unwholesome when you cast   135
    Your stinking greasy caps in hooting at
    Coriolanus' exile. Now he's coming,
    And not a hair upon a soldier's head
    Which will not prove a whip. As many coxcombs
    As you threw caps up will he tumble down   140
    And pay you for your voices. 'Tis no matter.
    If he could burn us all into one coal,
    We have deserved it.
ALL CITIZENS Faith, we hear fearful news.
FIRST CITIZEN   For mine own part,
    When I said banish him, I said 'twas pity.   145
SECOND CITIZEN And so did I.
THIRD CITIZEN And so did I, and, to say the truth, so did very many of
    us. That we did, we did for the best, and though we willingly
    consented to his banishment, yet it was against our will.
COMINIUS You're goodly things, you voices.
MENENIUS   You have made good work,   150
    You and your cry. Shall's to the Capitol?
COMINIUS O, ay, what else?

Exeunt [*Cominius and Menenius*]

SICINIUS Go, masters, get you home. Be not dismayed.
    These are a side that would be glad to have
    This true which they so seem to fear. Go home   155
    And show no sign of fear.

The tribunes hope that the news of Coriolanus is false. In Scene 7, the Lieutenant describes Coriolanus' popularity among the Volsce soldiers. He wishes Aufidius had not shared command of the army.

1 Staging Scene 7 (in pairs)

To gain a first impression of Scene 7 speak all the lines twice, changing roles so that both of you experience speaking as Aufidius and as his lieutenant. Then work on some of the activities below and on page 182.

a Why do you think Aufidius uses 'th'Roman' rather than 'Coriolanus' or 'Martius'?

b In lines 3–4, the Lieutenant uses the imagery of eating to describe Coriolanus' popularity. Turn to page 239 for other images of eating in the play.

c Is the Lieutenant reluctant to tell all he knows, or only too willing? To help you decide, speak his lines with many pauses, as if you were afraid to let Aufidius know everything. Then speak quickly and confidently.

d Lines 12–16 could be seen as a criticism of Aufidius' judgement. So just how does the Lieutenant tell his general that he thinks he's made a mistake?

e Imagine you are directing the play on an open stage with the minimum of scenery. You have decided to use only one prop or piece of stage furniture to signal the location of each scene. What will you use to indicate that the action of Scene 7 takes place at Aufidius' camp?

---

fly to favour
grace 'fore meat prayer before meals
means trickery
lame the foot/Of our design wreck our plan (to conquer Rome)

changeling fickle person
your particular your own sake
Joined in commission shared the command

FIRST CITIZEN The gods be good to us! Come, masters, let's home. I ever
    said we were i'th'wrong when we banished him.
SECOND CITIZEN So did we all. But come, let's home.
                                        Exeunt Citizens

BRUTUS I do not like this news.   160
SICINIUS Nor I.
BRUTUS Let's to the Capitol. Would half my wealth
    Would buy this for a lie.
SICINIUS   Pray let's go.
                                            Exeunt

ACT 4   SCENE 7
The countryside near Rome

Enter AUFIDIUS *with his* LIEUTENANT

AUFIDIUS Do they still fly to th'Roman?
LIEUTENANT I do not know what witchcraft's in him, but
    Your soldiers use him as the grace 'fore meat,
    Their talk at table, and their thanks at end,
    And you are darkened in this action, sir,   5
    Even by your own.
AUFIDIUS   I cannot help it now,
    Unless by using means I lame the foot
    Of our design. He bears himself more proudlier,
    Even to my person, than I thought he would
    When first I did embrace him. Yet his nature   10
    In that's no changeling, and I must excuse
    What cannot be amended.
LIEUTENANT   Yet I wish, sir –
    I mean for your particular – you had not
    Joined in commission with him, but either
    Have borne the action of yourself or else   15
    To him had left it solely.

Aufidius hints that Coriolanus has failed in certain duties to the Volsces. He predicts Coriolanus will capture Rome, sums up his character, and, as power defeats power, looks forward to overthrowing him.

1 Coriolanus' character (in small groups)

Use the following to help you prepare a presentation of Aufidius' lines.

Lines 17–26: Coriolanus, who appears to be serving the Volsces so well ('good husbandry' = valuable service), has 'left undone' something that will cause his downfall.

Line 28: He is a supreme soldier.

Lines 29–33: The Roman aristocracy love him and the plebeians will repeal his banishment.

Lines 33–5: He will capture Rome as easily and majestically as the osprey (fish hawk) catches a fish.

Lines 35–45: Although he served Rome well, his lack of stability caused his downfall, which may have come about through:

- pride, which comes from continued success ('daily fortune') and always corrupts men;
- lack of judgement, which causes political failure;
- his inflexible nature, unable to move from war ('th'casque' = helmet) to peace ('th'cushion' = the seat in the senate), always imposing rigid discipline ('austerity and garb').

Lines 45–9: Taints of these faults made him feared, hated, then banished. But his bravery ('merit') prevents talk of his faults.

Lines 49–50: So reputation changes according to circumstances. Different people, or times, change praise into condemnation.

Lines 51–3: To praise success is to bring about its failure.

Lines 54–5: One hero is defeated by a stronger person.

Lines 56–7: When Coriolanus has defeated Rome, I'll defeat him.

---

account reckoning
vulgar eye common people
carry capture
ere he sits down before he begins his siege
the repeal repealing his banishment

even with proper balance
taints corrupts
disposing of those chances seizing the opportunities
austerity and garb austere manner
spices flavours, traces

AUFIDIUS I understand thee well, and be thou sure,
        When he shall come to his account, he knows not
        What I can urge against him. Although it seems,
        And so he thinks, and is no less apparent   20
        To th'vulgar eye, that he bears all things fairly
        And shows good husbandry for the Volscian state,
        Fights dragon-like, and does achieve as soon
        As draw his sword, yet he hath left undone
        That which shall break his neck or hazard mine   25
        Whene'er we come to our account.
LIEUTENANT Sir, I beseech you, think you he'll carry Rome?
AUFIDIUS All places yields to him ere he sits down,
        And the nobility of Rome are his;
        The senators and patricians love him too.   30
        The tribunes are no soldiers, and their people
        Will be as rash in the repeal as hasty
        To expel him thence. I think he'll be to Rome
        As is the osprey to the fish, who takes it
        By sovereignty of nature. First he was   35
        A noble servant to them, but he could not
        Carry his honours even. Whether 'twas pride,
        Which out of daily fortune ever taints
        The happy man; whether defect of judgement,
        To fail in the disposing of those chances   40
        Which he was lord of; or whether nature,
        Not to be other than one thing, not moving
        From th'casque to th'cushion, but commanding peace
        Even with the same austerity and garb
        As he controlled the war; but one of these –   45
        As he hath spices of them all – not all,
        For I dare so far free him – made him feared,
        So hated, and so banished. But he has a merit
        To choke it in the utterance. So our virtues
        Lie in th'interpretation of the time,   50
        And power, unto itself most commendable,
        Hath not a tomb so evident as a chair
        T'extol what it hath done.
        One fire drives out one fire; one nail, one nail;
        Rights by rights falter, strengths by strengths do fail.   55
        Come, let's away. When, Caius, Rome is thine,
        Thou art poor'st of all; then shortly art thou mine. *Exeunt*

Looking back at Act 4

Activities for groups or individuals

Act 4 shows how Coriolanus (seated) sides with his greatest enemy, Aufidius, to lead a Volsce army against his homeland, Rome. It was fairly common practice in ancient times for an exile to join the enemy, even though the penalty for such treachery was death. But does Aufidius' suspicion of his new ally show in his face and body language?

1 Seven swift scene changes

Act 4 moves from Rome to Antium and to places between. Remind yourself of where each scene takes place, then propose a simple design that allows the stage action to flow quickly from scene to scene.

2 Seven scenes, different moods

For each of the seven scenes in Act 4 suggest two or three words that describe the dominant mood (or moods) you would wish the audience to experience in your production of the play. Which scene gives you most problems in accomplishing this task? Why?

3 Why? – a soliloquy for Coriolanus

Coriolanus arrives in Antium in Scene 4 with his mind made up to transfer his allegiance from Rome to the Volsces. But how and why does he change, rejecting all that his upbringing and education has taught him about loyalty and service to Rome? Write a soliloquy for Coriolanus that he might have spoken as he journeyed from Rome to Antium. In it he tells why he has decided to join the Volsces.

4 One fire drives out one fire …

At the end of Act 4, Aufidius reflects on Coriolanus' character and concludes that fame is transitory ('our virtues/Lie in th'interpretation of the time'). With the passage of time even the greatest reputation fades as people come to value a new hero or heroine. A leader will always be displaced by another leader, one strong man is defeated by another: 'One fire drives out one fire; one nail, one nail'. Give examples from your knowledge of what happens in sport (or entertainment, politics, business, or friendship), of 'One fire drives out one fire'. Why has the public reputation of your modern-day examples undergone great change?

5 Are ordinary people fickle?

The fickleness of ordinary people, their readiness to be swayed by smooth-talking politicians or by danger, is a feature of several of Shakespeare's plays. In Scene 6, the citizens, fearing Coriolanus' revenge, change their mind about their part in his banishment. Give your own view on what you think of Shakespeare's portrayal of ordinary people as fickle.

*Menenius refuses to go to Coriolanus to beg for mercy for Rome.
Cominius tells how he was rejected, and that Coriolanus will spare no
one. Menenius accuses the tribunes of bringing about Rome's destruction.*

1 Speak the scene (in groups of four)

Some time has passed since the last scene in Rome (Act 4 Scene 6), and
Coriolanus and his army are now besieging the city. The Romans hope
to persuade Coriolanus to show mercy, but he has already rejected his
old comrade-in-arms, Cominius. Now the tribunes want Menenius to
plead to Coriolanus.

To help you decide on staging, take parts as Menenius, Cominius,
Brutus and Sicinius and speak the whole scene. Menenius should
emphasise his contempt for the tribunes, for example as he tells them
to crawl on their knees to Coriolanus ('fall down and knee the way').

2 No name – 'nothing' (in pairs)

Coriolanus rejects all names, all identity: 'He was a kind of nothing,
titleless'. Talk about the state of mind of someone who refuses to be
called by any name, and seems not to know old friends. What image of
himself does Coriolanus wish to project?

3 Who?

Coriolanus sees war as a way of cleansing Rome. 'Chaff' is the worthless
remains (corn husks) of corn after it has been winnowed (using blasts
of air to separate grain from chaff). Before you turn the page, say who
Coriolanus thinks of as the 'chaff' and who as the 'grain' in lines 25–8.

---

dear particular warm personal
  friendship
coyed was reluctant
wracked for laboured to ruin
make coals cheap reduce Rome
  to ashes

memory memorial
minded reminded
bare petition empty plea
noisome musty chaff stinking
  mouldy corn husks
nose th'offence smell the offensive
  stuff

ACT 5 SCENE 1
Rome: the market-place

Enter MENENIUS, COMINIUS, SICINIUS and BRUTUS,
the two Tribunes, with others

MENENIUS No, I'll not go. You hear what he hath said
　　　Which was sometime his general, who loved him
　　　In a most dear particular. He called me father,
　　　But what o'that? Go, you that banished him;
　　　A mile before his tent fall down and knee　　　　　　5
　　　The way into his mercy. Nay, if he coyed
　　　To hear Cominius speak, I'll keep at home.
COMINIUS He would not seem to know me.
MENENIUS　　　　　　　　　　　　　　Do you hear?
COMINIUS Yet one time he did call me by my name.
　　　I urged our old acquaintance and the drops　　　　10
　　　That we have bled together. 'Coriolanus'
　　　He would not answer to; forbade all names.
　　　He was a kind of nothing, titleless,
　　　Till he had forged himself a name o'th'fire
　　　Of burning Rome.
MENENIUS [To the Tribunes] Why, so; you have made good work!　　15
　　　A pair of tribunes that have wracked for Rome
　　　To make coals cheap – a noble memory!
COMINIUS I minded him how royal 'twas to pardon
　　　When it was less expected. He replied
　　　It was a bare petition of a state　　　　　　　　　20
　　　To one whom they had punished.
MENENIUS Very well. Could he say less?
COMINIUS I offered to awaken his regard
　　　For's private friends. His answer to me was
　　　He could not stay to pick them in a pile　　　　　25
　　　Of noisome musty chaff. He said 'twas folly
　　　For one poor grain or two to leave unburnt
　　　And still to nose th'offence.

Coriolanus

The tribunes plead with Menenius that he should go to Coriolanus to beg mercy for Rome. After some reluctance, Menenius agrees, hoping that a good meal will soften Coriolanus' mood.

1 Menenius' motivation (in groups of three)

Menenius is persuaded to go to Coriolanus, but the actor playing the part must decide how to present Menenius in this scene. Use the following questions to help you explore how to play the episode on the opposite page.

a Does Menenius secretly wish all along to visit Coriolanus? Is he genuinely reluctant, or just putting on a show of reluctance?

b Is he confident that he can obtain mercy for Rome from Coriolanus, or is he secretly unsure, even pessimistic about the result of his mission?

c How influenced is he by Sicinius' lines 46–8, saying that even if he fails Rome will honour him, appropriate to his intention to succeed ('after the measure/As you intended well'). Menenius is a patrician, so what special appeal might Sicinius' words hold for him?

d Does Menenius really believe what he says in lines 52–9, where he argues that people are more likely to be pliable ('have suppler souls') after they have eaten? Do you?

2 'Our countryman'

Suggest one or two reasons why Sicinius, who led the call for Coriolanus' banishment, now calls him 'our countryman' in line 39. Is Menenius affected by this description?

Upbraid's reproach us
pleader advocate, defender
instant quickly recruited
grief-shot grief-stricken
hum at disdain, rebuke

unhearts discourages
unapt unready
prove test
Speed how it will however it turns out

MENENIUS For one poor grain or two!
                I am one of those. His mother, wife, his child,   30
                And this brave fellow too – we are the grains.
                [*To the Tribunes*] You are the musty chaff, and you are smelt
                Above the moon. We must be burnt for you.
SICINIUS Nay, pray be patient. If you refuse your aid
                In this so never-needed help, yet do not   35
                Upbraid's with our distress. But sure, if you
                Would be your country's pleader, your good tongue,
                More than the instant army we can make,
                Might stop our countryman.
MENENIUS   No, I'll not meddle.
SICINIUS Pray you go to him.
MENENIUS   What should I do?   40
BRUTUS Only make trial what your love can do
                For Rome towards Martius.
MENENIUS Well, and say that Martius return me,
                As Cominius is returned, unheard – what then?
             · But as a discontented friend, grief-shot   45
                With his unkindness? Say't be so?
SICINIUS   Yet your good will
                Must have that thanks from Rome after the measure
                As you intended well.
MENENIUS   I'll undertake't.
                I think he'll hear me. Yet to bite his lip
                And hum at good Cominius much unhearts me.   50
                He was not taken well; he had not dined.
                The veins unfilled, our blood is cold, and then
                We pout upon the morning, are unapt
                To give or to forgive; but when we have stuffed
                These pipes and these conveyances of our blood   55
                With wine and feeding, we have suppler souls
                Than in our priest-like fasts. Therefore I'll watch him
                Till he be dieted to my request,
                And then I'll set upon him.
BRUTUS You know the very road into his kindness   60
                And cannot lose your way.
MENENIUS   Good faith, I'll prove him,
                Speed how it will. I shall ere long have knowledge
                Of my success.   *Exit*

Cominius describes how Coriolanus sits in magnificent state, filled with an implacable desire for revenge. Only his mother and wife might make him show mercy. In Scene 2, the Volsce sentries are unimpressed by Menenius.

1 Modern examples? (in pairs)

Cominius is certain that Menenius' mission will fail because Coriolanus' sense of the wrong done to him rigidly controls any feelings of pity ('his injury/The gaoler to his pity'). Talk together about how vivid you find this description of Coriolanus and suggest several modern-day examples of people whose sense of grievance overwhelms their feelings of compassion and forgiveness.

2 Stage business (in pairs)

Show what Cominius does as he speaks 'Thus' at line 68. Then hold a piece of paper in your hand, representing Coriolanus' letter setting out his terms. Point to different parts of the 'letter' as you speak lines 68–70.

3 How alike? How different? (in pairs)

Step into role as Menenius and Cominius and talk about how you are like and unlike each other. Which of you most embodies the virtues of Rome?

4 'Speak with Coriolanus'

In what tone does the Second Watch imitate Menenius' words in line 11? Was Menenius wise to use the name 'Coriolanus' to a Volsce soldier?

---

injury sense of being wronged
gaoler prison warder
solicit plead with
fair entreaties favourable prayers

lots to blanks certain (winning lottery tickets to losing tickets)
passable acceptable

COMINIUS   He'll never hear him.
SICINIUS   Not?
COMINIUS I tell you, he does sit in gold, his eye
    Red as 'twould burn Rome, and his injury   65
    The gaoler to his pity. I kneeled before him;
    'Twas very faintly he said 'Rise', dismissed me
    Thus, with his speechless hand. What he would do
    He sent in writing after me, what he would not,
    Bound with an oath to hold to his conditions.   70
    So that all hope is vain
    Unless his noble mother and his wife,
    Who, as I hear, mean to solicit him
    For mercy to his country. Therefore let's hence,
    And with our fair entreaties haste them on.   75

Exeunt

ACT 5   SCENE 2
The Volsce camp near Rome

Enter MENENIUS to the WATCH or Guard

FIRST WATCH Stay. Whence are you?
SECOND WATCH Stand, and go back.
MENENIUS You guard like men, 'tis well. But, by your leave,
    I am an officer of state and come
    To speak with Coriolanus.   5
FIRST WATCH From whence?
MENENIUS From Rome.
FIRST WATCH You may not pass; you must return. Our general
    Will no more hear from thence.
SECOND WATCH You'll see your Rome embraced with fire before   10
    You'll 'speak with Coriolanus'.
MENENIUS   Good my friends,
    If you have heard your general talk of Rome
    And of his friends there, it is lots to blanks
    My name hath touched your ears. It is Menenius.
FIRST WATCH Be it so; go back. The virtue of your name   15
    Is not here passable.

Menenius claims that his reports have made Coriolanus' mighty reputation. The guards disbelieve him and say he cannot prevent the destruction of Rome because pleas for mercy are useless.

1 Understanding a spin doctor (in pairs)

In lines 17–25, Menenius' description of how he has been the chronicler of Coriolanus' deeds, enhancing his reputation, is rich in the imagery of books, bowling and coinage. Like a modern 'spin doctor' who tries to create a favourable image of a politician, Menenius claims he has painted a truthful picture of Coriolanus. Sometimes, like a bowler on a tricky bowling green ('subtle ground') he has overshot the mark ('tumbled past the throw'), that is, he has exaggerated, getting close to approving lies ('stamped the leasing').

To help your understanding of the lines, let one person step into role as Menenius. Speak the lines a short section at a time, accompanying each section with any actions, however exaggerated, to help make the meaning clear. The other person (who cannot see the script) listens to each section. If he or she understands, give the 'thumbs up' sign. If the listener does not understood, give a 'thumbs down', which is an invitation to the speaker to repeat the lines with other actions.

2 Class conflict

The guards are Volsce plebeians, Menenius is a patrician. Suggest ways in which each man could speak or act which bring out their different social class. For example, in what tone does Menenius speak 'fellow', and how does the guard speak 'sir'?

3 'Back'... 'Back'... 'Back!' (in pairs)

Is Menenius trying to force his way past the guard at lines 54–6? Or is the guard showing that although he is of lower social status, he is the master in this situation? Invent actions to accompany the lines.

---

lover greatest friend
haply amplified happily expanded
varnishèd shiningly portrayed
verity truth
lapsing slipping
factionary on the party working in support of

front his revenges oppose his vengeance
palsied intercession sickly intervention
dotant foolish old lover (dotard)
estimation respect

MENENIUS   I tell thee, fellow,
    Thy general is my lover. I have been
    The book of his good acts, whence men have read
    His fame unparalleled, haply amplified;
    For I have ever varnishèd my friends,   20
    Of whom he's chief, with all the size that verity
    Would without lapsing suffer. Nay, sometimes,
    Like to a bowl upon a subtle ground,
    I have tumbled past the throw and in his praise
    Have almost stamped the leasing. Therefore, fellow,   25
    I must have leave to pass.
FIRST WATCH Faith, sir, if you had told as many lies in his behalf as you
    have uttered words in your own, you should not pass here, no,
    though it were as virtuous to lie as to live chastely. Therefore go
    back.   30
MENENIUS Prithee, fellow, remember my name is Menenius, always
    factionary on the party of your general.
SECOND WATCH Howsoever you have been his liar, as you say you have,
    I am one that, telling true under him, must say you cannot pass.
    Therefore go back.   35
MENENIUS Has he dined, canst thou tell? For I would not speak with him
    till after dinner.
FIRST WATCH You are a Roman, are you?
MENENIUS I am as thy general is.
FIRST WATCH Then you should hate Rome, as he does. Can you, when   40
    you have pushed out your gates the very defender of them and in a
    violent popular ignorance given your enemy your shield, think to
    front his revenges with the easy groans of old women, the virginal
    palms of your daughters, or with the palsied intercession of such a
    decayed dotant as you seem to be? Can you think to blow out the   45
    intended fire your city is ready to flame in with such weak breath as
    this? No, you are deceived. Therefore back to Rome and prepare for
    your execution. You are condemned; our general has sworn you out
    of reprieve and pardon.
MENENIUS Sirrah, if thy captain knew I were here, he would use me   50
    with estimation.
FIRST WATCH Come, my captain knows you not.
MENENIUS I mean thy general.
FIRST WATCH My general cares not for you. Back, I say, go, lest I let forth
    your half-pint of blood. Back, that's the utmost of your having.   55
    Back!

Menenius claims the Guard will be severely punished for keeping him from Coriolanus. But Coriolanus is unmoved by Menenius' pleading for Rome and dismisses him.

1 Director's advice

Use these director's notes to help you deliver each character's lines:

Menenius: 'The first half of the speech is spoken triumphantly, even jeeringly, to the Guard, but you must make up your own mind whether he is serious in threatening the Guard with execution or torture. He may be joking. The second half, to Coriolanus, looks as if he's delivering an already prepared speech, learned by heart. It stresses father and son, but it is formal and elaborate, and he might even weep at line 68. He might speak it with half an eye on the Guard, to impress him. But however he speaks, it's an old actor's stagey performance.'

Coriolanus: 'His first word "Away!" is like a hammer blow. He's implacable, and begins by speaking like a god, or even a machine. His first two lines are very emphatic. His language seems involved, but he's saying that although revenge belongs to him alone ("Though I owe my revenge properly"), only the Volsces have power to pardon ("remission"). Ungrateful forgetfulness will poison his love for Menenius, rather than pity remember how great that love was. The second half of his speech, from line 83, might be softer in tone, even though he ends, as he began, with an awesome certainty as he speaks to Aufidius.'

Aufidius: 'Remember, this Volsce warrior intends no good to Coriolanus. His few words are ambiguous and ironic, because what Coriolanus hears might not be the same as Aufidius intends. So speak line 88 to remind the theatre audience of your violent intentions to Coriolanus, but so that he won't suspect.'

---

companion fellow
say an errand tell your story
estimation respect
Jack guardant Jack-in-office, bossy sentry
office order, obstruct
presently immediately

synod meeting
hardly moved persuaded with difficulty
assuage soften, diminish
varlet knave
Ingrate ungrateful
suits pleas for mercy

MENENIUS Nay, but fellow, fellow –

Enter CORIOLANUS *with* AUFIDIUS

CORIOLANUS What's the matter?

MENENIUS Now, you companion, I'll say an errand for you. You shall
know now that I am in estimation. You shall perceive that a Jack   60
guardant cannot office me from my son Coriolanus; guess but my
entertainment with him. If thou stand'st not i'th'state of hanging, or
of some death more long in spectatorship and crueller in suffering,
behold now presently and swoon for what's to come upon thee. [*To
Coriolanus*] The glorious gods sit in hourly synod about thy particu-   65
lar prosperity and love thee no worse than thy old father Menenius
does! O my son, my son! Thou art preparing fire for us; look thee,
here's water to quench it. I was hardly moved to come to thee, but
being assured none but myself could move thee, I have been blown
out of your gates with sighs and conjure thee to pardon Rome and   70
thy petitionary countrymen. The good gods assuage thy wrath and
turn the dregs of it upon this varlet here – this, who like a block hath
denied my access to thee.

CORIOLANUS Away!

MENENIUS How? Away?   75

CORIOLANUS Wife, mother, child, I know not. My affairs
Are servanted to others. Though I owe
My revenge properly, my remission lies
In Volscian breasts. That we have been familiar,
Ingrate forgetfulness shall poison rather   80
Than pity note how much. Therefore begone.
Mine ears against your suits are stronger than
Your gates against my force. Yet, for I loved thee,
     [*Gives him a letter*]
Take this along; I writ it for thy sake
And would have sent it. Another word, Menenius,   85
I will not hear thee speak. This man, Aufidius,
Was my beloved in Rome; yet thou behold'st.

AUFIDIUS You keep a constant temper.

Exeunt [*Coriolanus and Aufidius;*] *the Guard and Menenius* [*remain*]

FIRST WATCH Now, sir, is your name Menenius?

SECOND WATCH 'Tis a spell, you see, of much power. You know the way   90
home again.

The guards mock Menenius. He dismisses them as worthless. In Scene 3,
Coriolanus plans to besiege Rome. Aufidius acknowledges him as a true
servant of the Volsces. Coriolanus will hear no more mercy pleas.

1 Broken or unbowed? (in pairs)

What is the effect on Menenius of Coriolanus' rejection? Some
productions portray him as a broken man, pathetically trying to retain
some dignity. Others show him as defiant, giving the guards as good as
he gets. Take turns to speak lines 95–9 in different ways to discover
how you would present Menenius after his humiliating rejection.

2 'The rock, the oak'

Keep the description of Coriolanus (lines 101–2) in mind as you work
on Scene 3. Will he prove to be the immovable object that the Second
Watch thinks he is?

3 Staging the entry

Work out how you would stage the entrance of Coriolanus and Aufidius
to suggest their relationship. Although they are joint commanders,
Coriolanus' reputation overshadows that of Aufidius. One production
began the scene with Coriolanus seated in a magnificent chair of state,
with Aufidius standing beside him, recalling Cominius' description in
Act 5 Scene 1, lines 64–5: 'I tell you he does sit in gold, his eye/Red
as 'twould burn Rome …'

4 Questions of character (in pairs)

Why is Coriolanus so keen that Aufidius reports his behaviour to the
Volsce lords (line 3)? What difference does it make if Coriolanus is
thinking of himself, rather than Menenius, when he speaks 'with a
cracked heart' in line 9?

---

shent rebuked
slight insignificant
long for a long time
Set down our host place our
  besieging army

general suit public pleas for mercy
private whisper personal plea
godded worshipped me as a god
latest refuge last resort
grace honour

FIRST WATCH Do you hear how we are shent for keeping your greatness
back?

SECOND WATCH What cause do you think I have to swoon?

MENENIUS I neither care for th'world nor your general. For such things   95
as you, I can scarce think there's any, you're so slight. He that hath a
will to die by himself fears it not from another. Let your general do
his worst. For you, be that you are, long, and your misery increase
with your age! I say to you, as I was said to, 'Away'!

Exit

FIRST WATCH A noble fellow, I warrant him.   100

SECOND WATCH The worthy fellow is our general. He's the rock, the oak
not to be wind-shaken.

Exeunt

ACT 5   SCENE 3
The Volsce camp near Rome

Enter CORIOLANUS and AUFIDIUS with Volscian soldiers

CORIOLANUS We will before the walls of Rome tomorrow
    Set down our host. My partner in this action,
    You must report to th'Volscian lords how plainly
    I have borne this business.

AUFIDIUS   Only their ends
    You have respected, stopped your ears against   5
    The general suit of Rome, never admitted
    A private whisper, no, not with such friends
    That thought them sure of you.

CORIOLANUS   This last old man,
    Whom with a cracked heart I have sent to Rome,
    Loved me above the measure of a father,   10
    Nay, godded me indeed. Their latest refuge
    Was to send him, for whose old love I have –
    Though I showed sourly to him – once more offered
    The first conditions, which they did refuse
    And cannot now accept, to grace him only   15
    That thought he could do more. A very little
    I have yielded to. Fresh embassies and suits,
    Nor from the state nor private friends, hereafter
    Will I lend ear to.

The arrival of his mother, wife and child makes Coriolanus fear he might break his vow to hear no more Roman pleas for mercy. He declares he will be inflexible, but his self-doubt returns.

1 Staging the women's entry (in small groups)

Every production tries to present the stage direction of line 21 to great dramatic effect. Sometimes the women are veiled, and dressed in robes of mourning or tattered costumes (there may be clues to their costume at lines 39 and 94). Share views on how you think the women are dressed, then work out your own staging of lines 19–21 and the women's entry.

2 Private or public?

To whom does Coriolanus speak, and how much does Aufidius hear? Some of Coriolanus' lines may be soliloquies or asides, not intended for the hearing of anyone on stage. As you work through this scene, identify the lines which he intends as 'public' (to be heard by Aufidius and the other watching Volsces), and which are 'private' (spoken to himself – or possibly to his wife or mother). For example, does Coriolanus intend Aufidius to hear lines 27–9 and 40–2?

3 Coriolanus' changing moods (in pairs)

Coriolanus' mood switches often from certainty and determination to doubt and uncertainty (for example, in lines 20–1 he moves from 'Shall I be tempted …?' to 'I will not'). One person speaks everything Coriolanus says on the opposite page, pausing after each short section. In each pause, the other person says 'doubt' or 'certainty'. How many mood swings can you identify?

---

infringe violate, break
trunk body
bond and privilege of
  nature natural ties of affection
forsworn break their vows
Olympus Greek mountain, home
  of the gods

supplication humble begging
aspect of intercession pleading
  look
gosling young goose
knew no other kin rejected all
  family

Shout within

Ha? What shout is this?
Shall I be tempted to infringe my vow   20
In the same time 'tis made? I will not.

Enter VIRGILIA, VOLUMNIA, VALERIA, YOUNG MARTIUS,
with Attendants

My wife comes foremost, then the honoured mould
Wherein this trunk was framed, and in her hand
The grandchild to her blood. But out, affection;
All bond and privilege of nature, break!   25
Let it be virtuous to be obstinate.
                    [*Virgilia curtsies*]
What is that curtsy worth? Or those dove's eyes,
Which can make gods forsworn? I melt, and am not
Of stronger earth than others.
                    [*Volumnia bows*]
                              My mother bows,
As if Olympus to a molehill should   30
In supplication nod, and my young boy
Hath an aspect of intercession which
Great Nature cries 'Deny not.' Let the Volsces
Plough Rome and harrow Italy, I'll never
Be such a gosling to obey instinct, but stand   35
As if a man were author of himself
And knew no other kin.
VIRGILIA   My lord and husband!
CORIOLANUS These eyes are not the same I wore in Rome.
VIRGILIA The sorrow that delivers us thus changed
        Makes you think so.
CORIOLANUS   Like a dull actor now   40
I have forgot my part and I am out,
Even to a full disgrace. Best of my flesh,
Forgive my tyranny, but do not say
For that 'Forgive our Romans.'
                    [*They kiss*]
                              O, a kiss
Long as my exile, sweet as my revenge!   45

Coriolanus kneels to his mother, but she rebukes him and kneels to him, an action contrary to all his beliefs. He greets Valeria and hopes that his son will become a supreme soldier.

1 Four greetings (in groups of five)

Coriolanus greets in turn his wife, his mother, Valeria and his son. What actions accompany his words? Some are given in the stage directions: *They kiss* (what kind of kiss?), *Kneels*, and so on. Invent actions as you enact lines 40–76. In one production, Coriolanus playfully shadow-boxed with his son as he spoke lines 70–5.

2 Constancy

Each of Coriolanus' greetings expresses the theme of constancy: of remaining true and faithful. He uses 'virgined' (remained chaste) to Virgilia; speaks of the natural duty he owes to his mother; describes Valeria's chastity; and hopes that his son will never be dishonourable, but immovable 'Like a great sea-mark' (lighthouse).

Coriolanus' declarations of constancy stand in ironic contrast to his own behaviour. He has not remained true, leading an army against his own city. Identify how accurately lines 70–5 (addressed to his son) describe Coriolanus himself. Are his thoughts noble? Has he proved 'To shame unvulnerable' (impossible to dishonour)?

3 Why use hyperbole?

Volumnia may be speaking ironically or sarcastically in lines 52–6 in saying that she should kneel to Coriolanus. He accepts the rebuke ('your corrected son'), and uses hyperbole (exaggerated language) to show he recognises that by Roman tradition, a mother should never kneel to her son (for example, 'Murdering impossibility' means 'making all things possible'). Suggest one or two other reasons for Coriolanus' exaggerated comparisons in lines 58–62.

---

queen of heaven (in Roman mythology) Juno, goddess of marriage
prate prattle, talk idly
unproperly against all custom
corrected rebuked
Fillip strike

holp helped
Publicola a Roman consul
curdied congealed, frozen
poor epitome small likeness
flaw gust of icy wind
that eye thee who look on you as leader

Now, by the jealous queen of heaven, that kiss
I carried from thee, dear, and my true lip
Hath virgined it e'er since. You gods! I prate,
And the most noble mother of the world
Leave unsaluted. Sink, my knee, i'th'earth;   50
                              Kneels
Of thy deep duty more impression show
Than that of common sons.
VOLUMNIA   O, stand up blest!
                              [*Coriolanus rises*]
Whilst with no softer cushion than the flint
I kneel before thee, and unproperly
Show duty as mistaken all this while   55
Between the child and parent.
                              [*She kneels*]
CORIOLANUS   What's this?
Your knees to me? To your corrected son?
                              [*He raises her*]
Then let the pebbles on the hungry beach
Fillip the stars. Then let the mutinous winds
Strike the proud cedars 'gainst the fiery sun,   60
Murdering impossibility, to make
What cannot be, slight work.
VOLUMNIA   Thou art my warrior;
I holp to frame thee. Do you know this lady?
CORIOLANUS The noble sister of Publicola,
The moon of Rome, chaste as the icicle   65
That's curdied by the frost from purest snow
And hangs on Dian's temple – dear Valeria!
VOLUMNIA [*Indicating Young Martius*] This is a poor epitome of yours,
Which by th'interpretation of full time
May show like all yourself.
CORIOLANUS   The god of soldiers,   70
With the consent of supreme Jove, inform
Thy thoughts with nobleness, that thou mayst prove
To shame unvulnerable and stick i'th'wars
Like a great sea-mark, standing every flaw
And saving those that eye thee!
VOLUMNIA   Your knee, sirrah.   75
                              [*Young Martius kneels*]
CORIOLANUS That's my brave boy!

Coriolanus tells his mother not to try to persuade him from attacking Rome. She persists, so he asks the Volsces to listen. She explains his family's dilemma: either Rome or he must perish.

1 Emotional blackmail? (in small groups)

In spite of Coriolanus' instruction not to plead for mercy for Rome, Volumnia does precisely that. Between lines 86 and 182 she uses all her powers of persuasion in an attempt to save her native city. Relying on her son's love for her and for Rome, she employs a mixture of logic and emotional blackmail to help her succeed. Use the activities below and on the following pages to help you stage the lines.

a What is Coriolanus' emotional reaction to hearing his mother say that if her plea fails, he will be to blame (lines 89–91)?

b How can you intensify the dramatic effect of Coriolanus' invitation to the Volsces to listen (lines 92–3)?

c Describe the women's appearance. What do lines 94–6 suggest about their dress and bodily health?

d Explore different ways of speaking Volumnia's lines: quietly and reasonably, angrily and passionately, and so on.

e Identify all words or phrases Volumnia might stress because of the emotional impact she knows they will have on Coriolanus.

f Explore different ways of expressing the divided loyalties Volumnia declares in lines 104–11: the women's love for Rome, and their love for Coriolanus. They are unable to pray, because praying for the one means that the other must be destroyed. The swinging rhythm of her lines can help your explorations. As the scene develops you will find how Volumnia exploits that dilemma.

---

suitors pleaders
forsworn sworn
Be held ... denials be my
 rejection of you
capitulate negotiate

mechanics plebeians, workmen
T'allay to abate, cool
raiment clothes
bewray reveal
capital deadly
barr'st prevent us offering

VOLUMNIA Even he, your wife, this lady, and myself
    Are suitors to you.
CORIOLANUS   I beseech you, peace;
    Or, if you'd ask, remember this before:
    The thing I have forsworn to grant may never   80
    Be held by you denials. Do not bid me
    Dismiss my soldiers or capitulate
    Again with Rome's mechanics. Tell me not
    Wherein I seem unnatural. Desire not
    T'allay my rages and revenges with   85
    Your colder reasons.
VOLUMNIA   O, no more, no more!
    You have said you will not grant us anything,
    For we have nothing else to ask but that
    Which you deny already. Yet we will ask,
    That if you fail in our request the blame   90
    May hang upon your hardness. Therefore hear us.
CORIOLANUS Aufidius, and you Volsces, mark, for we'll
    Hear nought from Rome in private.
               [He sits]
                      Your request?
VOLUMNIA Should we be silent and not speak, our raiment
    And state of bodies would bewray what life   95
    We have led since thy exile. Think with thyself
    How more unfortunate than all living women
    Are we come hither, since that thy sight, which should
    Make our eyes flow with joy, hearts dance with comforts,
    Constrains them weep and shake with fear and sorrow,   100
    Making the mother, wife, and child to see
    The son, the husband, and the father tearing
    His country's bowels out. And to poor we
    Thine enmity's most capital. Thou barr'st us
    Our prayers to the gods, which is a comfort   105
    That all but we enjoy. For how can we –
    Alas! How can we for our country pray,
    Whereto we are bound, together with thy victory,
    Whereto we are bound? Alack, or we must lose
    The country, our dear nurse, or else thy person,   110
    Our comfort in the country.

Volumnia forsees certain disaster for Coriolanus: defeat and disgrace as a traitor, or victory by killing his family. She threatens that if he attacks Rome, she will die. She pleads for a peace treaty.

1 Private thoughts and feelings (in pairs)

One person steps into role as Coriolanus. The other speaks the following passages, pausing after each. In the pause, Coriolanus declares his feelings about what he has heard from his mother, wife and son.

Lines 111–18: 'We must ... blood' (You will either be paraded in defeat as a traitor to Rome, or victoriously ride in triumph, but having killed your family.)

Lines 118–25: 'For myself ... world' (If you attack Rome, it will be over my dead body.)

Lines 125–7: 'Ay ... time' (And I, your wife, mother of your son, will die too.)

Lines 127–8: ''A shall not ... fight' (But I'll survive to fight.)

2 Suicide?

Volumnia and Virgilia tell Coriolanus that by attacking Rome he will cause their deaths. Do they mean they will commit suicide, or be killed in the Volsce onslaught? In nineteenth-century productions, Volumnia sometimes produced a knife to show her intention. Modern productions rarely show that gesture. Invent your own actions for lines 120–7.

3 Seeking a compromise

In lines 132–40, Volumnia proposes a peaceful way out of the dilemma (does this sound to you like the Volumnia of earlier in the play?). She then threatens Coriolanus with how history will destroy his honour and reputation if he conquers Rome. Describe Aufidius' reactions as he hears the compromise proposal.

---

evident calamity certain disaster
foreign recreant traitor to Rome
bear the palm be applauded, be crowned victor
determine come to an end

all-hail universal acclamation, greeting of praise
dogged followed
chronicle history
abhorred loathed and detested

                                    We must find
An evident calamity, though we had
Our wish which side should win. For either thou
Must as a foreign recreant be led
With manacles through our streets, or else   115
Triumphantly tread on thy country's ruin
And bear the palm for having bravely shed
Thy wife and children's blood. For myself, son,
I purpose not to wait on fortune till
These wars determine. If I cannot persuade thee   120
Rather to show a noble grace to both parts
Than seek the end of one, thou shalt no sooner
March to assault thy country than to tread –
Trust to't, thou shalt not – on thy mother's womb
That brought thee to this world.

VIRGILIA   Ay, and mine,   125
That brought you forth this boy to keep your name
Living to time.

BOY   'A shall not tread on me.
I'll run away till I am bigger, but then I'll fight.

CORIOLANUS Not of a woman's tenderness to be
Requires nor child, nor woman's face to see.   130
I have sat too long. [*He rises*]

VOLUMNIA   Nay, go not from us thus.
If it were so that our request did tend
To save the Romans, thereby to destroy
The Volsces whom you serve, you might condemn us
As poisonous of your honour. No, our suit   135
Is that you reconcile them, while the Volsces
May say 'This mercy we have showed', the Romans
'This we received', and each in either side
Give the all-hail to thee and cry 'Be blest
For making up this peace'! Thou know'st, great son,   140
The end of war's uncertain, but this certain,
That if thou conquer Rome, the benefit
Which thou shalt thereby reap is such a name
Whose repetition will be dogged with curses,
Whose chronicle thus writ: 'The man was noble,   145
But with his last attempt he wiped it out,
Destroyed his country, and his name remains
To th'ensuing age abhorred.'

Volumnia tries all kinds of persuasive arguments to make Coriolanus change his mind: flattery, scorn, his wife and child, her own feelings, accusation and shame, kneeling to him, insult, resignation, prediction.

1 'Speak to me, son'

Volumnia switches from one attempt at persuasion to another. Match the list at the head of this page with particular lines, for example:

Flattery: lines 149–53 (Volumnia asks Coriolanus to imitate the all-powerful gods who show mercy in using lightning, not to destroy people, but only to split a tree.)

Scorn: lines 154–5 (a noble man does not harbour grudges), and so on.

Speak each separate section using different tones of voice.

'*They kneel*'. Every production tries to make the stage directions at lines 171, 177 and 182 into memorable moments of theatre. What advice would you give the actors about how to perform each stage direction?
See also Activity 1 on page 208.

affected ... honour acquired the most noble honour	**one i'th'stocks** a common criminal put to shame
wide cheeks o'th'air sky	**fond ... brood** desiring no more children
sulphur lightning	**restrain'st from** deny
bolt thunderbolt	**'longs** belongs
rive an oak split a tree	**dispatch** dismissal

                    Speak to me, son.
Thou hast affected the fine strains of honour,
To imitate the graces of the gods,   150
To tear with thunder the wide cheeks o'th'air,
And yet to charge thy sulphur with a bolt
That should but rive an oak. Why dost not speak?
Think'st thou it honourable for a noble man
Still to remember wrongs? Daughter, speak you;   155
He cares not for your weeping. Speak thou, boy.
Perhaps thy childishness will move him more
Than can our reasons. There's no man in the world
More bound to's mother, yet here he lets me prate
Like one i'th'stocks. Thou hast never in thy life   160
Showed thy dear mother any courtesy,
When she, poor hen, fond of no second brood,
Has clucked thee to the wars and safely home,
Loaden with honour. Say my request's unjust,
And spurn me back. But if it be not so,   165
Thou art not honest, and the gods will plague thee
That thou restrain'st from me the duty which
To a mother's part belongs. – He turns away.
Down, ladies. Let us shame him with our knees.
To his surname Coriolanus 'longs more pride   170
Than pity to our prayers. Down! An end;
                    [*They kneel*]
This is the last. So, we will home to Rome
And die among our neighbours. – Nay, behold's.
This boy, that cannot tell what he would have
But kneels and holds up hands for fellowship,   175
Does reason our petition with more strength
Than thou hast to deny't. – Come, let us go.
                    [*They rise*]
This fellow had a Volscian to his mother;
His wife is in Corioles, and his child
Like him by chance. – Yet give us our dispatch.   180
I am hushed until our city be afire,
And then I'll speak a little.
          [*He*] *holds her by the hand, silent*

                        207

Coriolanus fears that in yielding to his mother's plea for mercy for Rome he has sealed his own death warrant. Aufidius intends to regain his power by exploiting Coriolanus' change of heart.

1 Conflicting emotions, physical responses?

Coriolanus is silent throughout Volumnia's lines 131–82. But how does he react? Suggest how he responds to each section of her appeal. At what point does he take her hand? How long a pause before he speaks? Is he moved by her language or just the sight of his family?

2 'This unnatural scene'

Coriolanus probably means a number of things when he speaks of 'this unnatural scene' (line 185). Put the following interpretations in order of which Coriolanus considers most unnatural, down to least unnatural.

- a Roman who intended to destroy Rome;
- a soldier who goes against his nature;
- a Roman who has betrayed his promise to the Volsces;
- a conquerer yielding to a woman's pleas;
- a mother whose action condemns her son to death.

3 'I was moved withal'

Aufidius makes his intentions clear in his aside at lines 201–3, but what tone of voice does he use to Coriolanus when he speaks line 195?

4 *Exeunt*

Work out how everyone leaves the stage, to show what each thinks lies ahead, and their relationships with the other characters. For example, is Volumnia aware of the damage she has done to her son?

---

ope open
mortal deadly
true wars my promised attack on
 Rome
convenient appropriate
stead place
withal by it

sweat compassion weep tears of
 pity
Stand to support
former fortune return to my
 earlier power and status
confederate arms allies

CORIOLANUS O mother, mother!
　　　　What have you done? Behold, the heavens do ope,
　　　　The gods look down, and this unnatural scene　　　　185
　　　　They laugh at. O my mother, mother! O!
　　　　You have won a happy victory to Rome;
　　　　But for your son – believe it, O believe it –
　　　　Most dangerously you have with him prevailed,
　　　　If not most mortal to him. But let it come. –　　　　190
　　　　Aufidius, though I cannot make true wars,
　　　　I'll frame convenient peace. Now, good Aufidius,
　　　　Were you in my stead, would you have heard
　　　　A mother less? Or granted less, Aufidius?
AUFIDIUS I was moved withal.
CORIOLANUS　　　　　　　　I dare be sworn you were.　　　　195
　　　　And, sir, it is no little thing to make
　　　　Mine eyes to sweat compassion. But, good sir,
　　　　What peace you'll make, advise me. For my part,
　　　　I'll not to Rome; I'll back with you, and pray you
　　　　Stand to me in this cause. – O mother! Wife!　　　　200
AUFIDIUS [*Aside*] I am glad thou hast set thy mercy and thy honour
　　　　At difference in thee. Out of that I'll work
　　　　Myself a former fortune.
CORIOLANUS [*To the ladies*]　　　Ay, by and by.
　　　　But we will drink together, and you shall bear
　　　　A better witness back than words, which we,　　　　205
　　　　On like conditions, will have counter-sealed.
　　　　Come, enter with us. Ladies, you deserve
　　　　To have a temple built you. All the swords
　　　　In Italy, and her confederate arms,
　　　　Could not have made this peace.　　　　210

　　　　　　　　　　　　　　　　　Exeunt

Menenius is certain that the ladies' plea for mercy will fail because Coriolanus is implacable in his desire for revenge on Rome. A messenger warns Sicinius of danger

1 First read through (in groups of four or more)

Take parts as Menenius, Sicinius and the two messengers and speak the whole scene as a first step in preparation for staging it. When you have completed your first reading, talk together about dramatic irony. The audience have just seen Scene 3, and know that the ladies have in fact succeeded, but Menenius and Sicinius do not. How can you exploit this dramatic irony in your performance?

2 Character description

Suggest why Menenius uses 'Martius' rather than 'Coriolanus', then make a list of all the ways in which he describes Coriolanus in lines 9–24. Comment on how accurate you judge each description to be. Which descriptions do you think are wrong? Which may be true?

3 Humour in disaster

Identify lines which might produce laughter from an audience, and work out how to deliver them. What advice about humour do you think Shakespeare offered his actors in this scene?

4 'A thing'

Coriolanus is twice more described as 'a thing' (see page 176): 'more than a creeping thing', 'in his state as a thing' (like a statue of Alexander the Great). Advise Menenius whether or not he should pause before speaking 'thing' in lines 10 and 17, as if searching for a suitable word to describe Coriolanus.

---

quoin wedge-shaped keystone
stay upon wait for
condition character
tartness sharpness, bitterness
engine battering ram
a corslet body armour
knell funeral bell

hum ... battery anger is like cannonfire
state golden throne
thing ... Alexander statue of Alexander the Great, King of Macedonia (356–323 BC)
long of because of

ACT 5 SCENE 4
Rome: outside the Capitol

Enter MENENIUS *and* SICINIUS

MENENIUS See you yond quoin o'th'Capitol, yond cornerstone?

SICINIUS Why what of that?

MENENIUS If it be possible for you to displace it with your little finger, there is some hope the ladies of Rome, especially his mother, may prevail with him. But I say there is no hope in't; our throats are sentenced and stay upon execution. 5

SICINIUS Is't possible that so short a time can alter the condition of a man?

MENENIUS There is difference between a grub and a butterfly, yet your butterfly was a grub. This Martius is grown from man to dragon. He has wings; he's more than a creeping thing. 10

SICINIUS He loved his mother dearly.

MENENIUS So did he me; and he no more remembers his mother now than an eight-year-old horse. The tartness of his face sours ripe grapes. When he walks, he moves like an engine, and the ground shrinks before his treading. He is able to pierce a corslet with his eye, 15 talks like a knell, and his hum is a battery. He sits in his state as a thing made for Alexander. What he bids be done is finished with his bidding. He wants nothing of a god but eternity and a heaven to throne in.

SICINIUS Yes, mercy, if you report him truly. 20

MENENIUS I paint him in the character. Mark what mercy his mother shall bring from him. There is no more mercy in him than there is milk in a male tiger. That shall our poor city find. And all this is long of you.

SICINIUS The gods be good unto us! 25

MENENIUS No, in such a case the gods will not be good unto us. When we banished him, we respected not them; and, he returning to break our necks, they respect not us.

Enter a MESSENGER

MESSENGER Sir, if you'd save your life, fly to your house.
    The plebeians have got your fellow tribune 30

*Brutus has been attacked by the plebeians. News arrives that the ladies
have succeeded in persuading Coriolanus to show mercy to Rome.
Sounds of the citizens' rejoicing are heard.*

1 What happens to Brutus?

The Messenger reports how the citizens, fearful that Coriolanus may
destroy Rome, are dragging the tribune Brutus through the streets,
threatening to kill him if Volumnia's plea fails. Neither Brutus nor
Sicinius appear again in the script. Turn to page 214 to read how one
production memorably staged the final appearance of the tribunes.

2 Shakespeare's own experience? (in pairs)

Lines 42–3 describe how the citizens, joyful at the news of peace, burst
through the gates of Rome to greet the ladies. Perhaps the image comes
from Shakespeare's own personal experience. Sometimes, as he walked
over Old London Bridge, a very short distance from the Globe Theatre,
he saw the flooded River Thames ('the blown tide') pouring through
the arches of the bridge.

When you have time, find a picture of old London Bridge (it is in
many books about Shakespeare's life and times). Talk about how likely
it is that Shakespeare's own experience of the bridge is the source of his
image of the citizens pouring out of Rome.

3 Do they leave the stage?

The sounds of music and shouting anticipate the spectacle of the next
scene in which the ladies enter the city, joyously acclaimed. In the
theatre, the characters usually do not leave the stage at the end of Scene
4, but turn to watch the triumphal entry of the ladies in Scene 5. When
you have read the next scene and studied the illustration on page 214,
decide how you would stage the end of Scene 4 and the start of
Scene 5.

---

hale haul, drag
by inches by slow torture
are dislodged have lifted their
siege and left their camp
Tarquins kings of Rome, see
page 2
recomforted once more happy
citizens

hautboys oboes
sackbuts brass instruments like
trombones
psalteries stringed instruments like
zithers played by plucking
Tabors small drums
doit small coin

And hale him up and down, all swearing if
The Roman ladies bring not comfort home
They'll give him death by inches.

Enter another MESSENGER

SICINIUS What's the news?

SECOND MESSENGER Good news, good news! The ladies have
   prevailed,   35
  The Volscians are dislodged, and Martius gone.
  A merrier day did never yet greet Rome,
  No, not th'expulsion of the Tarquins.

SICINIUS   Friend,
  Art thou certain this is true? Is't most certain?

SECOND MESSENGER As certain as I know the sun is fire. 40
  Where have you lurked that you make doubt of it?
  Ne'er through an arch so hurried the blown tide
  As the recomforted through th'gates.
   Trumpets, hautboys, drums beat, all together
            Why, hark you!
  The trumpets, sackbuts, psalteries and fifes,
  Tabors and cymbals, and the shouting Romans 45
  Make the sun dance.
       A shout within
       Hark you!

MENENIUS   This is good news.
  I will go meet the ladies. This Volumnia
  Is worth of consuls, senators, patricians,
  A city full; of tribunes such as you,
  A sea and land full. You have prayed well today. 50
  This morning for ten thousand of your throats
  I'd not have given a doit.
      Sound still with the shouts
      Hark, how they joy!

SICINIUS [*To Second Messenger*] First, the gods bless you for your
  tidings.
  Next, accept my thankfulness.

SECOND MESSENGER Sir, we have all great cause to give great
  thanks.   55

SICINIUS They are near the city?

SECOND MESSENGER Almost at point to enter.

SICINIUS We'll meet them and help the joy.   *Exeunt*

The ladies are welcomed as they make a triumphal entry into Rome. In Scene 6, Aufidius declares his intention to accuse Coriolanus in front of the Volsce lords.

'Welcome, ladies, Welcome!' Many productions stage Scene 5 as a magnificent pageant, a spectacle full of action and sound. In one production, as the triumphal procession moved off stage, Sicinius was seen tending the battered body of Brutus who had been killed by the mob. Rehearse and perform your own staging of Scene 5. You may wish to write a speech for Volumnia: what would she say?

tribes political groups	**vouch** guarantee, assert
fires bonfires	**ports** gates
Repeal recall from banishment	**purge** cleanse, expiate
repair return, go	*faction* political group
commons' ears the hearing of the ordinary citizens	

ACT 5 SCENE 5
Rome: the city gates

Enter two SENATORS, *with* VOLUMNIA, VIRGILIA, *and* VALERIA,
passing over the stage, with other LORDS

A SENATOR Behold our patroness, the life of Rome!
    Call all your tribes together, praise the gods,
    And make triumphant fires. Strew flowers before them.
    Unshout the noise that banished Martius;
    Repeal him with the welcome of his mother.   5
    Cry 'Welcome, ladies, welcome!'
ALL Welcome, ladies, welcome!
        A flourish with drums and trumpets. [*Exeunt*]

ACT 5 SCENE 6
Corioles: a public place

Enter TULLUS AUFIDIUS, *with Attendants*

AUFIDIUS Go, tell the lords o'th'city I am here.
    Deliver them this paper.
        [*He gives a paper*]
              Having read it,
    Bid them repair to th'market-place, where I,
    Even in theirs and in the commons' ears,
    Will vouch the truth of it. Him I accuse   5
    The city ports by this hath entered and
    Intends t'appear before the people, hoping
    To purge himself with words. Dispatch.
                  [*Exeunt attendants*]

Enter three or four CONSPIRATORS *of Aufidius' faction*

                   Most welcome!
FIRST CONSPIRATOR How is it with our general?

Aufidius regrets the help he gave to Coriolanus. He lists his grievances, saying that Coriolanus patronised him, and treated him as a subordinate. The First Conspirator feels cheated of booty.

1 Plotting against Coriolanus (in small groups)

Just as the tribunes had earlier prepared the citizens of Rome, telling them how to bring down Coriolanus, now Aufidius plots with the Volsce conspirators. He knows he must find a way that can be interpreted by the Volsce citizens as honourable ('admits a good construction'), and in lines 20–40 he reviews the reasons for his grievance.

Work out a suitable staging for the 'conspirators' episode in lines 9–59. To help your preparation, consider the following:

a Do Aufidius and the conspirators whisper together, afraid of being overheard?

b Is Aufidius angry and passionate in his complaints against Coriolanus or does he list his grievances in a rational, calculating manner, or …?

c Why is Aufidius concerned about the reaction of the Volsce people (lines 14–15)?

d Does Aufidius tell lies in lines 20–5? Identify the claims he makes which have not been shown in the script.

e In what tone does the Third Conspirator correct Aufidius at lines 26–8?

f Aufidius resents that Coriolanus merely rewarded him with smiles ('waged me with his countenance'). Suggest an appropriate facial expression for Aufidius as he speaks line 39.

g Identify the images of growth and harvest in lines 22 and 35–6. What would you reply to an actor who wanted to replace 'dews of' with 'flowing', and 'did end' with 'stored up'?

---

alms charitable gifts
parties supporters
raised promoted
stoutness stubborn pride
lack of stooping failure to compromise
joint-servant equal partner

files ranks of soldiers
designments purposes
he did end all his he harvested for himself alone
mercenary a paid soldier
carried captured
spoil booty

AUFIDIUS   Even so   10
    As with a man by his own alms empoisoned
    And with his charity slain.
SECOND CONSPIRATOR   Most noble sir,
    If you do hold the same intent wherein
    You wished us parties, we'll deliver you
    Of your great danger.
AUFIDIUS   Sir, I cannot tell.
    We must proceed as we do find the people.   15
THIRD CONSPIRATOR The people will remain uncertain whilst
    'Twixt you there's difference, but the fall of either
    Makes the survivor heir of all.
AUFIDIUS   I know it,
    And my pretext to strike at him admits
    A good construction. I raised him, and I pawned   20
    Mine honour for his truth; who being so heightened,
    He watered his new plants with dews of flattery,
    Seducing so my friends; and to this end
    He bowed his nature, never known before
    But to be rough, unswayable, and free.   25
THIRD CONSPIRATOR Sir, his stoutness
    When he did stand for consul, which he lost
    By lack of stooping –
AUFIDIUS   That I would have spoke of.
    Being banished for't, he came unto my hearth,
    Presented to my knife his throat. I took him,   30
    Made him joint-servant with me, gave him way
    In all his own desires; nay, let him choose
    Out of my files, his projects to accomplish,
    My best and freshest men; served his designments
    In mine own person, holp to reap the fame   35
    Which he did end all his, and took some pride
    To do myself this wrong – till at the last
    I seemed his follower, not partner, and
    He waged me with his countenance as if
    I had been mercenary.
SECOND CONSPIRATOR   So he did, my lord.   40
    The army marvelled at it, and in the last,
    When he had carried Rome and that we looked
    For no less spoil than glory –

Coriolanus

Aufidius expresses contempt at Coriolanus' yielding to the ladies' tears, and vows to kill him. The Volsce lords agree that failure to capture Rome is inexcusable.

1 How many conspirators? (in pairs)

Shakespeare writes parts for three conspirators. But would the episode work just as well on stage with only one conspirator? Speak lines 9–59 with one person reading all the conspirators' lines. Discuss the advantages and disadvantages of staging the scene with only one conspirator.

2 Aufidius' letter

Just what did Aufidius write in his letter to the Volsce lords? The First Lord says that only the final fault – Coriolanus' failure to conquer Rome – is inexcusable. Make your own list of the charges Aufidius levels against Coriolanus, then write the letter.

3 'He', 'him', 'his' (in pairs)

Speak all the lines opposite emphasising each reference to Coriolanus. Why do you think none of the Volsces speak his name?

4 Corioles or Antium? (in pairs)

This edition of the play sets Scene 6 in Corioles. But should it be set in Antium, the Volsce capital? Many people think that Shakespeare began by setting the scene in Antium (and provided clues at lines 49, 60, 73 and 80), but realised, as he wrote, how much more dramatically effective it would be set in Corioles, scene of Coriolanus' great victory (see lines 52 and 92).

Take turns to step into role as Shakespeare and give your thoughts about where the scene is set.

---

my sinews ... him I'll use my full power against him
rheum tears
post mere messenger
at your vantage seize the opportunity
Ere before

along prostrate, dead
with heed perused carefully read
easy fines light punishment
levies troops
answering ... charge saying he followed our orders (or, making us no profit)

AUFIDIUS   There was it,
     For which my sinews shall be stretched upon him.
     At a few drops of women's rheum, which are   45
     As cheap as lies, he sold the blood and labour
     Of our great action. Therefore shall he die,
     And I'll renew me in his fall.

          Drums and trumpets sound, with great shouts of the people

                              But hark!
FIRST CONSPIRATOR Your native town you entered like a post
     And had no welcomes home, but he returns   50
     Splitting the air with noise.
SECOND CONSPIRATOR   And patient fools,
     Whose children he hath slain, their base throats tear
     With giving him glory.
THIRD CONSPIRATOR   Therefore, at your vantage,
     Ere he express himself or move the people
     With what he would say, let him feel your sword,   55
     Which we will second. When he lies along,
     After your way his tale pronounced shall bury
     His reasons with his body.
AUFIDIUS   Say no more.
     Here come the lords.

          Enter the LORDS *of the city*

ALL LORDS You are most welcome home.   60
AUFIDIUS I have not deserved it.
     But, worthy lords, have you with heed perused
     What I have written to you?
ALL LORDS   We have.
FIRST LORD   And grieve to hear't.
     What faults he made before the last, I think
     Might have found easy fines. But there to end   65
     Where he was to begin, and give away
     The benefit of our levies, answering us
     With our own charge, making a treaty where
     There was a yielding – this admits no excuse.
AUFIDIUS He approaches. You shall hear him.   70

Coriolanus reports success, claiming he has made an honourable peace treaty with Rome. Aufidius accuses him of treachery to the Volsces and speaks contemptuously of his unmanly behaviour.

1 Coriolanus' entry (in pairs)

The stage direction 'marching with drum and colours' (flags) accompanied by 'the commoners' (the ordinary people), suggests that Coriolanus enters in full military pomp, cheered on by the Volsce plebeians. Some productions present Coriolanus in splendid armour. To emphasise his popularity with the plebeians, in one production Coriolanus ran a 'lap of honour' around the stage, being kissed and embraced by the citizens. Prepare a set of notes to show how you would stage Coriolanus' entry.

2 Coriolanus makes his report (in pairs)

Coriolanus has to tell the Volsce Senators, in front of the Volsce plebeians, that he has returned, not with victory over Rome but with a peace treaty. Is his language in lines 71–84 similar to his language earlier in the play, or has it become toned down, more like a politician's speech than a soldier's? Speak lines 71–84 to each other several times then suggest how Coriolanus should deliver them on stage. Why does he switch from 'I' to 'we' as the speech develops?

3 Aufidius makes his accusation (in pairs)

Aufidius uses words and phrases (beginning with 'traitor') that he knows will anger Coriolanus and provoke him to a rash response. Identify all Aufidius' language that he knows will insult Coriolanus and challenge his image of himself as a man and a soldier. Then speak Aufidius' lines, putting as much contempt into your voice as you can.

---

infected with diseased by
subsisting continuing
prosperously … attempted
I have been successful
spoils booty
counterpoise … charges exceed
the costs by one third

Antiates Volsces (citizens of
Antium)
compounded on agreed
drops of salt tears
oath and resolution sworn purpose
pages young servants
heart courage

Enter CORIOLANUS *marching with drum and colours,*
the COMMONERS *being with him*

CORIOLANUS Hail, lords! I am returned your soldier,
　　No more infected with my country's love
　　Than when I parted hence, but still subsisting
　　Under your great command. You are to know
　　That prosperously I have attempted and   75
　　With bloody passage led your wars even to
　　The gates of Rome. Our spoils we have brought home
　　Doth more than counterpoise a full third part
　　The charges of the action. We have made peace
　　With no less honour to the Antiates   80
　　Than shame to th'Romans. And we here deliver,
　　Subscribed by th'consuls and patricians,
　　Together with the seal o'th'senate, what
　　We have compounded on.
　　　　　　　　　　[*He offers a document*]
AUFIDIUS　　　　　　　　　　Read it not, noble lords,
　　But tell the traitor in the highest degree   85
　　He hath abused your powers.
CORIOLANUS 'Traitor'? How now?
AUFIDIUS Ay, traitor, Martius.
CORIOLANUS 'Martius'?
AUFIDIUS Ay, Martius, Caius Martius. Dost thou think   90
　　I'll grace thee with that robbery, thy stol'n name
　　Coriolanus, in Corioles? –
　　You lords and heads o'th'state, perfidiously
　　He has betrayed your business and given up,
　　For certain drops of salt, your city Rome –   95
　　I say 'your city' – to his wife and mother,
　　Breaking his oath and resolution like
　　A twist of rotten silk, never admitting
　　Counsel o'th'war. But at his nurse's tears
　　He whined and roared away your victory,   100
　　That pages blushed at him and men of heart
　　Looked wondering each at others.
CORIOLANUS　　　　　　　　　　　　Hear'st thou, Mars?
AUFIDIUS Name not the god, thou boy of tears.
CORIOLANUS　　　　　　　　　　　Ha?
AUFIDIUS No more.

Coriolanus furiously threatens Aufidius, then mocks the Volsces, exultantly inviting them to kill him. The people call for his death, and in spite of the Second Lord's pleas, Coriolanus is killed.

When the actor Laurence Olivier (left) played Coriolanus, he modelled his stage death scene on the fate in 1945 of the Italian dictator Mussolini (right), who was shot, then hung by his heels on public display. For an activity on staging Coriolanus' death, see page 226, number 5.

first time ... scold (but is Coriolanus telling the truth?)
notion sense of the truth
stripes sword scars
Stain dishonour, bloodstain
edges sharp swords

writ your annals written your histories
blind fortune mere good luck
presently immediately
folds in ... earth covers all the world

CORIOLANUS Measureless liar, thou hast made my heart   105
    Too great for what contains it. 'Boy'? O slave! –
    Pardon me, lords, 'tis the first time that ever
    I was forced to scold. Your judgements, my grave lords,
    Must give this cur the lie; and his own notion –
    Who wears my stripes impressed upon him, that   110
    Must bear my beating to his grave – shall join
    To thrust the lie unto him.
FIRST LORD Peace, both, and hear me speak.
CORIOLANUS Cut me to pieces, Volsces. Men and lads,
    Stain all your edges on me. 'Boy'! False hound,   115
    If you have writ your annals true, 'tis there
    That, like an eagle in a dovecote, I
    Fluttered your Volscians in Corioles.
    Alone I did it. 'Boy'!
AUFIDIUS   Why, noble lords,
    Will you be put in mind of his blind fortune,   120
    Which was your shame, by this unholy braggart,
    'Fore your own eyes and ears?
ALL CONSPIRATORS   Let him die for't.
ALL PEOPLE Tear him to pieces! Do it presently! He killed my son! My
    daughter! He killed my cousin Marcus! He killed my father!
SECOND LORD Peace, ho! No outrage. Peace!   125
    The man is noble, and his fame folds in
    This orb o'th'earth. His last offences to us
    Shall have judicious hearing. Stand, Aufidius,
    And trouble not the peace.
CORIOLANUS   O that I had him,
    With six Aufidiuses, or more, his tribe,   130
    To use my lawful sword!
AUFIDIUS   Insolent villain!
ALL CONSPIRATORS Kill, kill, kill, kill, kill him!

    [*The*] *conspirators draw* [*their swords*] *and kill Martius, who falls;*
            Aufidius stands on him

Aufidius offers to explain to the Volsce senate why Coriolanus was such a danger. The First Lord decrees a dignified funeral. Aufidius, expressing remorse, orders the funeral march and promises a magnificent tomb.

1 Stage the closing moments (in large groups)

Many productions have enacted the closing moments with great spectacle. Sometimes they have taken up clues in the script, having a column of Volsce soldiers with trailed pikes (holding the weapons, reversed, point down), and a herald (an officer who followed the coffin) speaking of the deeds of Coriolanus.

Rehearse and act out the final lines and stage direction in which Coriolanus is borne off stage to the solemn music of a dead march.

2 Final image

What would be the very final image the audience would see as the lights fade on your own production of the play? To help your imagination, suggest what effect on the audience you think the following two productions were trying to achieve in their final image:

a Coriolanus' body carried out by Aufidius and the three conspirators through the gates of Corioles, the same gates he had entered in Act 1 to capture the city single-handedly.

b Aufidius struggling to free himself from the weight of Coriolanus' dead body, and holding out an arm imploringly, calling on other Volsces to 'Assist'.

3 Alternative ending?

Shakespeare ends the play with Coriolanus' former enemies proposing to honour him in death. Write an extra scene showing how the news of Coriolanus' death is reported in Rome and how Volumnia, Virgilia, Menenius, and the tribunes and plebeians respond.

---

did owe you threatened you with
deliver prove
censure sentence of punishment
herald official who proclaimed a
 dead person's deeds

urn final burial place, jar for his
 ashes
Trail your steel pikes carry your
 weapons as for a funeral

LORDS Hold, hold, hold, hold!

AUFIDIUS My noble masters, hear me speak.

FIRST LORD   O Tullus!

SECOND LORD Thou hast done a deed whereat valour will weep.   135

THIRD LORD Tread not upon him. Masters all, be quiet.
       Put up your swords.

AUFIDIUS My lords, when you shall know – as in this rage
       Provoked by him you cannot – the great danger
       Which this man's life did owe you, you'll rejoice   140
       That he is thus cut off. Please it your honours
       To call me to your senate, I'll deliver
       Myself your loyal servant, or endure
       Your heaviest censure.

FIRST LORD   Bear from hence his body,
       And mourn you for him. Let him be regarded   145
       As the most noble corpse that ever herald
       Did follow to his urn.

SECOND LORD   His own impatience
       Takes from Aufidius a great part of blame.
       Let's make the best of it.

AUFIDIUS   My rage is gone,
       And I am struck with sorrow. Take him up.   150
       Help, three o'th'chiefest soldiers; I'll be one.
       Beat thou the drum, that it speak mournfully;
       Trail your steel pikes. Though in this city he
       Hath widowed and unchilded many a one,
       Which to this hour bewail the injury,   155
       Yet he shall have a noble memory.
       Assist.

Exeunt, bearing the body of Martius. A dead march sounded.

Looking back at the play
Activities for groups and individuals

1 Is justice done?

Do characters get what they deserve? For example, does Coriolanus meet a fitting end? Consider each major character in turn and say whether you think they get their just desserts by the end of the play.

2 Hero? Tragedy?

Is Coriolanus a hero? Is *Coriolanus* a tragedy? Look up several definitions of 'hero' and 'tragedy' (don't expect them to agree on every point), then begin your reply by giving your own definitions.

3 Dramatic construction

All Shakespeare's plays are constructed so that each scene comments, often ironically, on the scene which immediately succeeds or follows it. Take any scene and suggest how it relates to the scenes before and after it in such a way as to heighten dramatic effect and understanding of story, character and themes.

4 Shakespeare's own beliefs?

What was Shakespeare's own attitude to the plebeians? Did he, like Coriolanus, believe in a sharply hierarchical society? Take sides and argue whether it is possible to discover Shakespeare's own political beliefs from the play.

5 Staging Coriolanus' death

'Like an eagle in a dovecote, I fluttered your Volscians in Corioles.' In the play's final scene, Coriolanus' reminder of how he attacked their city infuriates his enemies. Work out your own staging of Coriolanus' final moments from line 105. Does Coriolanus fight against his attackers, drawing his sword at line 131, or does he willingly accept his death?

6 Why are they silent?

The women in the play say nothing more after Coriolanus holds his mother's hand in Act 5 Scene 3. Why not? Step into role as Shakespeare and give your reply.

7 Triumphal entries: but victory over whom?

The women's entry to Rome in Act 5 Scene 5 contrasts ironically with Coriolanus' welcome in Act 2 Scene 1. He entered Rome in victory; the triumphal celebration of the women is for his defeat. Many productions stage the women's entry as a magnificent pageant, a spectacle full of action and sound. In one such production, Volumnia suddenly revealed the tiny figure of Coriolanus' son, young Martius, dressed in a full suit of black armour, an exact copy of what his father had worn in Act 1. It was a chilling reminder that she intended to bring up her grandson to be the same fighting machine as his father. Work out how to stage both entries to show how they relate to each other.

8 Memorial

'He shall have a noble memory' declares Aufidius at the play's end. 'Memory' could be a tomb or the epitaph carved on it relating Coriolanus' deeds. Design the tomb and write the epitaph (which can be in verse or prose). Remember that it is written by the Volsces, not by Coriolanus' fellow Romans or family.

9 What mood?

The play's mood has been described as one of 'bleak uncompromising pessimism'. How would you wish audiences to feel at the end of a production you have directed? Describe how you would try to achieve that response.

10 An affirmative play?

What evidence can you find in *Coriolanus* of honesty, kindness, warm and sincere human relationships, and hope?

11 A modern dress production

Work out how you could stage a production in modern dress, so that the audience would be reminded of parallels to the story in modern times.

12 Time lines

Create a graphic display to show how the plot unfolds. For example, you could use three 'time lines': line A shows events in Rome, line B indicates points where the action takes place among the Volsces, line C shows off-stage action.

What is *Coriolanus* about?

There is no single, simple answer to the question 'What is *Coriolanus* about?'. A first reply might be that it is the story of an heroic soldier whose downfall is caused by pride and inflexibility of character. The play focuses unremittingly on Coriolanus: there is no sub-plot, and even when he is not on stage he is the subject of conversation. A second reply might be that the play is about mother–son relationships: how Coriolanus is both created and destroyed by his mother, Volumnia.

But the play is about more than the story of one man or his family relationships. For example, you might choose to tell the story by structuring it into three phases: war, politics and betrayal. The play might then be seen to be about how war shapes Coriolanus, giving him success and identity; how politics brings him failure which results in his banishment from Rome; and how his betrayal of Rome by his defection to the Volsces causes his death.

Another view of *Coriolanus* is to see it as a particular type of play. For example, it has been regarded as a tragedy in which a flaw in the hero's character (pride) causes his downfall, and as a history play about the early days of the Roman Republic. It has also been seen as a kind of morality play: Shakespeare's dramatic adaptation of a story from Plutarch (see page 245) which Shakespeare's contemporaries read in order to learn lessons from the life of a particular individual.

Yet another perspective on the play is that it is Shakespeare's way of dramatising certain issues that preoccupied his contemporaries: the threat of civil disruption by an impoverished underclass protesting about enclosures and corn shortages, or the quarrels between King James I and Parliament over the right to make laws (see page 244).

A helpful way of answering the question 'What is *Coriolanus* about?' is to identify the themes of the play, some of which now follow.

Change – 'th'interpretation of the time'

Examples are: the fickleness of the mob; the shifting value of fame and reputation; Coriolanus' change of allegiance from Rome to the Volsces; the question of whether he becomes false to his nature.

Valour – 'the chiefest virtue'

For the Romans, 'valour' was bravery in battle. Coriolanus the man, and *Coriolanus* the play, embody the belief that honour lies in the glory that comes from courageous action in war. In his eulogy (speech in praise of Coriolanus), Cominius identifies valour as the quality that Roman patricians value most highly: 'It is held/That valour is the chiefest virtue' (Act 2 Scene 2, line 78).

Although the theme of valour is so evident in the play, Shakespeare invites you to make up your own mind about its value. In an earlier play (*King Henry IV Part 1*) he created a character, Falstaff, who memorably questioned its worth: 'Discretion is the better part of valour'. In *Coriolanus*, Shakespeare again provides opportunities for very different interpretations. Is the play a sustained critique of valour and its accompanying militarism and heroism, seeing it all as aggressive machismo? Or is the play sympathetic to the ideal of bravery, the glory of war, military society and the flawed hero?

To discover your own attitude to 'valour' it can be helpful to begin by considering your response to certain climactic moments in the play, for example when Coriolanus cries 'Make you a sword of me?' (Act 1 Scene 6, line 76), or when, facing certain death, he taunts the men who are about to kill him: 'like an eagle in a dovecote, I/Fluttered your Volscians in Corioles' (Act 5 Scene 6, lines 117–18).

Appearance and reality – 'I'll mountebank their loves'

Shakespeare explores the theme of appearance and reality in every one of his plays. In *Coriolanus*, his portrayal of people not being what they seem is often expressed through the imagery of acting. Volumnia urges her son to play a hypocritical part and conceal his true nature as he seeks the citizens' votes for the consulship. When he leads the Volsce army against Rome, Coriolanus tries to play the role of the implacable avenger, but is betrayed by his feelings for his family.

Throughout the play, appearances are deceptive. Coriolanus, for all his integrity and inflexibility, turns traitor to Rome. Aufidius pretends friendship, biding his time until he can topple Coriolanus. All the high-flown talk of the patricians about their ideal of service to Rome barely conceals the fact of their contempt for the great majority of Rome's inhabitants, the plebeians. The single short scene in which the Roman spy and traitor Nicanor appears (Act 4 Scene 3), sharply illustrates the theme of deception that runs through the play.

Politics: who shall rule? – 'One fire drives out one fire ...'

Coriolanus is perhaps Shakespeare's most political play. It is a sustained exploration of the question of government: who should hold power? The struggle between Coriolanus and the tribunes is often interpreted as the battle between oligarchy and democracy: the rule of an elite versus the rule of the people (although not in the sense that democracy is understood today as 'one person one vote').

The play portrays men and women as political animals. The patricians are concerned to keep power firmly in their hands. The tribunes, as representatives of the ordinary people of Rome, manoeuvre for a greater role in government. Coriolanus is fiercely hostile to any encroachment by the working class on the power of the elite to which he belongs.

Coriolanus exposes how people are manipulated by politicians who exploit and twist language to achieve their ends. Menenius and the tribunes alike are seen working on the emotions of the citizens. Menenius tells his fable of the belly, to persuade the plebeians that Rome is a united, harmonious society. The tribunes know which words to use to provoke Coriolanus' fury and subsequent downfall. Volumnia urges Coriolanus to dissemble, to play act, to gain political power. She assures him that honour and 'policy' (deceitful behaviour to gain power) can grow together 'like unsevered friends' (Act 3 Scene 2, line 43) in both war and peace.

Mothers and sons – 'O mother, mother! What have you done?'

Many of Shakespeare's plays explore the troubled relationships of fathers and daughters. In contrast, *Coriolanus* is concerned with a son's fraught relationship with his mother. Coriolanus' contempt for the plebeians is rooted in his mother's similar dismissive attitude to them as 'woollen vassals, things created to buy and sell with groats'. In spite of Coriolanus' devotion to personal honour and truth, she succeeds in persuading him to practise deceit, begging for votes in Rome's market-place.

The play shows how Coriolanus' patriotism and military prowess have been shaped and developed by Volumnia ('I holp to frame thee'), and how his attachment to his mother proves fatal when he cannot resist her plea that he spare Rome from destruction. The natural bond of son and mother triumphs over Coriolanus' feelings for revenge, as he '*holds her by the hand, silent*'.

Conflict – 'The present wars devour him!'

The play is characterised by strife and dissension at all levels. There are wars between the Romans and the Volsces, factional antagonism between patricians and plebeians, and family conflict as Volumnia makes her unwilling son plead for the citizens' votes. At the level of the individual, Coriolanus and Aufidius are personal enemies. Within himself, Coriolanus experiences emotional conflict. He renounces his life-long loyalty to Rome and then is doomed to destruction as his affection for his family overcomes his commitment to the Volsces' cause.

Individual versus society – 'What is the city but the people?'

The play explores the nature of social bonds: how far an individual is indissolubly tied to society by all kinds of bonds. The tribunes harness the collective action of the people, but Coriolanus thinks he can succeed 'alone' (one of his favourite words). The play exposes how his confidence in himself alone is undermined by his sense of obligation to his family and to Rome.

Ingratitude – 'You are a traitor to the people'

The citizens of Rome are not grateful for what Coriolanus has done to save them from the Volsces. They reward him, not with the honour of the consulship, but with the disgrace of banishment.

Pride – 'He's vengeance proud'

Coriolanus' pride, his haughtiness and inflated sense of self-esteem, is obvious through the whole play. He has scorn for everything and everybody he considers unworthy. Are there other characters you also think of as proud?

Service – 'What do you prate of service?'

The play portrays the very different notions of what 'service to the state' means to Coriolanus, the patricians, the tribunes, and the citizens of Rome.

Rome – 'Our renowned Rome'

Rome itself could be considered to be a theme of the play. Shakespeare's contemporaries were fascinated by Ancient Rome and felt that they could learn lessons for their own times from a study of Rome's history and characters. You can find more on Rome on pages 242–3.

Characters

Coriolanus is always centre stage in the play. If he is not physically present, other characters talk about him. There are only two brief episodes when he is not the subject of conversation (Menenius' description of himself, and his fable of the belly). But in spite of being relentlessly in the spotlight, Coriolanus reveals little of his innermost thoughts and feelings. He has few soliloquies, and each member of the audience is left to make up their own mind about why he is as he is, the roots of his motivations and personality.

What makes Coriolanus so contemptuous of the plebeians, always ready to revile them? What makes him unable to control his temper, so that he explodes at key moments? How can he seek honour in war, yet be offended by praise, and disdainful of material reward for his military exploits? What makes him cry 'I banish you', when the reality is that the people of Rome banish him? Why does he join the Volsces and seek to destroy Rome? And what finally makes him give in to his mother's plea?

There is no single key to Coriolanus' character. Right at the start of the play the First Citizen identifies four sources of his brave deeds: desire for fame, love of Rome, the wish to please his mother, and pride (Act 1 Scene 1, lines 27–30). Much later in the play, Aufidius locates three flaws in Coriolanus' character: 'pride', 'defect of judgement', and his inflexible 'nature' which made him act in peace time exactly as he had acted in war (Act 4 Scene 7, lines 37–45). But what is Coriolanus' 'nature'? Here are some descriptions of his personality that have been made by Shakespearian critics:

proud	arrogant	intolerant	violent	guileless
ungracious	irascible	courageous	scornful	noble
overbearing	blunt	absolute	honest	contemptuous
harsh	inflexible	stubborn	disdainful	modest
implacable	selfish	loyal	constant	isolated

Choose five of the adjectives above which you think express Coriolanus' nature most powerfully. Find a line or an episode in the play as an example of each, and use them to make up a presentation of some kind (for example, a dramatic enactment or an essay) titled 'Coriolanus'.

Coriolanus the warrior. But he is also son, father, husband, and would-be
politician. Step into role as each character in the List of Characters on
page 1. First, declare your view of, and feelings for, Coriolanus.
Then say how you think he feels towards you.

Volumnia – 'Anger's my meat'

Coriolanus' mother both creates and destroys him. She has brought him up with a taboo on tenderness: every human feeling must be suppressed other than the joy of serving Rome in war. Volumnia devotes her life to turning her son into a fighting machine ('to a cruel war I sent him'), rejoicing in his wounds and the honour they bring. She plans for Coriolanus to become consul, the most important political person in Rome.

Volumnia has been described as a politically skilled schemer, obsessed with bloodshed and wars. She knows how to manipulate her son through his pride, his sense of honour, and his feelings for her. She uses psychological blackmail on him to achieve her purposes. But, at the end of the play, her pleading for Rome is fatal for her son. He gives way to his feelings for his mother, and in doing so signs his own death warrant at the hands of Aufidius and his Volsces.

Like the men in the play, Volumnia is also a dramatic contrast to Coriolanus. He values constancy, and despises false appearance. But she is willing to embrace 'policy': deceitful pretence to achieve her goals. So she urges her son to act a part as he begs for votes in the market-place, and instructs him in the insincere gestures and expressions he can use to persuade the citizens (whom both son and mother hold in contempt). In the patriarchal society of Rome, women lack power, but Volumnia burns with ambition to place her son in the position of greatest power. Does she then intend to exercise power through him?

Virgilia – 'O Jupiter, no blood!'

Virgilia speaks only 36 lines, and Coriolanus calls her 'My gracious silence'. She may represent the compassionate and tender feelings which are lacking in the militaristic climate of Rome. Quickly read through all the lines she speaks in the play, then write several entries in the diary she keeps secret from all other characters. She will probably disclose what she feels about her mother-in-law.

Valeria – 'The moon of Rome'

Valeria speaks only 37 lines (in Act 5 Scenes 3 and 5 she does not speak), but is described by Coriolanus as 'The moon of Rome, chaste as the icicle/That's curdied by the frost from purest snow/And hangs on Dian's temple'. Remind yourself of Activity 2 on page 26, then suggest how she might behave in her two 'silent' scenes to show she symbolises the values cherished by the patricians.

Identify each character and choose a line from Act 5 Scene 3 as an appropriate caption.

Sicinius and Brutus: political enemies of Coriolanus

The tribunes of the people, unlike Coriolanus, are clever politicians. They are skilled in manipulating the citizens and in provoking Coriolanus to anger. Sicinius and Brutus can be played as sincere democrats, guardians of the citizens' rights, who wish to serve the people. They want Rome to be a peaceful community, enjoying the social justice so obviously lacking under the rule of the patricians.

Alternatively, the tribunes can be played as wily, self-seeking schemers who do not have the people's interests at heart, but their own. They can be portrayed as devious and hypocritical, cynically exploiting situations to bring about the downfall of Coriolanus.

Aufidius: military enemy of Coriolanus

Aufidius is Coriolanus' rival in war, a mirror-image of him as a great warrior with whom he has a love–hate relationship. Defeated by Coriolanus in war, envious of his honour, and jealous of his popularity with the Volsce soldiers, Aufidius deceitfully plans Coriolanus' death. One production of the play presented Aufidius as virtually the twin of Coriolanus. The two men looked alike, dressed alike, and used the same gestures and movements.

The citizens of Rome: class enemies of Coriolanus

The citizens are plebeians, working-class people. They stand in sharp dramatic contrast to Coriolanus, who, as a patrician, despises them as inferiors. Their concern is for group action in opposition to his extreme individualism. He loves war and fighting, but they are unwilling soldiers, pressed into military service. He sees them as cowards, more interested in looting than fighting. Individually, the citizens are shrewd and humorous, but as a group, they are fickle, easily swayed by the tribunes.

Menenius: a father-figure to Coriolanus?

Menenius contrasts with Coriolanus in his affability and love of pleasure, his pragmatism and his willingness to play a part, to talk and flatter his way out of difficult situations. Much more easy-going than Coriolanus, he is only too ready to compromise, and to hide his true feelings about the plebeians. Some critics have seen him as a surrogate father to Coriolanus, and have compared him to Falstaff, the loose-living, luxury-loving old companion of Prince Hal in *King Henry IV Parts 1* and *2*.

Activities on characters

1 Work on one or more of the following activities on Coriolanus:

a Improvise a scene from his childhood to show how Volumnia brought him up.

b Collect quotations to illustrate Coriolanus' 'journey through the play'.

c Give your reasons for agreeing or disagreeing with the following:

   • 'Coriolanus learns nothing in the course of the play'.
   • 'The word 'Alone' is the key to understanding Coriolanus'.
   • 'Coriolanus does not love Rome, or any character in the play'.

d In Act 1 Scene 9, Coriolanus promises to do justice to his new name to the utmost of his ability ('undercrest your good addition/ To th'fairness of my power'). An undercrest was a motto or picture at the base of a coat of arms. Design a coat of arms for Coriolanus showing the 'crest' (main symbol) and undercrest.

2 Is Volumnia the same person at the end of the play as she was at the start? Speak her first and last speeches (Act 1 Scene 3, lines 1–14 and Act 5 Scene 3, lines 131–82), then give your views on whether you think she has changed and what you think will happen to her in the future (for example, does she kill herself?).

3 The tribunes Sicinius and Brutus are guardians of the citizens' rights. Are their personalities different? Is one man more conciliatory than the other? To help you present them on stage, step into role successively as each tribune and state your aims, and say what you think of the citizens, patricians, and your fellow tribune.

4 Aufidius is a brave opponent of Coriolanus on the battlefield, but ends the play using conspirators to kill his old enemy. Why doesn't Aufidius face Coriolanus alone? Step into role as Aufidius and give your reasons. Do you genuinely feel the sorrow you claim in your final speech?

5 Names are of much significance in the play. 'Martius' is a reminder of Mars, the Roman god of war, and it is for his exploits in war that Martius is given the name of Coriolanus. But Shakespeare does not give names to the plebeians. Throughout the play they are treated as a mob by patricians and referred to in all kinds of insulting ways: 'rabble', 'curs', 'th'ignorant', and so on. Step into role as a plebeian, give yourself a name, and tell the story of the play from your personal viewpoint.

6 Cominius is at the centre of the action for much of first half of the play. How different is he from Coriolanus in the way he treats his troops, and in his language? Do you think the play displays a critical or sympathetic attitude to him?

The language of *Coriolanus*

Antithesis – 'Brave death outweighs bad life'

Coriolanus is full of conflicts: patricians versus plebeians, Romans versus Volsces, Coriolanus versus almost everybody. Shakespeare's language powerfully expresses conflict through its use of antithesis: the opposition of words or phrases against each other, setting the word against the word. Coriolanus' contemptuous diatribe against the citizens (Act 1 Scene 1, lines 151–60) contains many antitheses:

peace/war	affrights/proud	lions/hares	foxes/geese
fire/ice	hailstone/sun	worthy/subdues	greatness/hate.

Every page of the play contains antitheses. For example, 'My birthplace hate I, and my love's upon/This enemy town' (Act 4 Scene 4, lines 23–4) sets 'hate' against 'love', and 'birthplace' against 'enemy town'. Turn to two or three pages at random, identify the antitheses, and find some physical way of enacting them as you speak. You might for example 'weigh' them with your hands, or turn from side to side as you speak, or 'arm-wrestle' them with a partner.

Imagery – 'Struck Corioles like a planet'

Imagery is the use of emotionally charged words and phrases which conjure up vivid mental pictures in the imagination. In spite of its frequent harshness and lack of lyricism, the language of *Coriolanus* abounds in imagery. It intensifies and deepens imaginative effect, creating atmosphere and giving insight into characters' feelings and thoughts.

All Shakespeare's imagery uses metaphor or simile. A simile compares one thing to another using 'like' ('I go alone, like to a lonely dragon'), or 'as' ('As weeds before a vessel under sail'). A metaphor is also a comparison. It does not use 'like' or 'as' but suggests that two dissimilar things are actually the same. An example is Coriolanus' description of Aufidius: 'He is a lion/That I am proud to hunt'. The following are some of the clusters of repeated images which help build up a sense of the themes of the play.

Animal imagery 'You common cry of curs.' There are striking contrasts in the animal imagery used to describe patricians or plebeians. Coriolanus and his patrician class, the nobility of Rome, are the predators: lions, eagles, the osprey, dragon. The plebeians are the prey or vermin: hares, deer, geese, fish, mice, rascals (young deer), rats, curs. Coriolanus pictures the citizens of Rome as a hydra, a many-headed monster ('the beast with many heads'). He uses a similar unnatural image as he refuses to hear his deeds praised: 'my nothings monstered'.

Eating and food 'Anger's my meat.' Together with the animal imagery of predators and prey go a host of images of food and eating. The corn riot of the first scene evokes imagery of eating, and Menenius tells his fable of the belly. Volumnia describes Coriolanus in battle as a harvestman relentlessly reaping his enemies' lives. Coriolanus claims that without the patricians, the plebeians 'Would feed on one another' (Act 1 Scene 1, line 171), but it is war that finally devours Coriolanus himself.

Acting 'Like a dull actor now I have forgot my part'. The theme of false appearance is often expressed in images of acting and theatre. Coriolanus is unwilling to entreat the citizens for their votes: 'It is a part/That I shall blush in acting' (Act 2 Scene 2, lines 139–40). Volumnia tries to persuade him to conceal his real character and attitudes behind a friendly mask. She gives him a lesson in how to behave, urging him to 'perform a part/Thou hast not done before'. Although Coriolanus wishes to 'play the man I am' (Act 3 Scene 2, lines 16–17), he finally agrees to go to the plebeians and 'mountebank their loves' (line 133). Later he will play the part of traitor to Rome in Antium.

Disease and surgery 'infected with my country's love.' Images of sickness and medicine abound. Coriolanus' first words in the play express his contempt for the plebeians, who 'rubbing the poor itch of your opinion, Make yourselves scabs'. He heaps images of disease on his soldiers as they retreat at Corioles: 'All the contagion of the south light on you ... boils and plagues Plaster you o'er ... and one infect another Against the wind a mile!' Coriolanus is himself seen by Sicinius as a 'disease that must be cut away'.

The body and fragmentation 'tearing his country's bowels out.' Images of the body recur throughout the play. They symbolise the state as the body politic, but a body fatally divided against itself. The imagery in Menenius' fable of the belly is intended to reinforce the patrician ideology of Rome as a united body, with all its parts functioning harmoniously. But the body imagery that follows exposes that unity to be a fiction, showing the body parts to be at war with each other.

Coriolanus dismisses the plebeians as 'fragments', and calls the tribunes 'tongues o'th'common mouth'. Menenius' own imagery dismembers or fragments the united body, making the plebeians merely 'voices', 'tongues', 'mouths', 'breath', 'heart', 'hands'. He calls them 'the mutinous members', and their leader 'the great toe'. Such imagery of dismemberment, like the picture of Coriolanus' young son 'mammocking' (tearing apart) a butterfly, emphasises the disunity of Rome.

Key words

Certain words echo through the play, often repeated. Write out the following words as a list, putting those words which Coriolanus finds most offensive at the top, and those which are most appealing to him at the bottom. Then write the story of *Coriolanus* as briefly as you can to include each key word.

noble	voices	power	gentle	man	fame	deed	honour
home	Rome	corn	shall	boy	traitor	mildly	
must	will	alone	service				

Martial language – 'His sword, death's stamp'

The language of *Coriolanus* has been described as austere, martial, devoid of lyricism, and 'language looking for a quarrel'. T S Eliot's poem *Coriolan* expresses its hard, uncompromising nature:

> 'Stone, bronze, stone, steel, stone, oakleaves, horses' heels
> Over the paving ...'

Military language is still very much in everyday use. Collect and analyse examples of the language of sports commentators, politicians, and business people. How frequently do they use military metaphors, and what do you think is the purpose of such language?

Stage directions – '*Enter the army of the Volsces*'

Coriolanus has more stage directions than most other Shakespeare plays. Some people think that is because Shakespeare wrote the play after he had retired to Stratford-upon-Avon. Knowing he would not be present to advise actors in rehearsals in London, he added more explicit stage directions than are found in his earlier plays.

Like every Shakespeare play, the language of *Coriolanus* is filled with implicit stage directions, giving actors clues as to how they might behave. 'Action is eloquence' says Volumnia (Act 3 Scene 2, line 77) as she tells Coriolanus how to behave and what gestures to use when he meets the citizens. Her words provide a clue to performing Shakespeare. For example, suggest what gestures and expressions the First Citizen might use as he speaks the very first line of the play 'Before we proceed any further, hear me speak.' Then turn to any page of the script at random. Work out how to perform it using all the clues to action suggested in the language.

Inventing words – prefixes, nouns used as verbs

Shakespeare invents words to suit his dramatic purposes, often by using prefixes (for example, un-):

unchilded	unactive	disbenched	unshout	unsaluted
unclog	bemock	demerits	undercrest	

He turns nouns into verbs, adding to the concrete nature of the play's language:

godded, virgined, coffined, agued, horsed, servanted, monstered.

Write a short speech for Coriolanus that uses both techniques.

Language styles

Choose one of the following major ways in which language is used in the play. Collect lines to illustrate its use. Prepare a presentation to show your audience what the language style is like in practice.

persuasion	invective	eulogy (praise)
harangue	accusation	argument
manipulation	proverbial	exhortation (urging)

Verse and prose

In Shakespeare's time, the convention in plays was that high status characters spoke in verse, and that prose was used for comedy or by low status characters. So the plebeians' speeches are usually in prose, and Coriolanus' in verse. But Shakespeare never followed any convention slavishly, and his characters switch from prose to verse, probably depending on whether the situation is 'comic' or 'serious'. The high status Roman ladies use much prose in their first scene at home, as does Coriolanus in the 'voices' episode with the plebeians. Turn at random to three or four pages and suggest why Shakespeare writes in verse or prose on each.

Rome: patricians and plebeians

Coriolanus' Rome was a city state where warfare with its neighbours was mirrored by internal conflict between insecure patricians and rebellious plebeians, the leaders and the led. It was not a united community, but a city of factions, firmly divided into two classes, the patricians and the plebeians: the rulers and the ruled. Each faction feared the other, and Shakespeare often expresses their bitter strife in imagery of a dismembered human body.

The play is set around 490 BC, shortly after the birth of the Roman republic. The tyrant kings, the Tarquins, have recently been driven out, and Rome is struggling to establish a new form of government. It is not a democracy, because the great majority of the people, the plebeians, have no political power or real control over their lives. Virtually all power is in the hands of the patricians.

The patricians were obsessed with rank and esteem. In Rome's rigid patriarchy, women had little or no power, and social status was determined entirely by birth. The social class boundary was rigidly policed, and intermarriage between plebeians and patricians was prohibited by law.

The patricians suspected and feared kings, tyrants and foreign powers. They equally distrusted their own people, the plebeians, who they held in contempt. The patricians saw themselves as embodying the noble values of Rome, especially 'virtue', which for Romans meant bravery and honour, and the fame which went with such valour (see page 229). They therefore praised Coriolanus, seeing him as a perfect example of bravery, nobility and honour.

Power was exercised by the senate, and senators came from the ranks of the patricians. As a republic, Rome was deeply suspicious of the single leadership of a king, and therefore replaced it with the dual leadership of the consulate. Each year the senate nominated two consuls whose election was confirmed by the plebeians. The consuls led both the senate and the army. In *Coriolanus*, Shakespeare seems to suggest that there was only one consul. Perhaps he did this to make the focus on Coriolanus more intense and to heighten dramatic conflict.

In the growing republic, a few plebeians became more wealthy than some patricians, but they could not become members of the patrician class. It was inevitable that the plebeians demanded more power, a greater voice in governing the city. They were were granted tribunes, a change in government that Coriolanus is unable to accept. The tribunes' role was to protect the plebeians from false arrest and to act as the voice of the people. Although they took no real part in government, they were spokesmen with some power of veto. In the play, the tribunes appeal to the ancient rights of the plebeians, but it is not clear what such rights actually were.

Most plebeians were subject to military service. They could be called upon to serve in the army and to protect Rome against its enemies. But many plebeians were aware that Rome's wars were fought in the interests of the patrician class, not their own. As the play shows, Rome's citizen army was often very reluctant to fight.

The part that the ordinary people of Rome play in the election of Coriolanus as consul may reflect quarrels about political elections that raged in Shakespeare's time. Election to the English parliament was not by secret ballot, but by acclamation, a shout of assent to confirm a candidate already chosen by a tiny minority of the elite ruling group. But that system was increasingly challenged around the time that Shakespeare wrote the play. In his own county of Warwickshire there was a case of the electors revoking their original approval, just as, in Act 2 Scene 3, the tribunes urge the plebeians to do.

- Shakespeare's contemporaries were fascinated by Roman history, and they often compared London with Rome. London dominated England, just as Rome had come to dominate Italy. The Elizabethans and Jacobeans felt they could learn moral and political lessons from Rome's ideals, families, institutions and characters. What insights into today's society does *Coriolanus* afford? Imagine that a rich sponsor has promised you funds to mount a production of the play if you can convince her that *Coriolanus* is relevant to young people today. Convince her!

- The language of the play creates a strong physical sense of the city itself: halls, gates, ports, streets, conduits, temples, windows, roofs, leads, storehouses, mills, shops, stalls. In similar fashion it conveys an impression of the bustling life of Rome's people: mechanics, cobblers, tailors, apron-men, actors, orange-wives, faucet sellers, ballad makers, mountebanks. As a stage designer how would you create Rome ? Sketch and write your proposal for presenting Rome.

The sources for the story

Shakespeare's own times

Social structure Like Coriolanus' Rome, Shakespeare's England was a land of 'haves' and 'have-nots', the counterparts of Rome's patricians and plebeians: the powerful and the powerless. The great majority of the people were very poor; they faced a lifetime of ceaseless toil and grinding poverty. In England's acutely hierarchical society, King James I and the aristocracy clung to their privileges. Like Rome's patricians, they were obsessed with notions of honour and esteem, measured by rank, breeding and wealth. But the power of this small elite was increasingly challenged. A growing middle class was becoming prosperous, and wanted to gain a share in government.

Enclosures and corn riots Throughout Shakespeare's lifetime, land which had once been common was 'enclosed': claimed as the sole property of rich landlords. The enclosures resulted in a huge underclass of landless labourers whose misery was made worse by falling wages and rising prices. Resentment against enclosures grew, and after a series of bad harvests, riots broke out in 1607–8 in the English Midlands.

Known as the 'Midlands insurrection', the protests were directed against enclosures and the hoarding of corn by 'gentlemen'. In one riot almost fifty protesters were killed. Shakespeare must have had first-hand knowledge of the uprisings, because at this time he was a landowner in Warwickshire, and so was seen locally as a 'gentleman'. The riots find their echo in Act 1 of *Coriolanus* as the 'mutinous citizens' protest against the hoarding of corn by the patricians.

Crown versus parliament The conflict between the patricians and the tribunes reflects the bitter struggles for political power between King James I and the House of Commons. The Commons appealed to their right as the popular voice of the people, but the king asserted that by divine right (the will of God) he held supreme power. King James was deeply angered by the challenge to his authority, and in 1605 contemptuously spoke of members of parliament as 'the Tribunes of the people, whose mouths cannot be stopped'. In another echo of the play, one faction of the Commons wanted the argument with the king to be conducted 'mildly'.

The warrior-heroes of the time Some critics argue that Coriolanus is a portrait of Robert Devereux (1566–1601), Earl of Essex and a favourite of Queen Elizabeth, who was executed for rebellion. Others claim that Shakespeare had in mind Sir Walter Raleigh (1552–1618), another favourite of the queen. Raleigh was famous for his pride and his delight in war. He held a monopoly of the tin mines in Cornwall, and his exploitation made him hated by the miners.

Shakespeare's mother Is *Coriolanus* linked with the death in 1608 of Shakespeare's mother? Her death may have prompted him to write a play that explores the relationship of mother and son.

Shakespeare's reading – Plutarch

Shakespeare found the story of *Coriolanus* (and his other Roman plays, *Julius Caesar* and *Antony and Cleopatra*) in *The Lives of the Noble Grecians and Romans*. Written by the Greek biographer Plutarch (approx 46–120 AD), it was translated into English by Sir Thomas North, and first published in 1579. Shakespeare's dramatic imagination was fired by what he read in *The Lives*.

Plutarch compares pairs of famous men, telling anecdotes about their lives to illustrate a moral or historical lesson. In Shakespeare's time, North's translation of Plutarch was very popular among educated people, who believed they could learn valuable lessons from studying the lives of famous men.

Shakespeare followed Plutarch's 'Life of Caius Martius Coriolanus' closely, but he made all kinds of revisions to story and character, selecting and shaping in order to increase dramatic effect. He omits some historical events and invents others. He greatly expands the roles of Menenius, Aufidius and the tribunes, and makes the plebeians more dramatically lively than in Plutarch.

Where Plutarch stresses that Coriolanus' character was affected by neglect after his father's death, Shakespeare emphasises the crucial importance of Volumnia in shaping his personality. In Plutarch, Coriolanus has two children. Shakespeare gives him only one. Plutarch blames usury (money lending at high rates of interest) as the prime cause of the plebeians' rebelliousness, but Shakespeare makes the main grievance the hoarding of corn by the patricians.

• Step into role as William Shakespeare. Consider in turn each 'source' above and say how each influenced you as you wrote *Coriolanus*.

Critics' forum

Use the following comments to explore your own responses to the play. Remember, you don't have to agree with any view if you can justify your own interpretation.

> Notoriously the victim of his dominating and devouring mother, Coriolanus is an overgrown child. Anywhere except upon a battlefield he is, at best, a disaster waiting to happen ... he is anything but a great spirit. *Harold Bloom, 1999*

> Coriolanus is the champion of power, or might is right ... he resembles the bulk of the European nobility in Shakespeare's time in being fit for nothing except fighting ... The play is a striking exposition of how aggressive nationalism and acute social division not only may, but must, go together; the former not only as a means of hoodwinking the poor, but as a way for the rulers to throw dust in their own eyes and have a good conscience to bolster them ... The play is in many ways ... a study of aristocratic flattery and cajoling of the people for the purpose of duping them. *Victor Kiernan, 1996*

> *Coriolanus* stubbornly refuses to be reduced to the status of a political tract or manifesto, and for all the sharpness and precision of its presentation of political conflict, the unspeaking eloquence of Shakespeare's famous stage direction – 'holds her by the hand, silent' – in the play's most intense moment of human confrontation and self-awareness, reminds us of concerns and intuitions of an altogether different order from those of political argument. *Robert Smallwood, 1994*

> Coriolanus, though literally a patrician, is perhaps Shakespeare's most developed study of a bourgeois individualist, those 'new men' (for the most part villains in Shakespeare) who live 'As if a man were author of himself/And knew no other kin'. Ruthlessly self-consistent and self-identical, Coriolanus is as superbly assured in his inward being as Hamlet is shattered in his ... Coriolanus confers value and meaning on himself in fine disregard for social opinion ... Coriolanus is nothing but his actions, a circular, blindly persistent process of self-definition. He cannot imagine what it would be like not to be himself ... he is exactly what he is, and so a sort of blank tautology. *Terry Eagleton, 1986*

Coriolanus is a tragedy in that its protagonist does finally learn certain necessary truths about the world in which he exists, but dies before he has any chance to rebuild his life in accordance with them. Paradoxically, it is only in his belated recognition and acceptance of historical change, of that right of the commons to be taken seriously, which the other members of his class in Rome have already conceded, that he achieves genuine tragic individuality.   *Anne Barton, 1985*

Rome's inhabitants form parties rather than relationships. Their first question is 'What is in it for us?' ... its final impression of aridness and waste might well be considered a warning against that petrification of humanity which occurs when people think only in terms of parties and movements and manifestoes.   *D J Enright, 1954*

He is a thing complete, a rounded perfection. We can no more blame him for his ruthless valour than we blame the hurtling spear for finding its mark. And yet Coriolanus has no mark: that is his tragedy ... His wars are not for Rome: they are an end in themselves ... So he whirls about like a planet in the dark chaos of pride, pursuing his self-bound orbit: a blind, mechanic, metallic thing of pride and pride's destiny.
G Wilson Knight, 1951

... essentially the splendid oaf who has never come to maturity ... It is this, in fact, that makes his conduct, which would be intolerable in a responsible adult, so far acceptable as to qualify him for the part of a tragic hero.   *Granville Barker, 1947*

... the greatest of Shakespeare's comedies ... and comedy neither compromises the author nor reveals him.   *Bernard Shaw, 1903*

It is from first to last, for all its turmoil of battle and clamour of contentious factions, rather a private and domestic rather than a public or historical tragedy ... The subject of the whole play is not the exile's revolt, the rebel's repentance, or the traitor's reward, but above all it is the son's tragedy.   *A C Swinburne, 1880*

Staging *Coriolanus*

Shakespeare probably wrote *Coriolanus* around 1608, but there is no record of a production in his lifetime. The play appeared in print for the first time in 1623 in the First Folio (see page 252), but for the next 200 years very free adaptations were much more popular than Shakespeare's original.

The titles of the adaptations provide clues to their approach. In 1682 Nahum Tate (who rewrote *King Lear* with a happy ending) staged his version: *The Ingratitude of a Commonwealth, or the Fall of Coriolanus*. In Tate's revision, Menenius and young Martius are murdered, Valeria becomes a chatterbox and flirt, Aufidius dies, and Coriolanus is reunited with his family.

The adaptations were often written in response to threats to civil order. For example, versions of the play proved popular after the 1715 and 1745 Jacobite rebellions. In both rebellions, an army invaded England in an unsuccessful attempt to overthrow the Hanoverian monarchy and place an exile from the house of Stuart on the throne. *The Invader of His Country or The Fatal Resentment* (1720), a re-writing by John Dennis, was prompted by the 1715 rebellion. A version by James Thomson, reacting to the 1745 rebellion, became *Coriolanus: or The Roman Matron*. It was first performed in 1749 with almost 200 actors on stage.

Nineteenth-century productions of the play were much concerned with spectacle. They staged grand processions and battle scenes, and attempted to create the 'authentic' architecture of ancient Rome on stage. One production included a giant lighthouse at Antium in its scenery.

Adaptations have continued in the twentieth century. The German playwright and director Berthold Brecht, a committed Communist, prepared a left-wing adaptation of the play to criticise militarism. His version played down Coriolanus' nobility, and emphasised the strength and solidarity of the people under the tribunes. In the production performed after Brecht's death, the plebeians refused to fight until they were given corn, Macbeth's Porter appeared, and the play ended with the tribunes curtly dismissing a plea that Coriolanus' memory should be honoured.

Coriolanus enters Rome in triumph. A modern staging of the play at the
Old Globe Theatre, San Diego. Compare with the illustration on page 62
and make your own suggestion of how to stage the triumphal entry.

In another adaptation, the English playwright John Osborne wrote *A place calling itself Rome*, set in 1970s Britain, torn by labour disputes and demonstrations. But throughout the twentieth century Shakespeare's own play has become increasingly popular around the world. Modern productions have usually sought parallels to the political and social preoccupations of their time. Some explore the relationship of democratic, military and fascist values. Others are more concerned with the psychological relationships of mother and son, or Coriolanus and Aufidius. For example, one production, influenced by Freudian theory, portrayed a homoerotic relationship between the two men.

The power of *Coriolanus* to express current political anxieties is evident. In Paris in 1933 there were riots at every performance of the play. Right-wing factions hailed Coriolanus as a perfect hero who had been wrongly victimised. The disturbances led to the police closing down the production. The government dismissed the theatre's director and replaced him with an ex-chief of police.

The play was popular in Communist states, and was used to explore relations between individual and society. A production in Moscow in 1934 portrayed Coriolanus as a self-seeking leader who betrayed his people.

In Nazi Germany in the 1930s the play became a school text with an anti-democratic message. Students were urged to think of Hitler as being like Coriolanus, a strong leader unjustly treated. After the war the occupying American forces banned performances of *Coriolanus* from 1945–53.

The theatrical potential of Shakespeare's stagecraft ensures the play's attractiveness to actors and audiences. The tight focus on Coriolanus heightens dramatic tension, and there are great opportunities for theatrical spectacle in staging crowd protests, triumphal processions and battle scenes with all the noise of drums and trumpets. One production introduced battering rams to assault the gates of Corioles, another used siege ladders.

Modern performances have staged the play in all kinds of periods and costumes: Napoleonic, nineteenth-century Germany, pre-Civil War America, Mussolini's Italy of the 1930s, Al Capone's Chicago, Central America with Sandanista guerrillas, Vietnam, the Solidarity movement in Poland, the 1991 Desert Storm offensive in Kuwait. Battle scenes have been played in slow motion, and in Japanese martial arts style.

This Royal Shakespeare Company production portrayed the Volsces as
tribal primitives who made Coriolanus their god.

William Shakespeare 1564–1616

1564 Born Stratford-upon-Avon, eldest son of John and Mary Shakespeare.
1582 Marries Anne Hathaway of Shottery, near Stratford.
1583 Daughter, Susanna, born.
1585 Twins, son and daughter, Hamnet and Judith, born.
1592 First mention of Shakespeare in London. Robert Greene, another playwright, described Shakespeare as 'an upstart crow beautified with our feathers ...'. Greene seems to have been jealous of Shakespeare. He mocked Shakespeare's name, calling him 'the only Shake-scene in a country' (presumably because Shakespeare was writing successful plays).
1595 A shareholder in 'The Lord Chamberlain's Men', an acting company that became extremely popular.
1596 Son Hamnet dies, aged eleven.
Father, John, granted arms (acknowledged as a gentleman).
1597 Buys New Place, the grandest house in Stratford.
1598 Acts in Ben Jonson's *Every Man in His Humour*.
1599 Globe Theatre opens on Bankside. Performances in the open air.
1601 Father, John, dies.
1603 James I grants Shakespeare's company a royal patent: 'The Lord Chamberlain's Men' became 'The King's Men' and played about twelve performances each year at court.
1607 Daughter, Susanna, marries Dr John Hall.
1608 Mother, Mary, dies.
1609 'The King's Men' begin performing indoors at Blackfriars Theatre.
1610 Probably returned from London to live in Stratford.
1616 Daughter, Judith, marries Thomas Quiney.
Dies. Buried in Holy Trinity Church, Stratford-upon-Avon.

The plays and poems
(no one knows exactly when he wrote each play)

1589–1595 *The Two Gentlemen of Verona, The Taming of the Shrew, First, Second and Third Parts of King Henry VI, Titus Andronicus, King Richard III, The Comedy of Errors, Love's Labour's Lost, A Midsummer Night's Dream, Romeo and Juliet, King Richard II* (and the long poems *Venus and Adonis* and *The Rape of Lucrece*).

1596–1599 *King John, The Merchant of Venice, First and Second Parts of King Henry IV, The Merry Wives of Windsor, Much Ado About Nothing, King Henry V, Julius Caesar* (and probably the *Sonnets*).

1600–1605 *As You Like It, Hamlet, Twelfth Night, Troilus and Cressida, Measure for Measure, Othello, All's Well That Ends Well, Timon of Athens, King Lear.*

1606–1611 *Macbeth, Antony and Cleopatra, Pericles, Coriolanus, The Winter's Tale, Cymbeline, The Tempest.*

1613 *King Henry VIII, The Two Noble Kinsmen* (both probably with John Fletcher).

1623 Shakespeare's plays published as a collection (now called the First Folio).